LSWR CARRIAGES

VOLUME 4

Goods, Departmental Stock and Miscellany

LSWR CARRIAGES

VOLUME 4

Goods, Departmental Stock and Miscellany

G R Weddell

© Kestrel Railway Books and Gordon Weddell 2006

Kestrel Railway Books
PO Box 269
SOUTHAMPTON
SO30 4XR

www.kestrelrailwaybooks.co.uk

No part of this publication may be
reproduced, stored in a retrieval system,
transmitted in any form or by any means,
electronic, mechanical, or photo-copied,
recorded or otherwise, without the
consent of the publisher in writing.

Printed by The Amadeus Press.

ISBN 978-1-905505-01-2 (1905505019)

Front cover, top: 34ft 6in open goods wagon of 1899. (MS King collection)

Front cover, bottom: 34ft 6in open goods wagon of 1899.

Back cover, top: 20-ton crane No 1 of 1908. (Real Photographs Co)

Back cover, bottom: LSWR Servants' Coal Club wagon No 6, built October 1922. (Gloucestershire County Record Office)

Contents

Index to Individual Subjects vi

Introduction viii

Chapter 1 Goods Vehicles 1

Chapter 2 Travelling Gasholders 69

Chapter 3 Travelling Cranes 81

Chapter 4 Miscellany 117

Appendix 157

Index to Individual Subjects

Chapter 1 Goods Vehicles

Note: All LSWR goods vehicles that existed at the end of 1922 and that came into Southern Railway ownership were described and illustrated in *An Illustrated History of Southern Wagons, Vol.1* by Bixley, Blackburn, Chorley, King and Newton, published by OPC in 1984. Apart from one or two cases, those descriptions and illustrations are not duplicated here.

Item	Description	Page
1.1	22ft bar and rod iron wagon of July 1854	7
1.2	6-ton goods wagon of pre-1862	7
1.3	Open goods wagon of c.1863 (approximately 16ft)	8
1.4	8-ton goods wagon of 1865	9
1.5	8-ton goods wagon of 1872	10
1.6	10-ton goods wagon of 1877	11
1.7	10-ton goods wagon of c.1881	13
1.8	34ft 6in wagon for Signal Department of 1898	15
1.9	34ft 6in open goods wagon of 1899	16
1.10	21ft 5in platform truck of c.1877	17
1.11	15ft 6in platform truck of 1893	18
1.12	15ft 4in wagon for Southampton Docks of 1900	18
1.13a	16ft road van truck of 1876	19
1.13b	16ft 10-ton road van truck of c.1890	21
1.14	17ft road van truck of c.1900	21
1.15	18ft road van truck of 1902	23
1.16	15ft 4in covered goods wagon of 1877	24
1.17	14ft 6in gunpowder van of 1888 and 1900	26
1.18	15ft SCR high-sided goods and cattle wagon of 1862	27
1.19	15ft cattle wagon of 1863	28
1.20	16ft 9in cattle wagon of 1876/78	30
1.21	18ft cattle wagon of 1880	31
1.22	18ft 8½in cattle wagon of c.1895	32
1.23	18ft 3in special cattle wagon of 1888	34
1.24	18ft 3in special cattle wagon of 1891	35
1.25	22ft special cattle van of 1910	38
1.26	15ft 4in meat van of 1873	39
1.27	15ft 4in stone wagon of 1870	40
1.28	15ft 4in stone wagon of 1875	41
1.29	Ballast wagon, pre-1863	42
1.30	11ft 8in timber wagon of 1861	44
1.31	12ft timber wagon of 1876	45
1.32	23ft "rail and batten" wagon of 1878	45
1.33	13ft timber wagon of 1892	47
1.34	Goods guard's vans before 1875	48, 49
1.35	18ft 6in goods guard's vans of 1874 and 1876	52
1.36	18ft 6in goods guard's van of 1878	54
1.37	18ft 6in goods guard's van of 1882	56
1.38	China clay wagon of 1913	58

1.39 to 1.49   These are photographs only, no drawings.

Chapter 2 Travelling Gasholders

Item	Description	
2.1	Travelling gasholders numbers 1, 2, 3, etc of 1896	70
2.2	Travelling gasholders numbers 5, 8, and 9 f 1896	72
2.3	Travelling gasholders numbers 10 and 11 of 1898	75
2.4	Travelling gasholders numbers 118S and 119S of 1921	77

Chapter 3 Cranes

Item	Description	
3.1	3-ton crane of c.1860 (later goods crane No 2)	82
3.2	4-ton crane of c.1860 (later goods crane No 3)	84
3.3	Breakdown cranes numbers 2 and 4 of 1875	85
3.4	22ft Nine Elms breakdown van of 1878	88
3.5	Breakdown crane No 3 (formerly No 1) of 1885	90
3.6	20-ton breakdown cranes numbers 1 and 5 of 1908/9	95, 96
3.7	36-ton breakdown crane No 6 of 1918	100
3.8	36-ton breakdown crane No 7 of 1922	100
3.9	Goods crane No 4 of 1901	102
3.10	Goods crane No 1 of 1903	102
3.11	Goods crane No 5 of 1911	103
3.12	Goods crane No 6 of 1901	104
3.13	Goods crane No 7 of 1885	105
3.14	Goods crane No 8 of 1897	105
3.15	Engineer's Crane No 9 of 1910	106
3.16	Engineer's Crane No 12 of 1900	106
3.17	Loco department shops crane	107
3.18	Carriage department steam crane M76	108
3.19	Carriage department shops crane R12	109
3.20	Carriage department shops cranes 1 and 2	109
3.21	Carriage department shops crane Y15	110

Chapter 4 Miscellany

Item	Description	
4.1.1	LSWR structure and load gauge	116
4.1.2	LSWR loading gauges used in goods yards	118, 119
4.2	Road vehicles (pair-horse meat van of c. 1893)	120
4.3	Goods yard cranes	128
4.4a	Shunting truck No 336 of 1898	133
4.4b	Shunting truck No 336 of 1908	134
4.5.1	Platform items (luggage barrow)	136
4.5.2	Platform items (long bow barrow)	139
4.5.3	Platform items (large platform trolley)	139
4.5.4	Platform items (parcels barrow)	140
4.5.5	Notices and gas lamp	141, 142
4.5.6	Water Crane	142
4.6.1	18ft Pooley weighing machine van of 1895	144
4.6.2	21ft Pooley weighing machine van of 1899	145
4.7	Engineer's inspection train	146
4.8	LSWR Employés Coal Company Ltd	147
4.9	"Skew" brake gear	150
4.10	LSWR buffer stop	153

INTRODUCTION

All that was written for the Introduction to *LSWR Carriages, Volume 3* applies here, but I would like to repeat that several photos included in this volume are of rather poor quality, because they are enlargements taken from the background of locomotive or station views. However, they are all that I have been able to find for those subjects.

Several photographs have either no credit, or are shown as "Author's collection", because so many that were purchased many years ago from very many sources had nothing written on the back as identification. If anyone recognises one of their photos, I trust they will accept my apologies and thanks for having made them available to the public.

Virtually all of the goods vehicles that were built by the LSWR, and which survived to become the property of the Southern Railway in 1923 (as well as one type that didn't – the 1881 covered wagon) have been very well described and illustrated in *An Illustrated History of Southern Wagons, Volume 1* (here referred to simply as *Southern Wagons, Volume 1*) so they will not be duplicated in this work. Chapter 1 deals with all the earlier goods vehicles for which evidence can still be found, although it will be evident from the text that many types or versions existed for which neither drawings nor photographs are known to have survived.

As with the previous volumes, I wish to thank all those who have helped with information, photographs, and sometimes even with questions that have made me look deeper into some points. Particularly, however, I thank Mr R Chorley and Mr HV Tumilty, without whose work I should never have started on these books, and my wife Margaret, whose patience has been stretched by the many hours that I have spent on the subject.

Gordon R Weddell

Photo]   *[Mr. E. S. C. Betteley*
THE ORIGINAL TERMINUS AT GODALMING, NOW THE GOODS STATION.

CHAPTER 1

GOODS VEHICLES

This chapter cannot give, and is not intended to give, the whole story of goods vehicle development by the LSWR. It cannot, because so little information has survived, and it is not intended to, because all of those goods vehicles that survived into Southern Railway ownership have already been very well described and illustrated in *An Illustrated History of Southern Wagons, Volume 1* by Bixley, Blackburn, Chorley, King and Newton, published by Oxford Publishing Co in 1984 (ISBN 0-86093-207-9) and reissued in 2000. This book will be mentioned several times and for convenience the title will be abbreviated to just *Southern Wagons, Volume 1*. Apart from one or two cases, those vehicles will not be dealt with again here.

Official records contain relatively little information. The only remaining diagram books show vehicles that were built after 1909, with numbering details, but little else. Relatively few official drawings have survived, indeed none from before 1854 and few from before 1870. The earlier ones are mainly of wagons built by the Metropolitan Carriage and Wagon Co, but several other companies provided wagons from time to time, apart from those built by the LSWR at Nine Elms or Eastleigh. By their nature most wagons had a fairly short life, fifteen years or so being quite common, but the LSWR quite often salvaged the metal parts from scrapped wagons for use in their replacements.

Regrettably there are very few photos that show goods vehicles at all clearly, the situation is even worse than it is with passenger carriages. Photographers seem to have taken considerable care to avoid anything with a revenue earning capability, or of real interest, appearing in their photos of locomotives. In a few cases, where wagons were in the background, there appears to be evidence of retouching to either remove them or to create a kind of misty background! It is inevitable, therefore, that there are far too few photographic illustrations to this chapter, and some are unavoidably of rather poor quality, since they have had to be grossly enlarged from background areas. The drawings have had to be based on the assumption that, because the official drawings were retained, the vehicles almost certainly appeared as shown. Purists might be a little unhappy about this, but it is necessary to either accept this or have next to nothing.

When the London & Southampton Railway first opened, there seems to have been little clear idea of what traffic (apart from upper class passengers) might be expected. The first reference to actual goods traffic was in the report to the half-annual General Meeting of Proprietors (shareholders) on 31st August 1838, shortly after the opening to Woking Common, when it was stated that so far no goods or cattle had been carried, but that the means for so doing were in active preparation. The first records of goods vehicles are in the accounts when, on 21st August 1838, J Braby was paid £321 4s 0d for trucks, and on 28th December 1838 William Beattie of Liverpool was paid £600 for wagons; there were then some further similar payments. Of the payments made to Joseph Wright some specified carriages, but some did not, leaving room for speculation. Apart from these bare facts there is no other information at all about them. In March 1839 the Traffic and General Purposes Committee (T&GPC) fixed a flat rate for goods of 6d (2.5p) per ton per mile, reduced to 5d for common carriers. A month later there was a report of a complaint about the detention of a load of mackerel at Farnborough, for which compensation was sought.

That there was some uncertainty over the policy of carrying goods is shown by minutes of the T&GPC in July 1839 when it discussed the subject of attaching goods wagons to passenger trains and agreed that it was undesirable, but did not issue any instructions.

In the following September, William Allcard was paid £1280 for wagons whilst Messrs Allcard and (William) Beattie tendered for the construction of 25 goods wagons to Mr Beattie's design, (probably meaning Joseph Beattie's design). In November W Beattie was paid £2709, presumably for more wagons, and in December, it was stated that six hopper wagons were being built, but with no other details.

At a meeting in January 1840 the T&GPC expressed the opinion "that wagons with falling down sides like those built by the London & Birmingham Railway are the best for the present purpose", and a fortnight later Allcard and Beattie submitted tenders. It was then agreed that Beattie should supply twenty at £66 10s 0d (£66.50) each.

In February, the shareholders were told that less goods had been carried in the previous six months, due largely to the cost and delay of transferring goods between road and rail, but that it was hoped that matters would improve following the completion of the line to Southampton (completed 11th May 1840). They were also told that the outlay on sufficient trucks, horseboxes, wagons, etc would have to be much beyond what had formerly been contemplated.

Joseph Beattie reported to the T&GPC in July 1840 on the supply of coal wagons, and submitted some plans of his own; these were referred to the Engineer, Joseph Locke. In his reply he agreed that they should provide sufficient for two trains, one for each end of the line, and that all other coal wagons should be built according to Mr Locke's own plans. In the meantime, the Court of Directors had ordered the provision of ten to twenty merchandise wagons.

Despite the comments of the T&GPC in July 1839, the mixture of passenger and goods vehicles continued. In April 1841, the Directors agreed that the carriage of passengers by goods trains on Sundays could be abandoned, whilst in the following June, it was agreed that a first class carriage should be added to the up evening goods train from Southampton. However, in January 1842, the company wrote to the Board of Trade stating that they had discontinued the practice of conveying third class passengers by the goods trains.

Through this period, the accounts frequently show payments for unspecified quantities of wagons to W Allcard, W Beattie, C Twynham and others. It was also decided to try to buy a quantity of second-hand contractor's wagons from Mr Brassey, and the minutes record the latter's agreement to supply a second batch of two hundred wagons for £6 6s 0d each! At this price one wonders what state they were in and for what purpose they were used.

At the end of 1842, the Directors called for tenders for the construction of ten or twenty wagons to Joseph Beattie's specification but, as usual, there is no further information.

The foregoing summarises the facts recorded in the early minutes books and accounts, but Sam Fay and RA Williams mention some interesting items (although, unfortunately without quoting their sources). RA Williams, in Volume 1 of his *History of the London & South Western Railway* states that in March 1843, goods guards were ordered to ride in the last vehicle of their train, and were provided with moveable seats that could be taken from wagon to wagon. This suggests that there were still no special wagons or vans fitted with brakes for the use of the guard. Sam Fay, writing in his book *A Royal Road* in about 1881, when he was a Traffic Clerk for the LSWR, says that at first all waggons (sic) were attached to the last passenger trains of the day, but that after the opening to Basingstoke, a separate goods train was run in the care of three youths of less than sixteen years old. Not surprisingly, they were soon replaced by a man who, however, had no brake van but was provided with "a Noah's Ark" (a vehicle with two swing doors in one side and a sloping roof) in which he carried small packages to and from stations along the route. This suggests the origin of the expression "road van" or "road box". He goes on to say that the ordinary goods wagons were about twelve feet in length, and very roughly finished, with dead buffers, unsprung drawbars and no side chains, as a result of which broken couplings caused many delays. Whether this referred to the vehicles bought from such builders as Allcard and W Beattie, or to those bought second-hand from Mr Brassey is not at all certain.

Returning to official facts, the Directors agreed in March 1844 to order ten sets of Joseph Beattie's patent wheels (sometimes referred to as "wheelbarrow" wheels), but instructed that initially they were only to be used on wagons. Little more is known about wagon wheels until the 1850s and 1860s when drawings from the Metropolitan Carriage & Wagon Co show the open-spoke type, which then continued to be used until at least 1909.

At about the same time, Mr Locke recommended that the coal wagons should be restricted to only carry 4 tons each. This seems to be related to the particularly frustrating statement in the Directors' minutes for 19th September 1845, that plans of the existing wagons and those of an improved make, being lower in the sides and longer in the body, were laid before the Board. It is frustrating, because these plans have not survived. The lower-sided wagons were approved and William Beattie's tender for building one hundred was accepted. A year later, it was instructed that the old high-sided goods wagons were to be cut down into coal wagons as they came in for repair, but as late as 1858, instructions were being issued to Station Agents that, "No sleepers or any other heavy substances should be loaded more than half way up to the top of the old high goods wagons. If these wagons be loaded nearly to the top, the centre of gravity is raised so high it renders them unsafe to travel".

In November 1846, William Beattie was awarded a further contract for one hundred wagons at £85 15s 0d each, and then shortly after that the Directors decided to order three hundred more and to enquire about the cost – in that sequence! Beattie got the contract for two hundred of these as well.

From then on, the authorisations and orders for wagons came fairly thick and fast. It would be boring to detail them all, but a few extracts might be of interest. In March 1847, it was decided to order one hundred merchandise wagons, one hundred long coal wagons, one hundred short coal wagons and

GOODS VEHICLES

fifty ballast wagons to the designs of Joseph Beattie. Tenders were sought from several builders: CC Williams of Bristol, W Beattie of Liverpool, Woolferston and Tiges (both of Salisbury), Lloyd Foster of Wednesbury, the Haigh Foundry of Wigan and a Mr Pace (or Pare). This latter was probably another of the former road coach proprietors like Joseph Wright and William Chaplin who had moved from the road to the rail business. The contract for most of these orders went to William Beattie. The short coal wagons (numbers 41 to 80) were delivered by the following November when they were paid for at £86 10s 0d each.

A notice to staff, issued in June 1847, instructed that the first choice of wagons when loading goods should be from those with fixed cloths. No goods were to be loaded in low sided or coal wagons – these were to be used exclusively for the carriage of coals. This notice is rather tantalising, since nothing further has come to light to describe these wagons with fixed cloths, so they remain among the many mysteries.

An accident report gives some interesting details about a goods train. It left Southampton on the night of 24th September 1847, hauled by Elephant, and arrived at Nine Elms at 4.35 the following morning. When it left Woking (in fog) it had 51 wagons, but on arrival at Nine Elms, the Guard found that 13 wagons, including the brakesman's van, were missing. A pilot engine took him back down the line to Wimbledon cutting where he found that the up Mail had run into the stationary wagons, destroying many of them, and killing the brakesman. At the inquest, it was found that the centre draw chain between two wagons had not been properly coupled, and both ends were on the same wagon. The side chains alone had been coupled, but had broken, possibly when the locomotive slipped, and then pulled again. It was stated that, "There was every reason to suppose that the brakesman was asleep in his box, otherwise he would have gone back with fog signals". From this it would appear that the guard, who was in charge of the train, must have been somewhere near the front, and presumably with poor lookout facilities, whilst his junior, the brakesman, was in the more important position at the rear of the train.

Reference to a brakesman does not necessarily imply that there were proper brake vehicles by this date, since the first mention of such vehicles was on 11th February 1848 when Mr Beattie submitted drawings for a proposed brake wagon for goods trains to the Traffic and Carriage Committee. Therefore, it seems most likely that hitherto, the brakesman's duty was to descend at the top and bottom of inclines, and apply or remove scotches to the wagon wheels. It is not certain whether or not handbrakes, as we know them, were commonplace by then. Mr Beattie also reported on a further proposal to fit a screw brake and lookout on the road boxes, leaving one to wonder whether this referred to the "Noah's Arks" mentioned earlier. The matter was apparently not fully resolved, because a week later, there was a further letter from Mr Beattie regarding the adaptation of the present wagons to the purpose of brake wagons. These are more tantalising statements for which there is no authenticated explanation.

Another interesting point is the mention of the centre draw chain not having been properly coupled. Was it a chain properly attached at one end or a loose chain? This query is because of a Traffic Committee recommendation of 13th September 1855 that each of the goods and coal wagons should have a coupling chain fixed at both ends. Mr Beattie was then instructed to carry it out by degrees. Despite this, the Traffic Department was still complaining in 1858 that, "There is a shortage of carriage couplings at Waterloo, caused by Station Agents permitting carriage couplings to be taken from intermediate stations, and unnecessarily used by the Goods Guards to couple goods wagons together. Station Agents are to send spares to Waterloo, and not permit their use for wagons." Then, in April 1861, Mr Beattie queried the continuance of the fitting of side chains to wagons since the Brighton Company had refused to take on some of the wagons at Havant that were without these chains. The Traffic Manager was told to discuss this with the LB&SCR, but later that month it was reported that it was because of cases where the couplings had got loose and had torn up the tie rods of points at Havant. Mr Beattie was told to see if they could be made more safe!

Later, in November 1865, a rather vague reference to an Officers Committee minute implies that they wanted couplings with hooks to be standardised, and it was agreed to replace the existing screw couplings on wagons. Nevertheless, a notice to staff in August 1868 told them to check all screw couplings, and change them if there was any doubt, but this might have referred to carriages. It went on to require that both coupling chains must always be used, or the screw of one and the chain of the other. Also that side chains must always be used on wagons as well as on carriages and on engines.

A return of all rolling stock as at the end of June 1848 is listed in Table 1 (in each category I have totalled those shown in the return as in good repair, awaiting painting or repairs, damaged, and so on).

LSWR CARRIAGES VOLUME 4

Table 1: Return of all rolling stock as at the end of June 1848	
Goods wagons	615
Coal wagons	375
Goods guards vans, having been lately fitted up	4
Covered wagons, used for passengers luggage in third class trains, much worn	3
Covered wagons, used for parcels in goods trains, considerably worn, being old	16
Timber trucks	56
Wagons used for transit of carriers of goods and also adapted for carriage of cattle	26
Wagons adapted for carriage of cattle, manure, coals, hay, etc	25
Skeleton wagons used to run between other wagons in goods trains	40
Ballast wagons	50

Shortly after this, in June 1849, it was agreed to alter twelve more goods wagons to guards' brake vans, again leaving it questionable as to whether these were open or covered vehicles.

Once again, the nineteen covered wagons mentioned here are open to conjecture. Since they were described as much worn and old in 1848, they must have been in service since the earliest years, but no other mention of them has come to light, unless they were the ones described in 1847 as "wagons with fixed cloths".

One small item contained in a notice of 24th July 1848 is that the practice of marking wagons with chalk was forbidden, and regular wagon labels were to be affixed. As many readers will know, chalk was still in common use well into the British Railways era!

The Traffic, Coaching and Locomotive Committee recommended the Directors to agree to a proposal from the Officers Committee in May 1849 that spring buffers should be fitted to goods wagons. They also recommended that the cost should be charged to capital. Both points were approved.

The next Return of Carrying Stock, which was included with the report to the shareholders in February 1852, showed among other vehicles, 4 luggage carriages, 26 luggage vans and 1411 goods wagons at 31st December 1851; the 4 luggage carriages had been built in the previous six months. This again raises the question of what were the distinctions and applications of these descriptions.

Before the coming of railways, coal was little used at more than a short distance from the coastal towns and ports or from canals, since it was so expensive to convey by road wagon. The situation was changed dramatically by the railways, and as might be expected, the demand grew for more and more coal wagons. As we have seen, by the end of the first ten years there were already 375 in use. Of course, this trade was hard on the wagons, and they probably had quite short lives, but for a long time there were repeated orders for quantities of one or two hundred at a time. For example, in July 1850, the Traffic, Coaching & Loco Committee recommended that an order should be placed for one hundred, to be constructed by Mr Beattie, following the extension of the wharf at Nine Elms. Again, in November 1852, an order was placed with William Worsdell for one hundred at £38 10s 0d each, the wheels and axles to be supplied by the LSWR. Then, in May 1853, a further hundred were ordered from him on the same terms, to be delivered on the rails at Birmingham.

A special traffic arising at this time was salt, and it was to cause slight problems later on. In October 1853, Messrs Clay & Newman of Droitwich approached the South Western with a proposal to send a considerable traffic in salt over the line via the North and South Western Junction line, provided the LSWR agreed to charge ¾d per ton per mile from Kew Junction when sending quantities less than 50 tons to one station at a time, and ⅝d per ton per mile when sending 50 ton lots. Messrs Clay & Newman would provide the wagons and sheets. This was agreed to in respect of all stations except, for no stated reason, Nine Elms. Evidently, the salt took its toll on the wagons, presumably seeping through the floors and setting up corrosion of the running gear. After a number of minor incidents involving either derailments or stoppage after inspection, it was decided, in 1861, to increase the charges to cover the increased risks, and inspectors were warned to take particular care before allowing these wagons on to the line. These increases were not implemented, but after several further incidents involving wagons 76, 187 and 520 belonging to Clay & Newman, as well as to No 176 belonging to Mr Corbett, it was decided in April 1870 to refuse the

GOODS VEHICLES

Table 2: Goods Stock as in October 1870

	Van truck	Goods guards van	Timber truck	General goods wagon	General goods wagon	Goods wagon	Coal wagon	Covered wagon	Cattle wagon	Ballast wagon
Interior dimensions of floor	16ft x 7ft 6in	15ft 8in x 7ft	11ft 6in x 7ft 2in	12ft 1in x 7ft 1in	14ft 8in x 7ft	15ft x 7ft 2in	14ft 8in x 7ft 2in	14ft 4in x 7ft 2in	13ft 3in x 7ft	13ft x 7ft
Length over buffers	19ft 9in	19ft 9in	15ft 3in	16ft 3in	18ft 9in	19ft 1in	18ft 9in	18ft 9in	17ft 9in	17ft 1in
Height of side (inside)	10in	5ft 6in to 5ft 9in & 7ft to 7ft 3in	n/a	2ft 5½in	2ft 10½in	3ft 2½in	2ft 4in	5ft 9in to 6ft 4in	6ft 2in	1ft 4in
Interior capacity (cubic feet)	Large furniture vans	15ft 8in x 7ft	Planks	230	375	513.5	244	628	571	171
Wheel centres	9ft	9ft	6ft 9in	7ft 6in	9ft	9ft	9ft	Figures unclear – could be 8ft or 10ft	8ft	8ft
Journals	6in x 3in	6in x 3in	6in x 3in	6in x 3in	6in x 3in	7in x 3½in	6in x 3in	6in x 3in	6in x 3in	6in x 3in
Maximum load (tons)	6	n/a	6	5	6	8	6	unknown	5	unknown
Maximum speed (mph)	20	20	20	20	20	20	20	20	20	20

Note: the interior capacities do not always tie up with the stated dimensions.

acceptance of any more salt vans onto the line. Salt vans certainly continued to travel over the line but there is no further mention in the minutes.

In an LSWR Correspondence Book covering 1869 to 1878 (P.R.O, RAIL 411/469) there is a list of Goods Stock as in October 1870 (see Table 2).

Appended to the half-year report to the Board by WG Beattie, dated 23rd January 1872, there is another summary of the quantities and sizes of stock. Although not so stated, the dimensions appear to be internal (the notes in brackets are the author's):

Covered wagons
- 265 @ 14ft 9in x 7ft, height: 5ft 9in to 6ft 4in, doors: 5ft 9in high and 6ft 6in wide, load: 6 tons
- 30 @ 14ft 9in x 6ft 11in, height 6ft 7¾in to 7ft 3¼in, doors: 6ft 1in high and 5ft 4in wide, load: 6 tons

Open wagons
- 595 @ 15ft x 7ft 2in, 3ft 2½in side, load: 8 tons
- 2440 @ 14ft 10in x 7ft, 2ft 10½in side, load: 6 tons

Low-sided trucks
- 325 @ 11ft 6in x 7ft, no sides, load: 6 tons (possibly timber trucks)
- 20 @ 22ft x 7ft, 9in sides, load: 10 tons (the bar and rod iron wagons of 1854)
- 20 @ 16ft x 7ft 8in, 9in sides, load: 6 tons (possibly road vehicle trucks)

Coal, coke or mineral wagons
- 888 @ 14ft 10in x 7ft, 2ft 4in sides, load: 6 tons
- 24 @ 15ft x 7ft, 2ft sides, load: 10 tons

Cattle wagons
- 50 covered @ 14ft x 7ft, height 5ft 10in, doors: 5ft 10in x 5ft 4in
- 50 covered @ 16ft 6in x 7ft 6in, height unknown, doors: 6ft x 5ft 6in
- 176 uncovered @ 14ft 2in x 7ft, height unknown, doors: 5ft 11in x 4ft 11in

Note how few of these dimensions agree with those given in October 1870!

There is no official, or contemporary written, evidence on the subject of the colour of early wagon stock. However an early contemporary painting of Bletchynden station, later Southampton West, shows a grey wagon. Some fairly early photos show wagons and vans that are almost certainly LSWR in a fairly light shade, presumably grey, and some with black ironwork on the body. They will be shown here at appropriate points. They include a very much-enlarged detail of Tonbridge yard (SER) which shows one of the 1872 wagons on which the lettering can just be made out as L&SWRC° 63. Incidentally, this raises the question of whether it was just a replacement for one of the 1847 coal wagons (numbers 41 to 80, mentioned earlier) or whether, as with the carriages, the LSWR had a separate number series for each of the different types of goods vehicle.

Another photo, of Wimbledon up yard in the mid-1870s, shows eleven wagons and a van, most of which are LSWR, again in a fairly light shade, mostly with black strapping. Two other photos, one at Dorchester around 1860 and another at Exeter, of unknown date but showing a Beattie well tank in gleaming condition, include parts of hatch roof vans with corrugated metal sides, again in a very light shade.

The first indication of colour in the minutes books is when the storekeeper wrote to the Locomotive and Stores Committee on 14th January 1887 referring to the trial by the Carriage Superintendent (Mr Panter) of zinc brown for painting wagons, and seeking authority to keep a supply, which was then authorised. Jumping ahead a long way, Surrey Warner gave details of the painting of wagons in *Modern Railway Working*, published in 1912. After due preparation, the bodies were painted dark brown outside and lead colour inside. The underframes were similarly brown outside, but all attached ironwork was black. The fact that only one coat of brown was used, and none of varnish, accounts for the fairly rapid lightening in the appearance of LSWR goods vehicles.

The inference from the above is that grey remained the predominant colour right up to at least 1887, that is, right through the Beattie and the Adams periods of responsibility for carriages and wagons.

Much the same vagueness applies to lettering, and the very few photographs available seem to show that in the Beattie period wagons were marked "L&SWRC°" in small characters. This was probably simplified to "L&SWR" fairly early in Mr Adams' time in office, and again simplified to LSWR by March 1884, when that style was recorded by the Railway Clearing House. However, in that RCH list, the wagon sheets were still shown as L&SWR.

Now that we have had a quick look over the earlier years we can go back and start looking at some vehicles type by type, but before that, here is a quotation from an article in the June 1911 special LSWR number of *The Railway Magazine*:

"The South Western Railway takes an important part in this work (supplying the alimentary needs of London's millions), and an examination of the contents of the freight-carrying vehicles on the various London trains would disclose Brixham soles and Dartmoor rabbits, Cornish herrings and Devon beef and cider, Dorset pork and butter and Hampshire mutton and game; cream, cheese and watercress from Somerset and Wilts, vegetables and fruit from Surrey and Middlesex, and even West Indian turtles. These are conveyed in such vast quantities as to necessitate the frequent running of special trains, and the climax is reached when the Hampshire strawberries ripen."

Bar and Rod Iron Wagons

Though several undated Joseph Wright drawings show goods vehicles built for the LSWR before 1863, the earliest definite date is for a wagon to carry bar and rod iron. This was proposed by the Traffic Committee in May 1854, and Mr Beattie was asked to contact Mr Evans of Dowlais Iron Works for advice. Acting on his report, it was decided to order twenty such wagons, each to be 22ft long on the floor. In July, Joseph Wright & Sons provided their drawing, and the order for twenty was approved. In the 1872 list of stock, their load was shown as 10 tons.

As will be seen from the present drawing (figure 1.1) it had three distinct peculiarities, the centre axle had flangeless wheels, the handbrake only operated on one of these wheels and the floor planking ran lengthways. One can imagine the first feature causing a lot of problems, but no mention of this has come to light. Perhaps the wheelbase of 7ft + 7ft was short enough to avoid derailments.

Another slightly unusual feature is in the actual Joseph Wright drawing. One half of the plan view is shown as from above, in the usual way, while the other half is as seen from below; the accompanying figure is also shown this way.

In these wagons, and in many of the others that follow, it was very common for internal members of the underframe to be less deep than the solebars or headstocks. With the headstocks usually 12in deep, the other members could be anything from 4in to the full 12in. Naturally, the tops of some members had to be flush with the tops of the solebars in order to

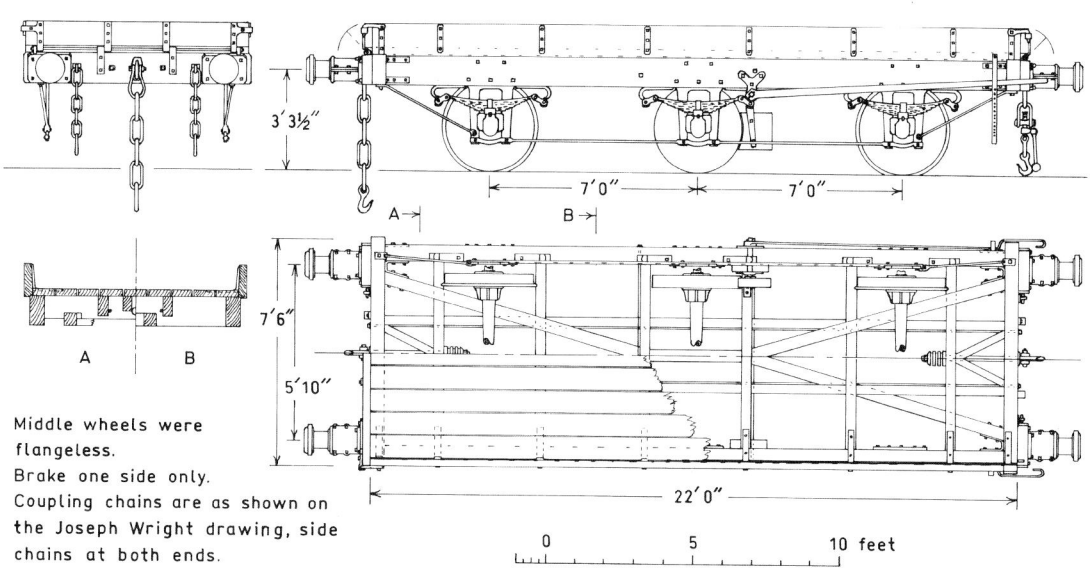

Figure 1.1. 22ft bar and rod iron wagon of July 1854.

support the floor, but others were often fitted lower down and half-jointed into upper ones. Sometimes longitudinals or semi-diagonals would slope from the tops of headstocks to the bottom of transverse members near to the centre.

Open Goods Wagons

The earliest open wagons that can be illustrated are two types that were built by Joseph Wright and by the Metropolitan Company (formerly Joseph Wright). The former, shown here as figure 1.2, was 15ft long over headstocks, and looked remarkably similar to those that became the "standard" LSWR type many years later. Although described here as pre-1862, it might be a Joseph Beattie design of early 1859, of which several batches were built by both Wright's and Brown Marshall – the minutes are not precise enough for positive identification.

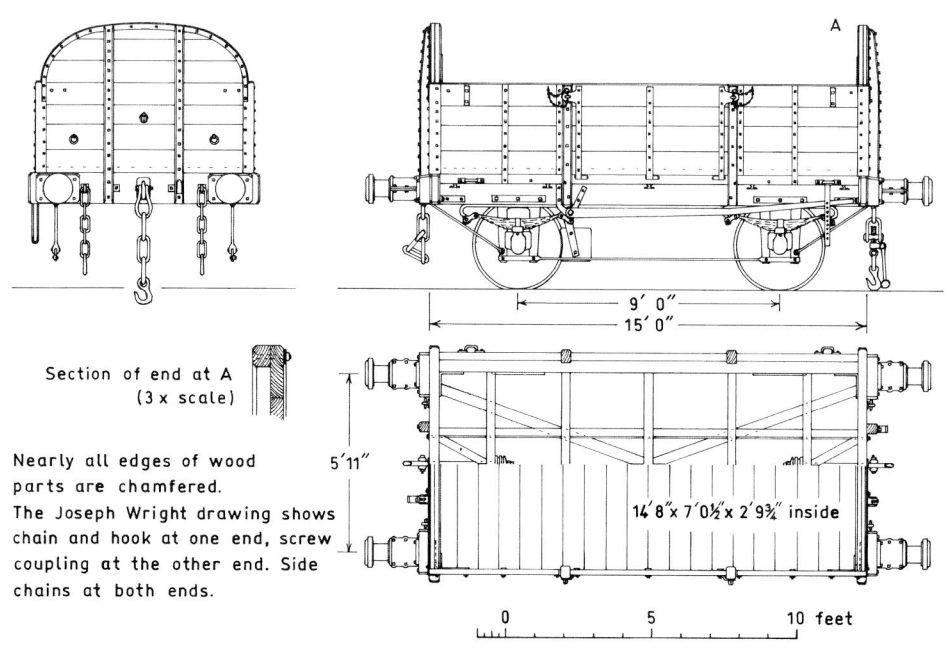

Figure 1.2. 6-ton goods wagon of pre-1862.

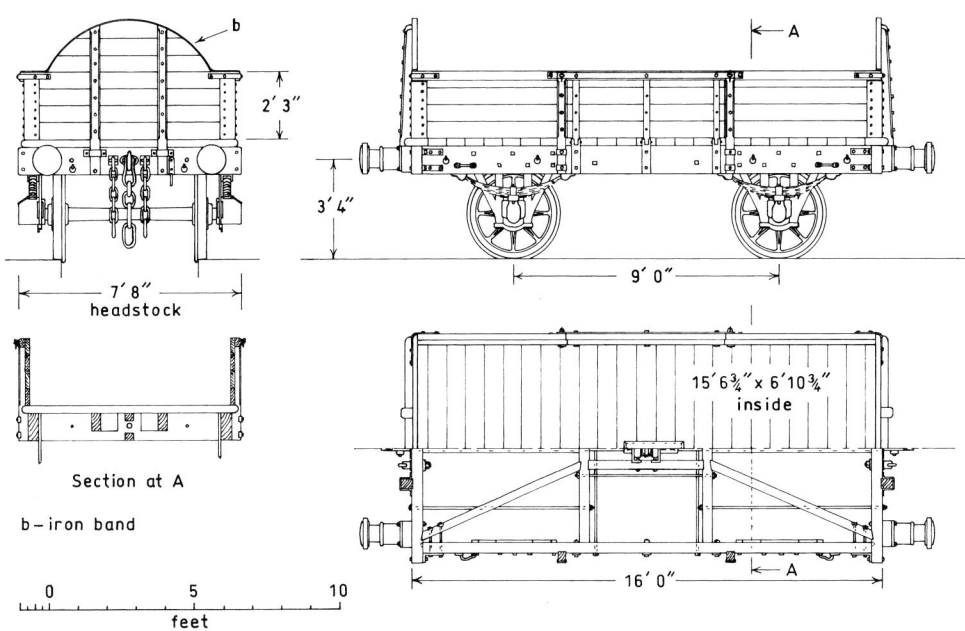

Figure 1.3. Open goods wagon of c.1863 (approximately 16ft).

Perhaps the most curious feature is the couplings. Apart from the usual side chains, the works drawing shows a screw coupling at one end and a long chain and hook at the other – so long that the hook would clearly drag along the track if not properly coupled to the next vehicle or hooked up on itself. This length was necessitated by the length of the buffers (around 2ft 3in), though this included wooden blocks about 6in thick on the headstocks. The reason for this apparently unnecessary and troublesome length is far from clear. It will be seen later that similar couplings and buffer mounting blocks were provided on most goods vehicles for several years. It was probably this type of coupling that, in mid-1861, caused complaints about couplings having got loose from their hooks and having torn up the tie rods of points at Havant and other places. As a result, Mr Beattie was requested to consider the best means of securing them!

An interesting statement was made during the Royal Commission into railway accidents in 1877, when a London & North Western Railway foreman shunter was invited to comment on wagon couplings that he experienced. He gave his opinion that three long links were best, adding that LSWR ones were very heavy, and that the very large buffers (presumably meaning long) on those wagons made matters worse.

The other wagon type (shown here as figure 1.3) is a trifle problematic. The Metropolitan drawing is dated December 1863, and is clearly marked "L&SW", but it is surprisingly different from the previous one in practically all respects. Seemingly of a much weaker construction, there was no crib rail and the floor planks ran right to the outside where they were rounded off. The sides and ends stood on the floor, only being supported by the end pillars and the pillars on either side of the doors. 150, presumably of the earlier type, had been ordered from Wright's in October and November 1862. Another 200 were needed in early 1863, and the £54 10s tender of the Railway Carriage Co of Oldbury was accepted. Then, when another 100 were wanted in November 1863, the Oldbury company's revised tender of £56 10s was accepted. In July 1864, the Oldbury company wanted to increase the price by another £2, but Metropolitan offered to build them at the Oldbury company's former price and got the order. It might be that the present drawing actually originated from the Oldbury version. Certainly some wagons to this drawing were supplied to the Great Eastern Railway, but it is not clear which firm built them.

Both of the types just described were probably intended to carry 6 tons, judging from the 1870 stock list, but the next version (figure 1.4) was built to carry 8 tons. The prices now quoted jumped considerably to £98 12s 6d, although outwardly the wagons looked very similar to the pre-1862 ones, apart from a few inches increase in size and with larger axle journals for the increased load. The outside length and breadth of 15ft 4in by 7ft 6in virtually became the LSWR standard for open wagons from then on.

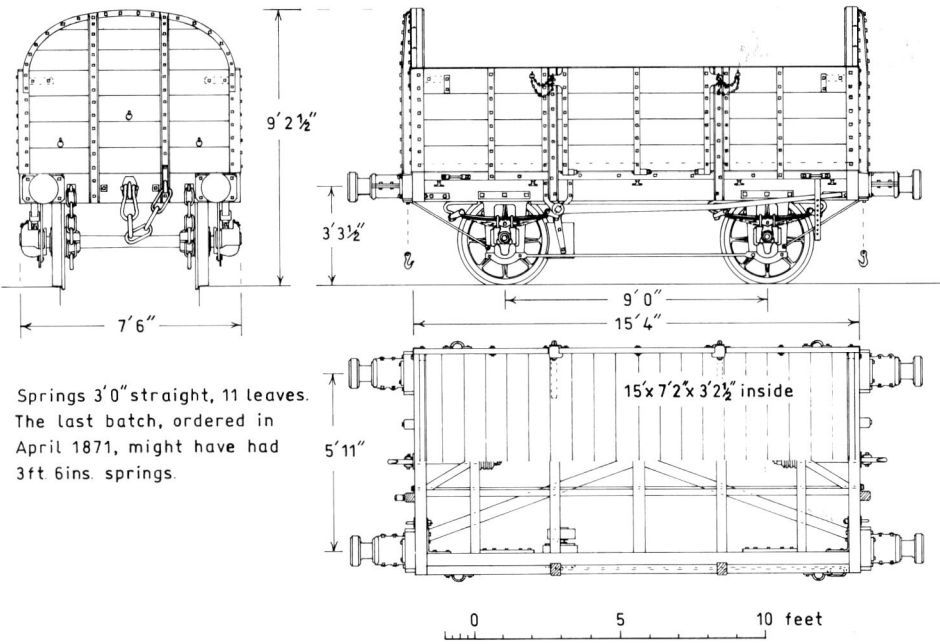

Figure 1.4. 8-ton goods wagon of 1865.

The first batch was of 200 ordered from the Railway Carriage Co in November 1865. These were followed by 100 ordered from Metropolitan in October 1868, and another 50 from them in December 1869. The Oldbury company got another order for 100 a year later, and Metropolitan got a further order for 50 in April 1871 at the reduced price of £90 each, but the works drawing had a written note that for this order the springs were to be 3ft 6in long instead of the 3ft of the earlier orders (and as shown here). However, there is another Metropolitan drawing dated May 1871 showing the earlier springs, so there is some doubt over this detail.

The next design, referred to once again as Mr Beattie's design, but now presumably meaning Mr WG Beattie, was placed with Metropolitan in October 1872 with an order for 200. As will be seen from figure 1.5, this was very similar to the earlier ones, but with diagonal strapping to the sides lapping round on to the ends, which probably added greatly to the support of them, axleguards in the so-called W shape and more compact buffer units. Once again, they were to carry 8 tons. On the earlier wagons, the drawbars pulled against the crossbeams through rubber pads, so that the pull was carried through the underframe. In this design, the two drawbars were connected together by a rod, making it effectively a continuous drawbar, so that the underframe was not subjected to any load from the vehicles behind it. Of course this drawbar had to move so as to permit the springing through the rubber pads, and for this, the coupling hooks did not seat directly against the washer plates on the headstocks, but had about a couple of inches clearance.

It is one of these wagons that appears in plate 1.5, apparently in virtually new condition, in Tonbridge (SER) yard in the 1870s. The lettering in the door panels can just be seen as L&SWRC° to the left and the number 63 to the right. The lightness of the grey paint and the black of the ironwork are apparent. Compare the high ends of the LSWR wagon with the even higher ends of the SER wagons in view. The colour of the latter, incidentally, was a fairly light red but this has shown up much darker than the LSWR grey. Another of the same type is shown in later condition as plate 17 in *Southern Wagons Volume 1*.

100 more were ordered from Metropolitan at the end of 1874, and as in previous repeat order cases, the drawings were marked for slight alterations of half an inch or so here and there, none of them appreciably affecting the appearance or performance of the vehicle, so one must wonder why they bothered.

It must be noted that throughout this period, batches of wagons were being ordered from various different builders, but because of the statements in two or three places that the vehicles were to be to Mr Beattie's design (both Joseph and William), it seems fair to assume that the bought ones, at least, were similar to those depicted here, whichever builder they came from.

Plate 1.5. Third from left is LSWR 8-ton wagon of 1872 in very new condition at Tonbridge (SER). (Tonbridge Historical Society)

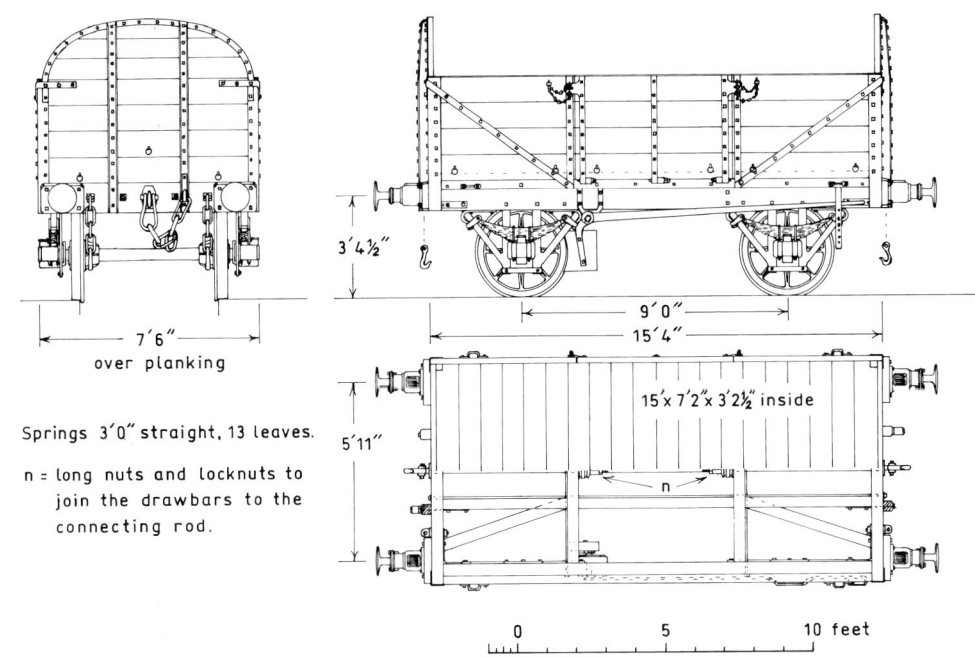

Figure 1.5. 8-ton goods wagon of 1872.

GOODS VEHICLES

There were also several references during this period to the shortages of wagons and to the LSWR having to hire from various companies, largely from Metropolitan and the Lancaster Wagon companies, such as 50 from Metropolitan for £5 5s per month in April 1870, another 50 from somewhere in the November, 50 more 8-tonners from Metropolitan in October 1872, and a further 10 from them in September 1874. Another 100 were hired from the Lancaster company in October 1876, followed by a batch of 50 from the Birmingham Wagon Co in March 1877.

In 1880, it was decided to end hiring, and to build any new requirements at Nine Elms. Despite this, further hirings had to take place until it was stated that none were still on hire in January 1886. This was not the end of hiring, of which more will be mentioned later.

Going back to the 1870s, there were also occasional mentions of orders for coal wagons. One of these orders is interesting, because in July 1874, the Traffic and Locomotive Committee recommended the purchase of 200 additional coal wagons, but at their next meeting it was stated that the Officers' Committee had recommended that they should be goods wagons and not coal wagons, so there clearly was a difference. The 1872 report shows open wagons having 3ft 2½in or 2ft 10½in sides, while on coal wagons they were 2ft 4in or 2ft 0in. Presumably, coal wagons would not have high raised ends, but unless some old photographs turn up showing the loads, we can only guess! It might or might not be relevant that on the South Eastern Railway, coal wagons had 4ft wide side doors as compared with ones 5ft wide on ordinary merchandise wagons, and that this difference was maintained until around 1905.

Next there are some slight puzzles, because in April 1876, an order was placed with the Midland Carriage and Wagon Co for "fifty long goods wagons", but there is no further evidence as to their actual dimensions or appearance. Then, in March 1877, it was decided to buy "fifty or sixty 10-ton wagons", followed three weeks later by a decision to buy 75 wagons from the Birmingham Carriage & Wagon Co, these having spring buffers, as already mentioned.

Shortly afterwards, in April, Metropolitan's tender was accepted for 100 open wagons. Their drawing, which also bears a barely decipherable LSWR drawing number that fits in neatly with the date of 1877, shows a 10-ton wagon but regrettably without any buffers! For the purpose of figure 1.6, it is assumed that they were the same as on a cattle wagon of about the same date. The length and width were the same as before, but the internal and overall heights were reduced. This might seem odd with an increased load capacity, but the main point here was the increased size of the axle journals from 7in x 3½in to 9in x 3½in. The overall height was slightly reduced, and the curvature of the ends simplified from three to two radii. Perhaps rather surprisingly, the continuous drawbar idea was dropped, reliance for load transfer being placed on tie rods between the crossbeams. A little later Metropolitan recorded another order but the date and quantity is not clear.

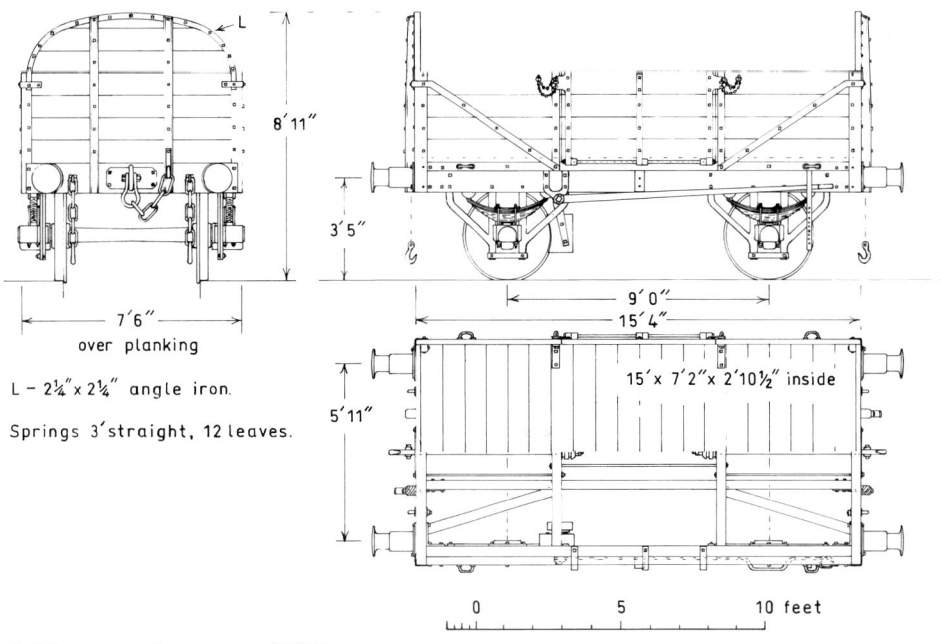

Figure 1.6. 10-ton goods wagon of 1877.

A special report on rolling stock in November 1878 states that in the previous ten years, 1037 8-ton wagons had been built, and a similar number of 6 ton ones had been broken up. This report was presented by William Adams, who had been appointed Locomotive and Carriage Superintendent (which included responsibility for goods stock) in January 1878, but it is evident from the minutes that improvement of the locomotive and carriage stock had a higher priority than making any changes between the wagons, so it is probable that the order for 100 round end wagons from Cravens in October 1878 for £50 each was of the same type as those just mentioned.

The next order went to the Birmingham Carriage & Wagon Co for 300 at £63 each in February 1880, after the General Manager had reported that the company was hiring 480 goods vehicles, and recommended that this practice should end by the end of June. These 300 were part of the ensuing order for replacement vehicles.

The increased price might suggest that these were to the new design for 10-ton open wagons that was published in the *Railway Engineer* for June 1881, shown here as figure 1.7. Once again, the sides were slightly lower than on the 1877 version, but more obviously, the ends were again lower and shaped on two radii. The axle journals were also slightly larger at 9in x 4in. Although the length outside the end planking was still 15ft 4in the length of the side was 15ft 10¼in. This was because the corner reinforcing posts were placed outside instead of inside the ends. This, together with the arrangement of the iron reinforcing knees either side of the door openings so that the vertical limb was outside the planking, meant that the interior was entirely clear of any obstructions. The solebars were strengthened by having ⅜in steel flitch plates bolted on the outside.

For the first time (so far as can be established) a tarpaulin bar was provided. This consisted of a length of timber, 3½in thick by 3in wide, with a metal tongue at each end that fitted into sockets on the outside of the end planking. Retaining chains were fitted so that the bar could be lifted off and laid along the top of one of the sides during loading.

Although the axleboxes look, at first glance, like those fitted after about 1906, they were different in that the boss and bolt on the right side was noticeably larger than that on the left. More unusual is that while the front cover sloped outwards from top to bottom, it was also angled in plan view, the right side being nearer to the wheel than the left. There is no very obvious reason for these peculiarities. One other unusual feature is the retaining ring on the open-spoke wheels, similar to those fitted on Mansell wheels.

By November 1880, Mr Scott reported that although 460 hired wagons had been given up, he had still been compelled to rehire 100 from Metropolitan for one year at £7 each. Then again, in the following March, he reported the hire of another 50, and so the Traffic Committee recommended that 100 should be either bought or built. Presumably, they were, but this cannot be confirmed. Anyway, the subject came up again in October when he was authorised by the Traffic Committee to hire another 100 8-ton wagons from the Lancaster Wagon Co for £8 each.

All ordinary open wagon designs after 1881 have been described and illustrated in *Southern Wagons, Volume 1*, and will not be repeated here, but some notes might be of interest.

In February 1882, Mr Adams reported on 100 second-hand wagons that had been offered by the Birmingham Wagon and Carriage Co. He stated that, although they were in fair condition, there were many differences from the South Western vehicles, and so the maintenance costs would be high. He added that an order for 100 standard type 10-ton wagons was being prepared. This materialised when the Traffic Committee approved an order for 100 "high-sided open wagons" in the following July.

The 1880/81 wagon design included a wooden tarpaulin bar, but in May 1895, the Locomotive and Stores Committee approved the adoption of Mr Williams' patent supports for goods wagon sheets, and it was noted that the rights to make and install them could be purchased for £250. This type of bar can be clearly seen in many photos of LSWR open wagons from this period onwards, particularly in the book *Southern Wagons Volume 1*.

Following the approval in December 1885 for the construction of 500 additional wagons at Nine Elms, Mr Panter obtained the authority of the Locomotive and Stores Committee in the following February to build some of them of oak and to fit them with laminated steel springs, at an estimated saving of £6 per wagon. The use of oak to help reduce the cost seems a little strange today, but the use of the fairly new steel springs can be seen in the reduced number of plates for the same, and in increased loads.

It was at a meeting of the Locomotive and Stores Committee in May 1892, that it was agreed to order 100 sets of pressed-steel wagon underframes as a trial from Leeds Forge Co. They were to be to LSWR dimensions, and to cost £17 a set. They proved satisfactory, and a year later, another 500 sets were ordered. From then on, many more were

GOODS VEHICLES

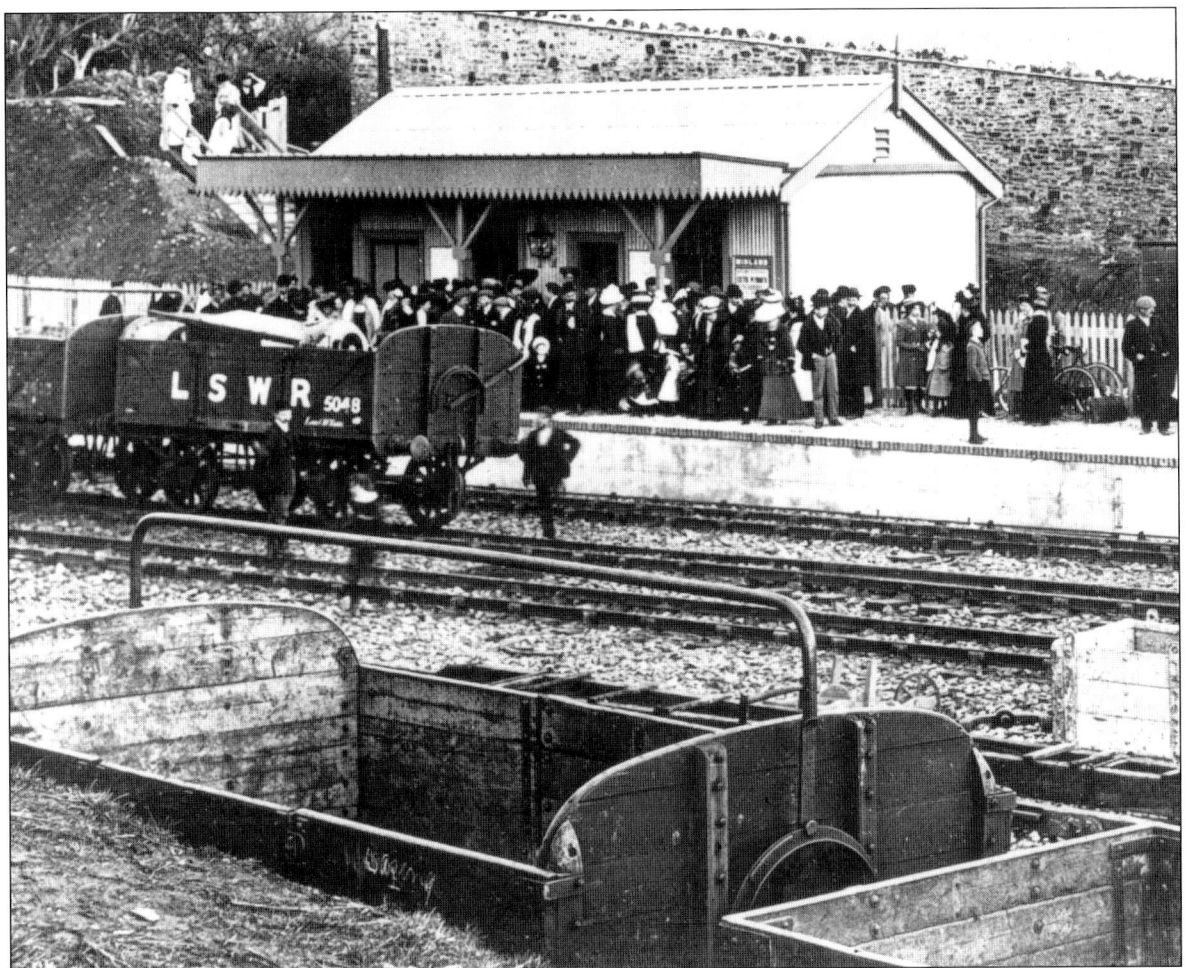

Plate 1.7. 10-ton wagon of 1881 showing side support pillars outside the ends. The original timber sheet rail has been replaced with the Williams pattern.

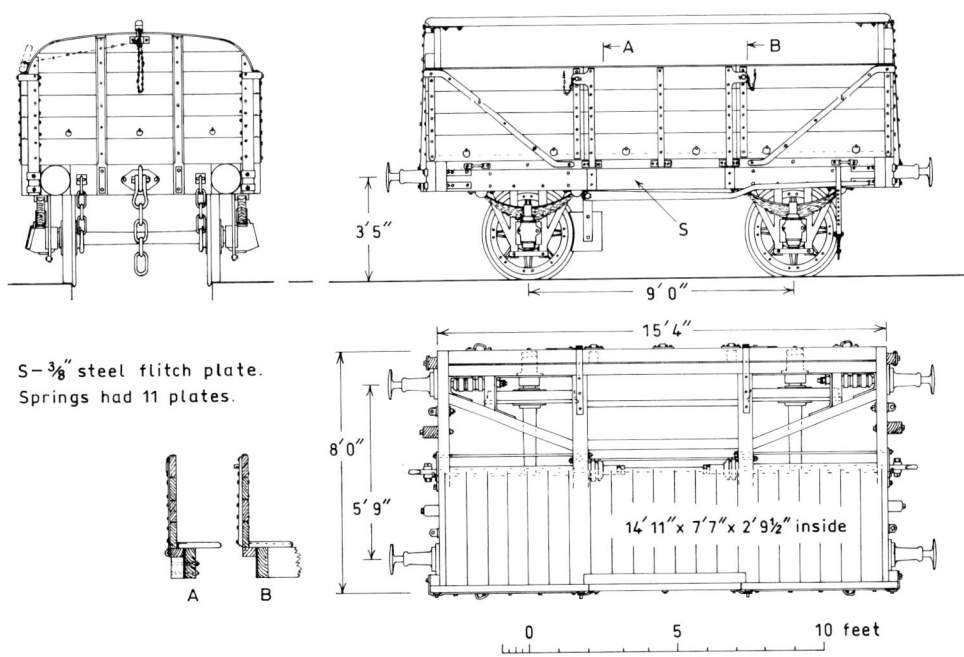

Figure 1.7. 10-ton goods wagon of c.1881.

ordered, and several vehicle types were built in both steel and wooden underframed versions.

The LSWR did not go in for many bogie goods vehicles. With one exception, the only ones were for the use of the Signal and Permanent Way departments. The latter had two types, one primarily intended for the carriage of rails and the other as ballast hopper wagons. Both are illustrated in *Southern Wagons, Volume 1*. The solitary wagon for the Signal Department was authorised at the end of October 1898 as a special wagon about 36ft long for "the carriage of signals, point lockbars and other parts". In the event it was built as a two-plank wagon, 34ft 6in long, with a small covered well near the centre. It was given the Traffic Department number 11813, but at some unknown later date, it was transferred to the Engineering Department and renumbered 46. It is shown here as figure 1.8. The purpose of the well is not entirely clear, particularly since it appears from the works drawing to have been partially obstructed by longitudinal frame members and tie rods. Unfortunately no photographs are available to confirm the details of this wagon.

Shortly after this, in 1899, a solitary open goods wagon of the same length, using the same type of bogie, was built. There is no reference to this in the minutes, and one might imagine that it was in the nature of an experiment and built under one of the block renewal orders, such as that of November 1898 for 400 long goods wagons. Whereas the Signal Department wagon was built on the normal wagon principle of having crib rails outside the solebars to carry the sides, this one had the solebars at the full width with the five side planks directly on top of them. Rounded ends and a tarpaulin rail were provided as in many other LSWR open wagons. Mr Panter's cross-lever handbrake was fitted, working on one wheel-set of one bogie. This wagon was numbered 12213, but clearly did not find favour with the Goods Department as no more were built. Here it is shown as figure 1.9.

Another type of open wagon that was literally a very open one was the platform truck. The first to be mentioned was in the minutes of the Locomotive Committee for 5th January 1854, when a letter from Mr Hedger was read requesting the provision of a 12-ton wagon for the conveyance of screw propellers and large and heavy machinery for the steamships at Southampton. Mr Beattie was instructed to prepare plans for two. These plans were approved at the next meeting, but no details have survived. The next reference was in the half-year report of January 1876, when it was stated that one platform truck had been delivered by contractors.

There was an LSWR drawing dated 26th April 1877 (shown here as figure 1.10) of a vehicle obviously designed to carry heavy loads, though no load figure is shown. Whether it was an LSWR copy of the contractor's drawing for the 1876 vehicle, or it was prepared in advance of discussions next mentioned is not at all certain, although from its construction, the latter seems the most probable. A meeting of the Locomotive Committee in May 1878 noted a letter from Mr Mills (possibly of the Goods Department) about the need for a 20-ton wagon for the conveyance of heavy pieces of machinery on the line. Mr Adams was instructed to consult with Mr Mills and to make arrangements to obtain the most suitable class of truck.

Only the headstocks and solebars were made of wood, and in all cases these were clad on both sides with $^5/_{16}$-inch plating. All the transverse beams were made of channel section reinforced with plating. Additional angle irons were placed either

Plate 1.9. 34ft 6in open goods wagon of 1899. (MS King collection)

GOODS VEHICLES

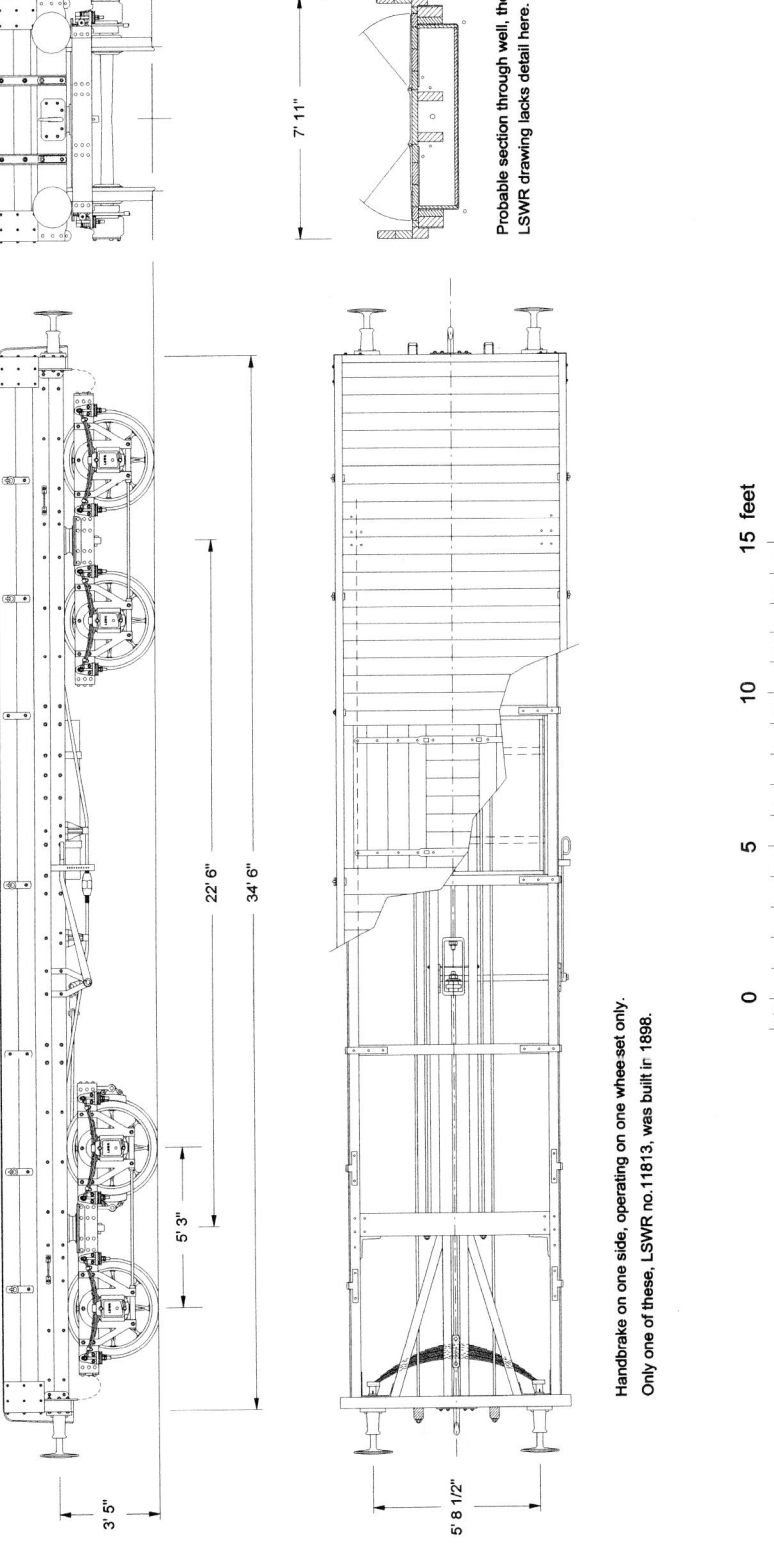

Figure 1.8. 34ft 6in wagon for Signal Department of 1898.

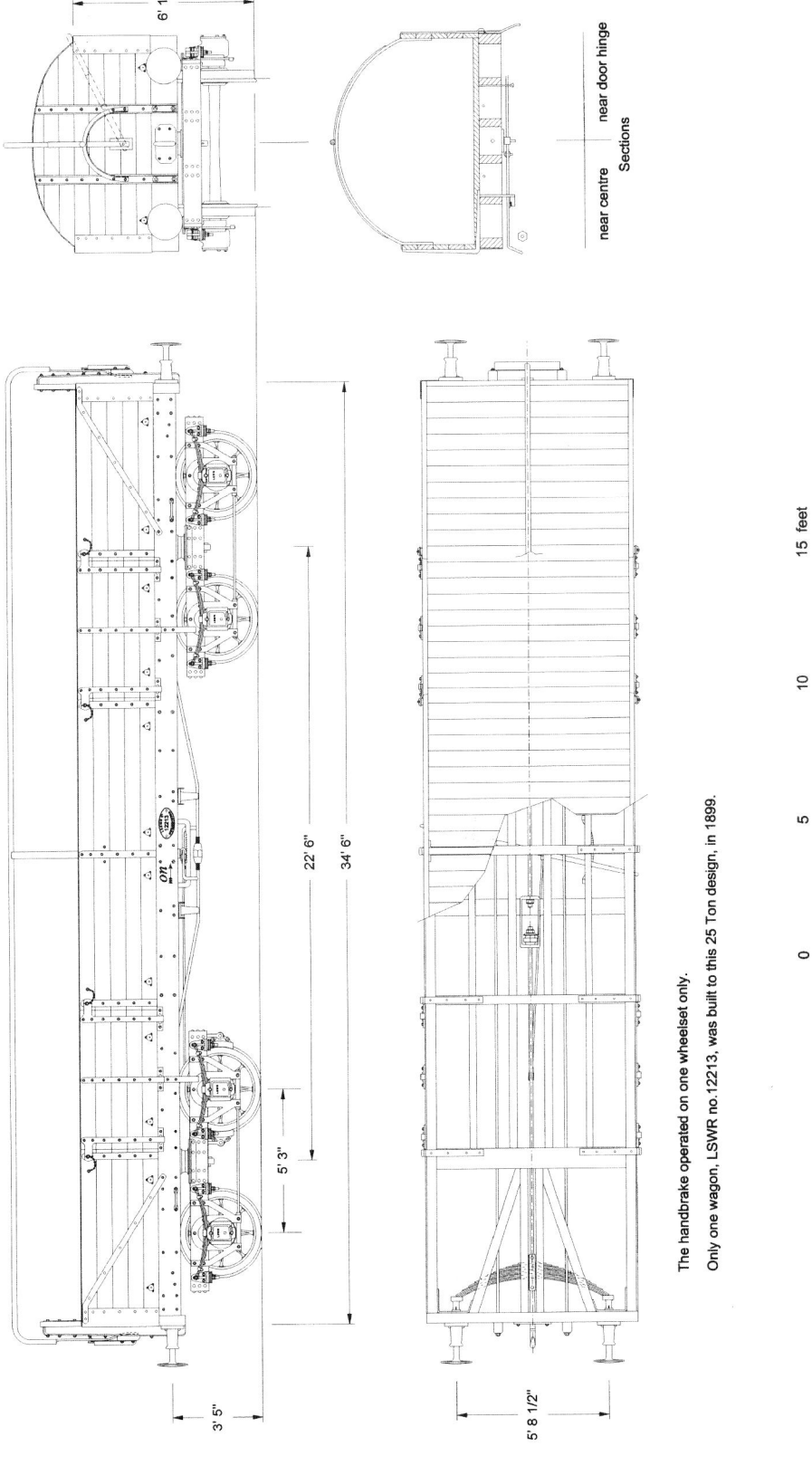

Figure 1.9. 34ft 6in open goods wagon of 1899.

GOODS VEHICLES

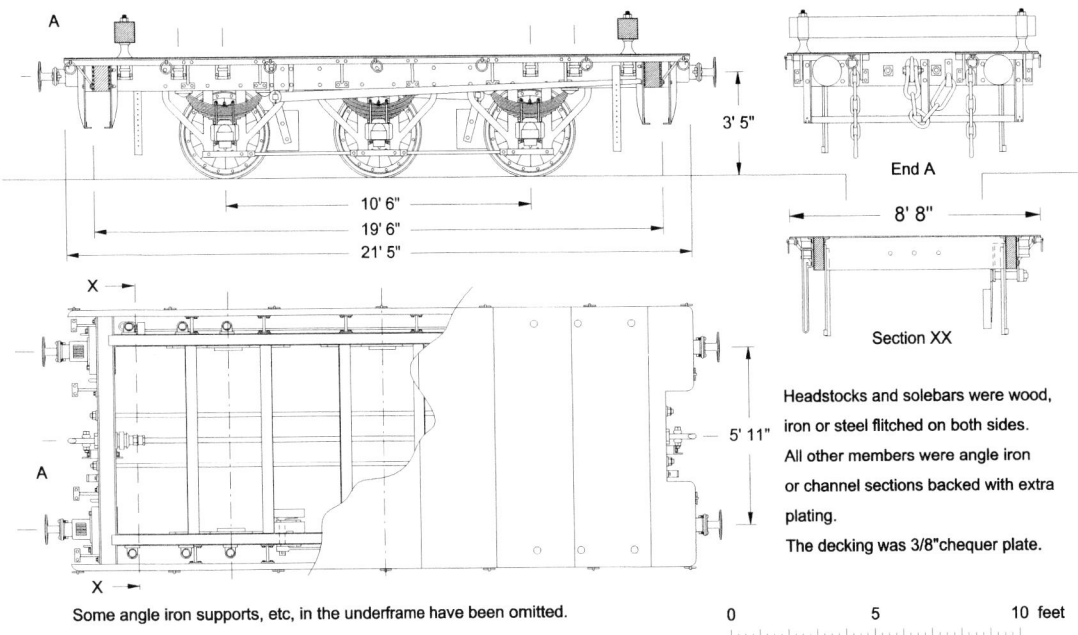

Figure 1.10. 21ft 5in platform truck of c.1877.

side of the solebars, outside the headstocks, and at the deck edges. The overhang of the deck at the ends and sides was supported by brackets. The width of the deck made it one of the widest LSWR goods vehicles at 8ft 8in, or 8ft 10½in over the securing ring brackets. The deck itself was of ⅜inch chequer plate. The two beams that, on a carriage truck, would be called the wheel bars, were also wooden and plated all round with ³/₁₆-inch iron or steel, presumably for protection against chains or wires. When not required, these bars could be housed on brackets underneath the frame.

The next recorded appearance of such vehicles was in LSWR drawings 412 and 414 of October 1893, allied to a minute of the Locomotive and Stores Committee of that month ordering that 50 wagons be built, from old materials where possible, and at an estimated cost of £25 each, for transfer purposes in Southampton Docks. The former drawing shows one in fair detail, and it is drawn here as figure 1.11. The other drawing is really three sketches entitled "Diagrams of wagons without sides and ends". They all appear to have been created using old underframes, or parts from old underframes, as authorised. The one shown here appears to have used parts of a 15ft 4in wagon underframe, although the headstocks might even have been from an old carriage. The buffers are of the c.1877 pattern (as is the brake) and the axleguards and axleboxes are 1880/90s style. A decking of 2½-inch planks was laid on the frame, overhanging it by one inch at each side and each end. The drawing gives no indication of any means of securing the load by ropes, for example.

A similar authority was issued in December 1899 by the Locomotive, Carriage and Stores Committee for 100 extra wagons to be built for Southampton Docks only. Drawing No 918 was prepared, titled "Wagon for Southampton Docks". These are mentioned in *Southern Wagons Volume 1,* but not illustrated, so they are shown here as figure 1.12. Although the LSWR numbered them 12494 to 12593, it is not at all certain that as many as 100 were built to this design, though 67 to drawing 918 were recorded in 1922, and many of this general description survived to be shown as Southern Railway diagram 1303. It is quite likely, however, that as had happened before, the opportunity was taken to transfer some older or damaged wagons to the docks department, and to build new ones to a current design to replace them in the traffic department.

Drawing 918 shows every indication of using recovered materials from earlier wagons, so there may well have been differences between wagons according to what was available. The journals are quoted as 7in x 3½in at 6ft 6in centres, suggesting that use was intended to be made of wheel-sets taken from the 8-ton wagons built in 1872 (shown as figure 1.5) whilst the buffers and drawbars appear to

LSWR CARRIAGES VOLUME 4

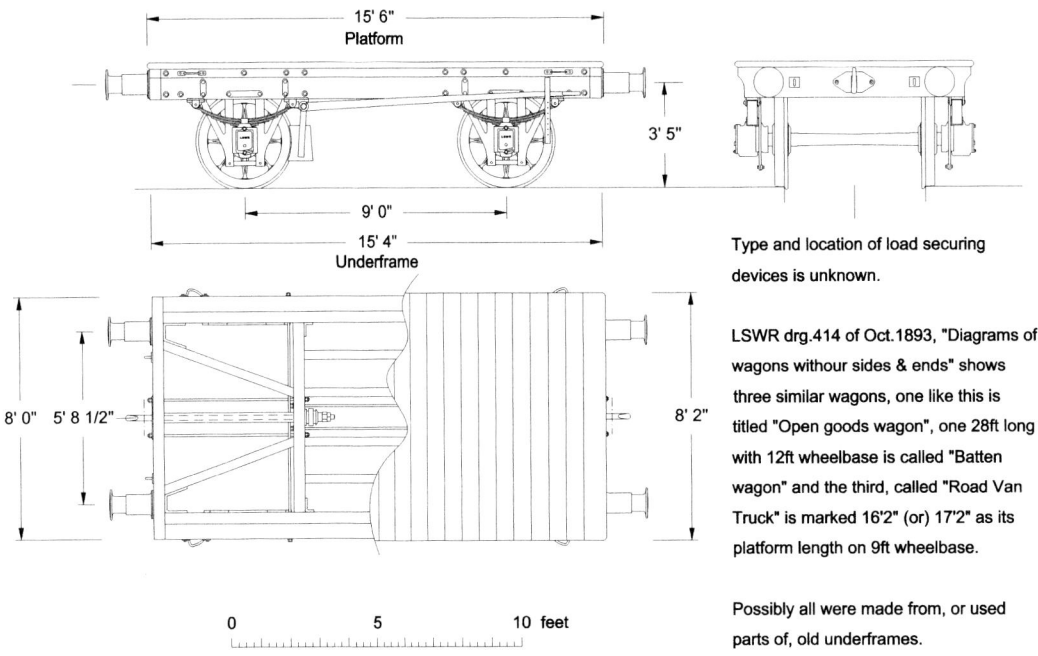

Figure 1.11. 15ft 6in platform truck of 1893.

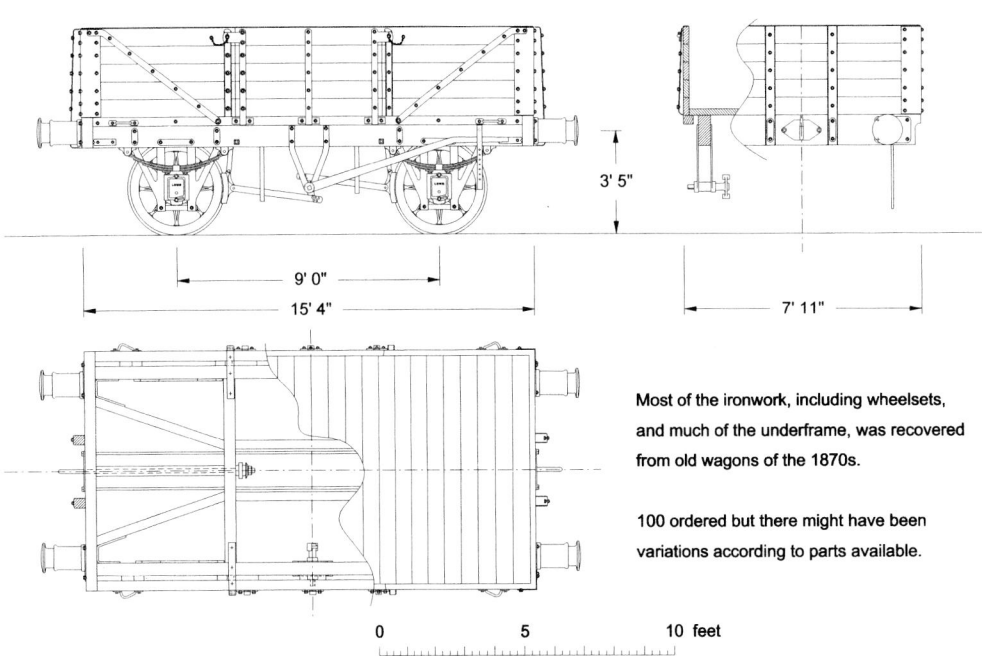

Figure 1.12. 15ft 4in wagon for Southampton Docks of 1900.

GOODS VEHICLES

be of the 1877 variety. The springs and axleboxes appear to date from around 1890.

As a note for model makers, the Appendix to the Working Time Table (WTT) for January 1892 states that:

"Wagons loaded with wool, hops, hay, straw, hemp, flax, and other bulky goods (also empty packages liable to take fire) must be thoroughly covered to protect them from wet and fire. When two sheets are used, the first sheet must overlap the other. Wagons loaded with hay, straw, or other inflammable material must be attached next in front of rear brake of train, and when at stations must be kept as far as possible from main line and station buildings."

"Open wagons must be cleared of loose straw, sawdust, &c. when they are unloaded."

"Wagons loaded with engines, anchors, boilers, armour plates, long timber, steam ploughs, rails, ironstone, coal, or heavy machinery, or other articles exceptionally heavy or lengthy; and boiler wagons, whether empty or loaded, must not be conveyed by fast or through goods trains. Through coal trains may be used."

Implying the continued existence of dumb-buffered wagons is another instruction:

"Mixed goods and passenger trains – No Goods or Cattle Wagons, except they have spring buffers, must in future be attached to Passenger Trains, and must be restricted as far as possible. In the case of Trains shown to the Public as Goods and Passenger Trains, the number of Goods Wagons on these Trains should not exceed 35 in addition to the Passenger Carriages."

Van Trucks

In Chapter 4 of *LSWR Carriages, Volume 3*, it was stated that open carriage trucks were among the earliest vehicles built for the line. These were intended for private road vehicles of the gentry, but as early as August 1839, it was agreed to build six trucks to carry heavier road vehicles, presumably mainly the Post Office Mail coaches, but possibly also some types of goods vehicles.

The next recorded order was for ten such trucks in August 1856, and then in June 1862, it was agreed to order from Joseph Wright 20 additional van trucks for the conveyance of road vans and agricultural implements. No drawings of these have survived, but figure 1.13a illustrates a 16ft van truck, of which a batch of twenty was built by the Metropolitan Co in late 1876. Although no details of the preceding batch have come to light, it will be noted that the 1876 dimensions tally with the listing of vehicles in October 1870, so presumably they were very similar. These earlier ones, of which there were 20, were rated to carry 6 tons, to run at

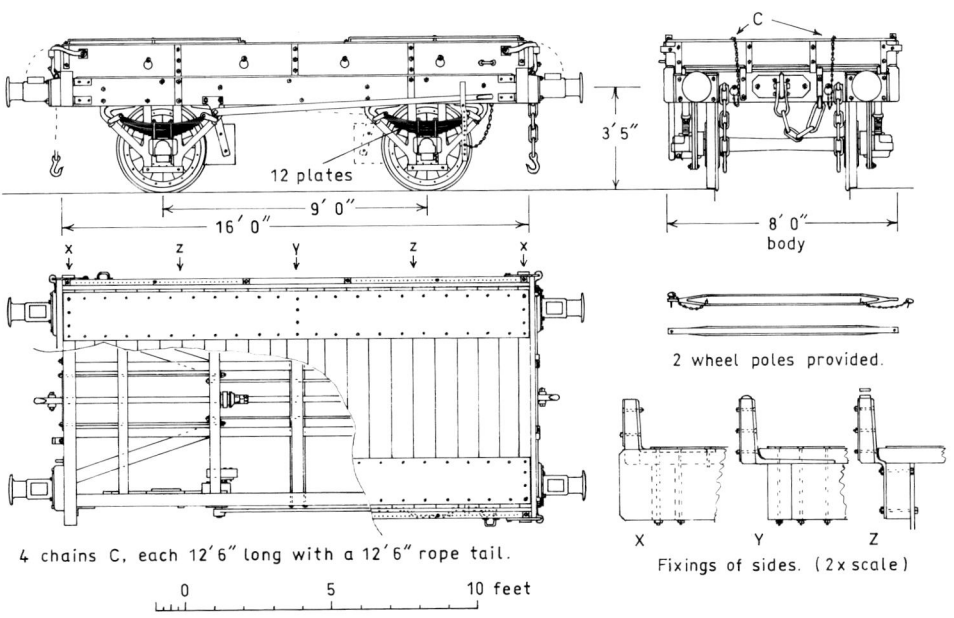

Figure 1.13a. 16ft road van truck of 1876.

the common maximum speed of 20 mph, and with their capacity noted as "large furniture vans".

There is a slight oddity about the sequence of events, in that the order for 20 was placed on 26th September 1876, with a stipulated delivery date of 28th November, the Metropolitan drawing was dated 26th October 1876, and included the LSWR drawing number 2230. However, the Nine Elms drawing 2230 had rather more details on it, but was dated 9th December 1876. Once again, it raises the question of who actually designed the vehicle.

Van trucks came up again in January 1883, when it was decided to order 25 more "precisely the same as the last van trucks". It seems a little unlikely that there was a fresh design within the preceding seven years, so these were probably also intended to be to LSWR drawing 2230. In the event, the contract went to the Midland Carriage and Wagon Co on their tender which, although for £64 12s each as compared with Metropolitan's offer of £60 5s each, promised quicker delivery by the next 13th November.

The next record of an order is for 25 in March 1892. For some years the LSWR had again been building most of its own vehicles, first at Nine Elms and then at the new Eastleigh Works. There is a drawing marked "No 45W" and "Copy drawing no 6267" signed by Mr Panter, dated Jan 28th 1890, showing a 16ft road van truck to load 10 tons. The LSWR diagram book of 1922 shows 58 of these surviving to December 1922, but described as being to drawing 262 – which is not available. The diagram looks just like the above-mentioned drawing, and on the assumption that they were effectively the same thing, figure 1.13b is shown here. (This drawing came to light at a late stage before submission to the publisher, so the figure had to be numbered in this way to avoid a wholesale renumbering of figures, plates and text right through this chapter.)

After that order in 1892, all further references in the minutes were to "long" van trucks for meat vans, illustrated in figure 39 of *Southern Wagons, Volume 1*. The first was in November of that year when the General Manager brought up the need for more meat vans to cater for the American traffic that was expected to result from the transfer of the Inman Line's ships to Southampton. As well as recommending the construction of 50 ordinary railway meat vans with AVB (also covered in *Southern Wagons, Volume 1*) he also recommended building 50 vans "of similar construction to the Company's ordinary road vans, but of different dimensions and interior arrangements ... and

Plate 1.13. Army exercises with a 4.7in gun and limber at Lydd Camp, using an LSWR 16ft road van truck. (Author's collection)

GOODS VEHICLES

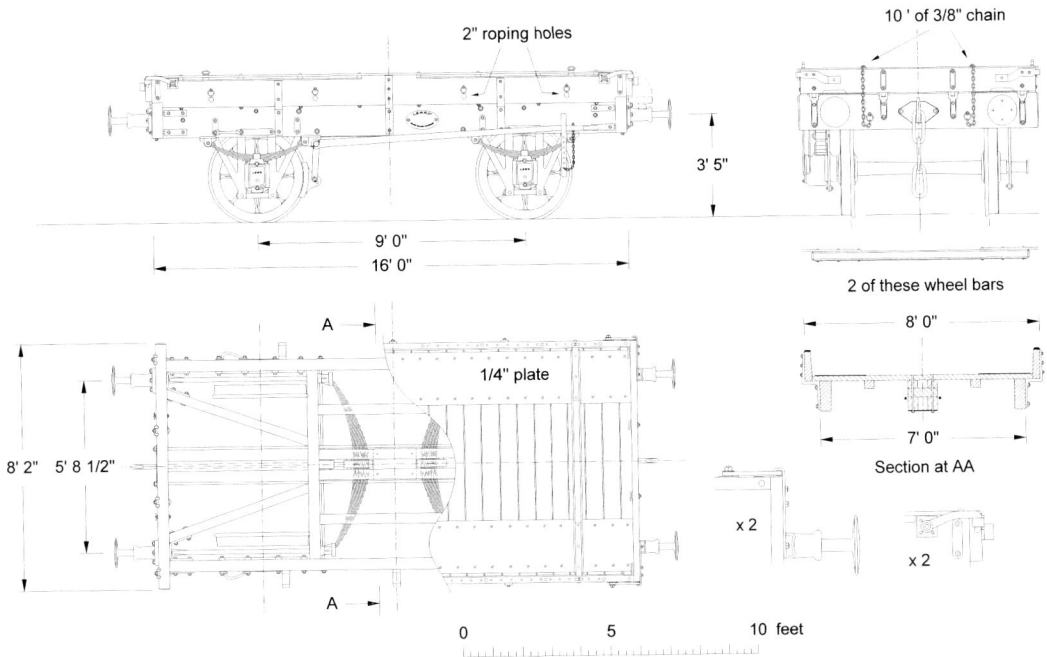

Figure 1.13b. 16ft 10-ton road van truck of c.1890.

fourteen long van trucks capable of holding two vans". We shall return to the road meat vans in Chapter 4.

Despite the lack of references in the minutes, those 28ft road van trucks (RVTs) were certainly not the only ones to be either designed or built after 1892; more 17ft and 18ft ones were certainly built at various dates. The 58 17ft RVTs (figure 1.14) that survived to the Grouping appear in the SR records with building dates between 1893 and 1901. However, their drawing is number 970 which, though undated, would seem to fit in at about 1900, implying that they were built by the workshops as renewals, and only graced with a drawing at a later

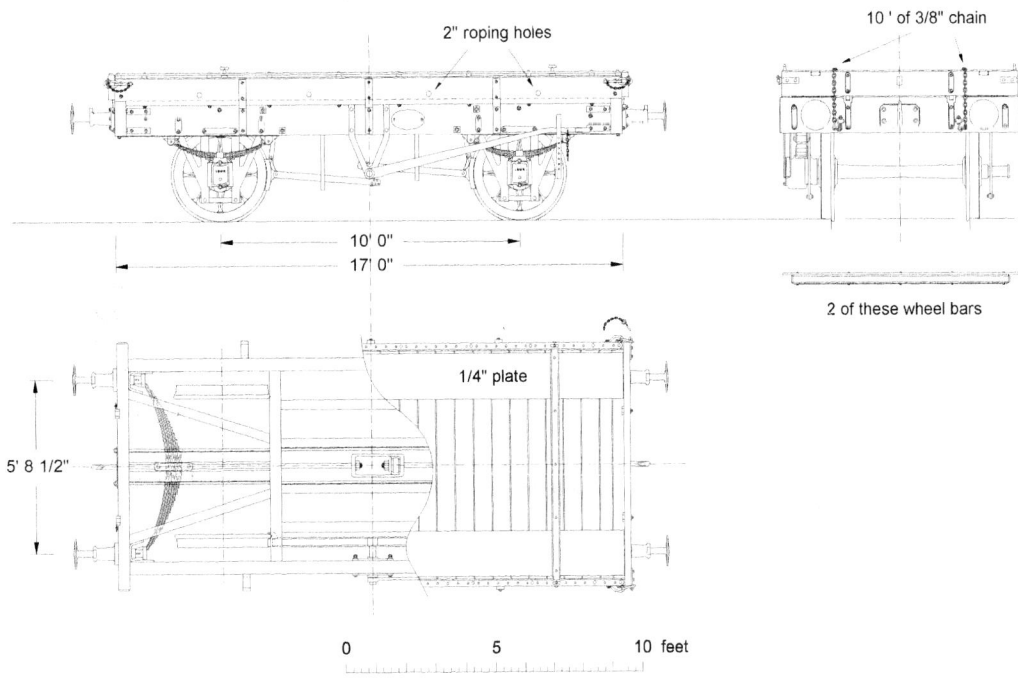

Figure 1.14. 17ft road van truck of c.1900.

Plate 1.14. T9 No 724, Exeter–Plymouth leaving Okehampton in September 1923. In the foreground are various road vehicle trucks and an open carriage truck with wheelbars and chains lying around. (LCGB/Ken Nunn collection)

stage. As before, they were on wooden underframes, whereas the next type was built on pressed-steel underframe members.

The 18ft RVTs were built to LSWR drawing 1124, which was issued around 1902, and by the Grouping there were 36 of them in existence. They were much like the previous RVTs in general form, but with the main difference that they were built on steel underframes (see figure 1.15). Apart from their length, these underframes were practically identical to those used for open and covered wagons at this period. The sides, falling ends and floor were made of timber, and in common with the earlier RVTs, in place of the open sides of open carriage trucks, these had solid sides with four holes, well smoothed at the edges, for use with securing ropes. The two ringbolts at each end both had 10 feet of ⅜in chain terminating with 12 feet of ¾in diameter rope to secure the load. The ends were again gouged out to allow them to clear the buffer castings, and provide a level run for vehicles, and the floorboards were spaced ⅜in apart to permit drainage. A double-block handbrake was provided on one side only.

Covered Vans

The rather conjectural origin of covered or closed vans was indicated earlier, but the first specific mention of building closed wagons is in a minute of 14th March 1851, when the Commercial and Traffic Committee agreed to a recommendation of the Officers' Committee that ten closed trucks, costing less than £100 each, should be built for the safe conveyance of specie. Mr Beattie was asked to prepare a scheme for converting some of the existing wagons, but it is not stated whether this was carried out. The logical extension of this idea followed that August, when the same committee approved the construction of 250 wagons, 180 being closed for £85 each, together with 40 cattle wagons and 30 timber trucks. Most of these were to be built by W Beattie at Liverpool, but it was agreed that Joseph Beattie should build 50 of the closed wagons at Nine Elms. In fact, William Beattie's tender was not the lowest, but he offered the best deliveries and was supported by a testimonial from Mr Henson of the LNWR. This latter point might be significant in connection with the design of these wagons. Shortly after this, William Beattie died, and although efforts were made by his son John Beattie to fulfil the orders, it looks as though most of those for the South Western ended up being built at Nine Elms.

At the General Meeting in February 1853, the Chairman reported that covered wagons had been brought into use to reduce the expenditure on tarpaulins.

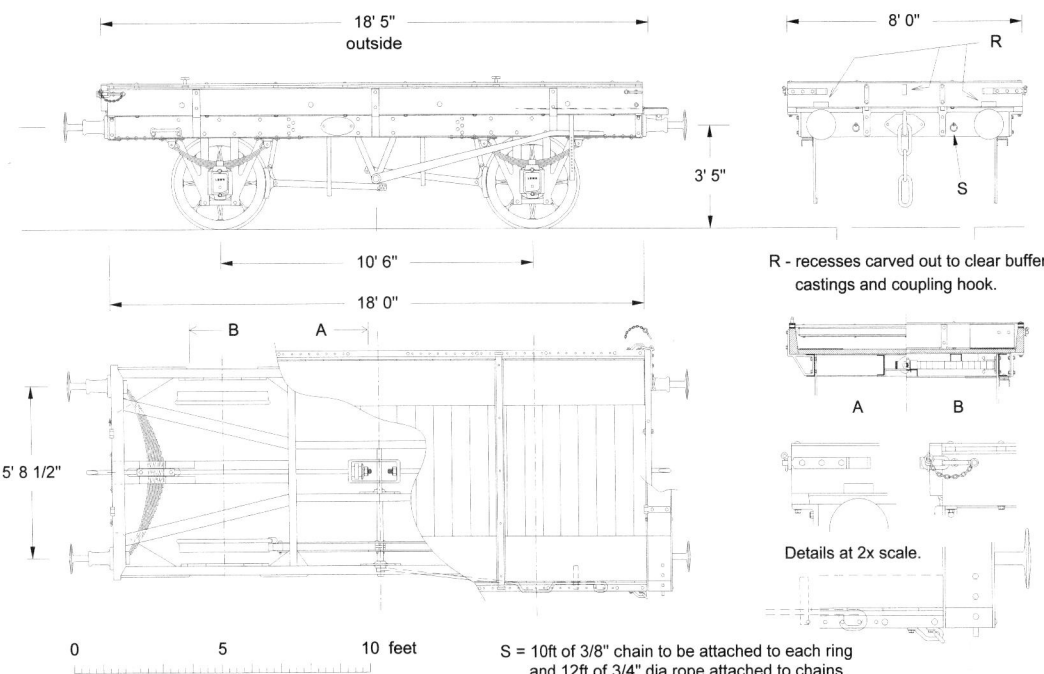

Figure 1.15. 18ft road van truck of 1902.

It is not clear just when covered vans with sliding hatches in the roof were first ordered although on 1st July 1858, an order was approved for the purchase of 100 "covered wagons with slides", with the remark that Mr Beattie and Mr Scott should discuss the form of construction. As usual, there is no evidence of the result of that discussion, but sliding roof hatches were certainly already in use because an instruction to Station Agents at an unknown date prior to May 1858 stated:

"Goods Wagons – These sustain damage at stations by porters leaving the roof and side doors open. They are also damaged by improper opening and shutting of the doors of box or covered wagons. The top slide should remain partly open and clear of the doors until they are secured, when the top slide should be pulled down upon them. Also, the top slide should be pushed back before any attempt is made to open the doors."

A later notice of 10th May 1866 stated:

"Station agents are instructed not to permit loading of livestock into box wagons as when the roof slide is left open the doors become insecure. Box wagons ought never to be placed in trains without the roof slide being closed and the doors securely fastened. These wagons are not adapted for conveyance of livestock. Signed Archibald Scott."

It may well be that the corrugated iron van seen here at plate 1.34 (part A) is one of the 1858 variety, and the photo at plate 1.39 might be of similar but later type since, from the little that can be seen of the former, the second looks to be slightly longer. They are both built on the style of early carriages, apparently having double solebars with the transverse bearers extending to the outside of the body. Regrettably no dimensions are known. Another is seen distantly in plate 1.40, in this case without corrugated sheeting, and yet another in plate 1.51, which will be discussed near the end of this chapter.

In March 1861, the Locomotive Committee accepted a recommendation from the Traffic Committee that a few of the box wagons should have hooks suspended from the roof in order to hang carcases of sheep, so as to save packing them into hampers. The senders at Exeter had refused to pack the carcases into hampers except when the weather was cold!

The West India Royal Mail Company complained in early 1864 that specie was still being conveyed in wagons that were not iron lined. The Locomotive Committee then agreed that 30 additional box wagons should be lined with iron at the ends at a cost not exceeding twenty shillings per wagon. It seems strange that they should have mentioned lining just at the ends, when lining all round would appear to be more satisfactory. It should be mentioned that when this shipping company and others, as well as the Post Office, referred to the carriage of specie they did not mean just money or jewellery, but all manner of valuable goods, and in particular, consignments of precious metals and of mail to and from the rest of the world. In the Post Office records, there are copies of numerous letters to the LSWR advising them of the intention to despatch, on the following day, quantities of boxes of mail for one or another of the shipping companies, and requiring the provision of sufficient wagon accommodation. Although there is no indication of the size of these boxes, it may be assumed that 120 boxes for Australia via Southampton, for example, probably required several wagons.

The shortage of suitable wagons was reflected in a complaint from the Post Office to Mr Scott in March 1867 that "It has been represented to me that Horse Boxes are frequently used for the conveyance to Southampton of the Foreign and Colonial Mails instead of the proper Specie Wagons. As it is necessary that this practice should at once cease I shall feel obliged if you will give the matter your immediate attention. I may mention that some time back I had occasion to make a similar representation to the Company." No doubt the LSWR replied with suitable promises.

That the wagons adapted for specie, and apparently others as well, were intended to run in passenger trains is apparent from an order of the Officers' Committee in September 1869 that cord communication should be completed as soon as possible in a range of classes of vehicles, including "Specie and Box wagons". This subject is also mentioned in Chapter 1 of *LSWR Carriages Volume 3*, under Luggage Vans.

The half-year report of January 1872 recorded that 30 covered goods wagons had been received from contractors, and in January 1875 Brown Marshall's tender for building 50 covered goods wagons to Mr Beattie's design was accepted. The January 1876 half-year report showed another 35 received from contractors, but in none of these cases do we have any information about what they looked like.

A tender from the Oldbury company for the construction of 100 covered wagons was accepted by the Traffic and Locomotive Committee on 17th May 1877, and at last they can be identified. They were 15ft 4in long wagons to LSWR drawing 2295, shown here as figure 1.16. The structure, like that of the similar meat van of 1873 (described in a later section) looks relatively flimsy compared with later vans, although there were internal angle irons joining the sides and ends, also iron diagonal bracing strips inside the fixed parts of the sides like the external ones on the sliding doors. The planking and framing members of the doors were flush on the

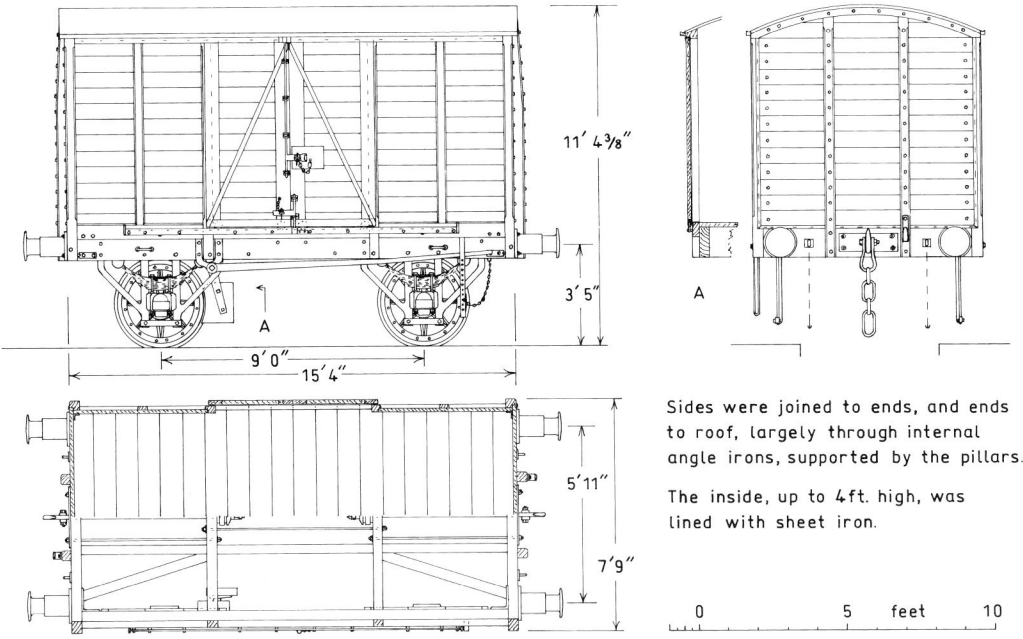

Figure 1.16. 15ft 4in covered goods wagon of 1877.

outside with the bracing strips on top. A particularly interesting detail is that the insides of the sides, ends and doors were lined with 18SWG (1.2mm) sheet iron to a height of 4 feet, presumably to make them acceptable for the carriage of specie in view of the earlier demands of the Post Office and the shipping companies.

The original of drawing 2295 has pencil sketches on it showing outside double diagonal framing, some changed dimensions, extensions to the door frames to make them roll more freely and the later form of axleguards. These sketches were clearly made in preparation for a new drawing in 1880 that appeared in *The Railway Engineer* for June 1881, described as "a covered goods wagon designed by Mr William Adams". This is reproduced as an appendix to *Southern Wagons, Volume 1*. Perhaps that claim was slightly exaggerated when it was clearly an upgrading of Mr Beattie's version.

One of the pencilled alterations that was not actually adopted was the provision of a false roof about 5½ in above the real one, carried on wooden blocks. Whether this was intended as a further means of security protection or as heat insulation in a manner similar to the false roofs applied to the "Eagle" saloons when they were converted to ambulances in Palestine during the first World War, is far from clear. Why it was even considered is one of the little unsolved mysteries.

In late 1878, an order for a further 50, presumably to the same design, was placed with the Craven company, along with several other types of goods vehicles.

The Traffic and Locomotive Committee decided to get tenders for a variety of wagons in January 1880, including fifty covered box wagons. It seems probable that the wagons described by *The Railway Engineer* in 1881, and mentioned above, were this batch, but there is no record of who built them, though it was probably Nine Elms Works.

A further 50 that were ordered to be built as replacements for a similar number of old ones that were to be broken up at the end of 1884 was probably to a new design, the drawing of which has not survived, although the evidence from the Southern Railway records suggests that it was substantially the same as the Eastleigh drawing number 264 of about 1892. This was for an 18ft van on a 10ft 6in wheelbase, with single sliding doors and double diagonal outside framing.

There were subsequently several variants of this design over the following years, and most are described and illustrated in *Southern Wagons, Volume 1*. The 1892 version is not shown; it had the old form of single brake shoe operated by a very long lever, but was otherwise like plate 46 in that book, though without any form of ventilation.

A note in the WTT for 1892 states that the following covered goods wagons were signwritten "To be returned to Southampton": numbers 1384, 1469, 1680, 3867, 4750, 5639.

One specialised use for covered wagons was the carriage of explosives. One of the early regulations of the LSWR was that gunpowder must not be conveyed on the railway under any circumstances, but there had been a few cases reported where packages containing gunpowder had been smuggled onto trains under some more innocuous description. The Traffic Manager therefore recommended, on 29th September 1853, that one of the covered vans should be converted to a powder magazine, "as it seemed impossible to avoid carrying gunpowder either openly or in disguise, and that it would therefore be better to fit a wagon for the purpose, the wagon to be painted a distinguishing colour and to be always used when powder was to be conveyed".

Recommendations of this sort in the minutes were normally confirmed unless there was some further negative minute, so presumably the van was duly converted, but there is no further mention as to the colour. Some more must have been similarly treated because in August 1868, it was decided that six of the box wagons should be converted to gunpowder vans, as those then in use were not sufficient.

In July 1879, the Traffic and Locomotive Committee ordered that eight of the new box wagons should be lined with lead to make them suitable for the carriage of Gunpowder. As before, there is no mention of any special markings.

The next reference was on 29th September 1897, when the Loco and Stores Committee noted that the Schultze Gunpowder Co would be granted a licence to place a gunpowder factory at Redbridge. Although not commented on, this would clearly bring more of this traffic to the LSWR.

The only drawings of gunpowder vans available so far show a simple body only (plus wheelbase), dated 11th October 1888 and signed by William Panter, and another very similar but slightly taller one in more detail which, by its drawing number, would have been prepared before or about 1900. One of the 1888 type, No 1379 (and cyphered as 01379 when a new 1379 was built in 1912, see below) became SR 61213, and was withdrawn in the first half of 1928. There is no register record of the later type, but the drawing has a written note that the spring retaining blocks were "to be bolted on in

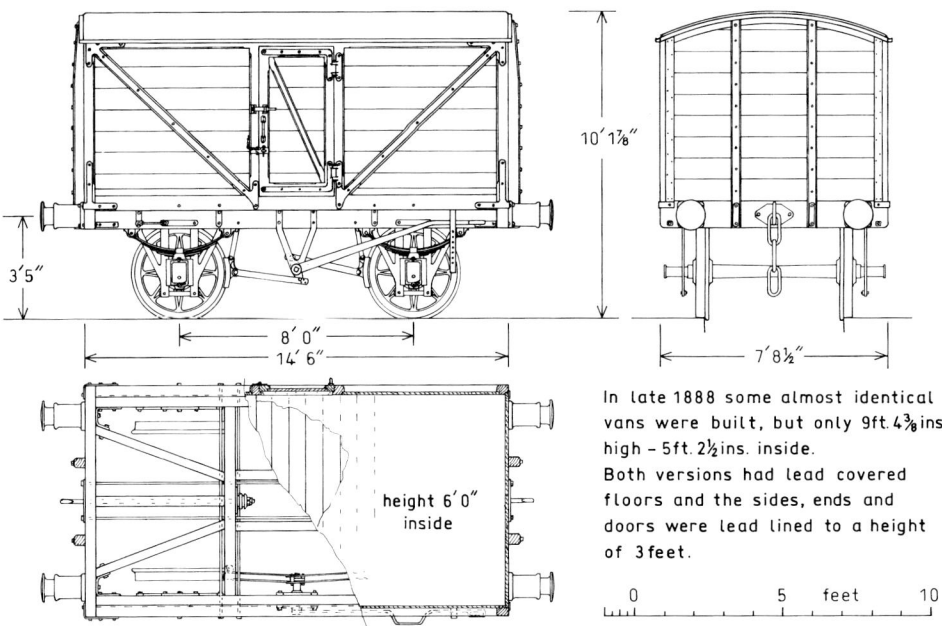

Figure 1.17. 14ft 6in gunpowder van of 1888 and 1900.

future". It is therefore felt justifiable to show them here in figure 1.17. Both versions were 14ft 6in long on an 8ft wheelbase, and both were noticeably lower in height than most other vans. Both were lined inside with lead sheet up to a height of 3 feet.

The Appendix to WTT for January 1892 instructed that gunpowder wagons, when empty, must be returned to Nine Elms without delay.

Their disappearance before the Grouping was probably due to a combination of their small size compared with the much better design mentioned below, and to the fact that the LSWR sold many wagons and vans to the War Office during the first World War. It seems quite likely that they got rid of a lot of their older and less profitable vehicles that way, old vans designed for the carriage of explosives being an obvious choice.

In 1904, and again in 1911, orders were placed with GR Turner for six gunpowder vans; at the latter date a price of £172 10s each was noted. The bodies of these vans were very similar to those of several other railways, such as the GWR iron minks of 1904, and were presumably an RCH standard. Naturally, the underframes incorporated LSWR fittings. The bodies, of ⅛in plate, were completely lined inside with wood, ⅜in for the roofs. In addition, the floor, sides and ends were lined to a height of 2ft with sheet lead fastened to the casing timber with copper nails. The 1911 drawing shows alterations to the brakes; it is fairly evident that the 1904 batch had a hand lever on one side only, borne out by the photo of 2134 (shown here in plate 1.43) the later batch having either-side levers, but still with brake shoes on one side only.

The author took several paint samples from the body of one in 1971. Next to the metal they appeared to be distinctly reddish-brown, then dark grey or black, red-brown again. Then, on the leeward side, what might have been very dark Southern Railway brown, and on the weather side (south-westerly) something that might have been either very dark grey or even black. Altogether not very helpful! A good drawing of these vans is included in *Southern Wagons, Volume 1*, so it will not be repeated here.

Wartime notices in the Public Record Office LSWR files for 1915, 1916 and 1917 include the numbers of many improvised gunpowder vans, for example, 263, 2665, 5929 and many more, but in the absence of any complete LSWR wagon records, there is no way of knowing what they were.

Cattle Wagons

As observed earlier, the stock return for June 1848 used the rather curious descriptions:

Wagons used for transit of carriers of goods and also adapted for carriage of cattle: 26
Wagons adapted for carriage of cattle, manure, coals, hay, etc: 25

GOODS VEHICLES

One can only guess what these vehicles looked like, although a slight clue is given in a note that the Traffic Coaching and Locomotive Committee recommended, in May 1849, that thirty long wagons should be converted to cattle carriages by having railed sides and moveable ends added.

In August 1851, the Locomotive Committee approved an order for William Beattie to build 130 closed wagons for £70 each and 40 cattle wagons for £60 each, from which we might deduce that the cattle ones were open. Mr Beattie's tender was supported by a testimonial from Mr Henson of the LNWR; the order was actually placed in the following December.

The Traffic Committee asked for 25 more cattle wagons to be provided in April 1855, but nothing was done and they repeated the request in the November, again with no evident response, although it is just possible that they were included in an order for wagons from Messrs Worsdell and Evans. Certainly, 20 were authorised in August 1856.

The opening of the line to Gillingham on 1st March 1859 provided a reason for building 50 more, and these were authorised by the directors in December 1858. It was agreed that these should be fitted with oil axleboxes as a trial instead of grease ones. The lowest tender was that of Brown Marshall at £58 10s each. They also got a follow-on order for another 50 in September 1859 at £63 each, and had delivered a total of 75 from the two orders by the end of December.

The board had clearly been approached by the War Office in mid-1861, because it was decreed in the August that, in future, cattle wagons should be 15ft 3in long and that they should be covered. This was to make them suitable for the transport of military horses.

In April 1863, the Officers and Traffic Committees agreed that a sample new cattle wagon should be built similar to one on the Somerset Central Railway (SCR), but with a roof and improvements as suggested by Mr Beattie. Fortunately, the Metropolitan drawing for the SCR one still exists, so it is possible to illustrate this open topped "high-sided goods and cattle waggon" of 1862 as figure 1.18. Apparently, the SCR ordered 30 of these around October 1862. Mr Beattie's version, also from the Metropolitan C&W Co, is shown as figure 1.19. It can be seen that they were both only 15ft long outside, so both companies clearly ignored the War Office request mentioned above!

Although there are clear similarities, it is obvious that Mr Beattie thought of many "improvements", although as he often did, he might have gone a little beyond what was strictly necessary

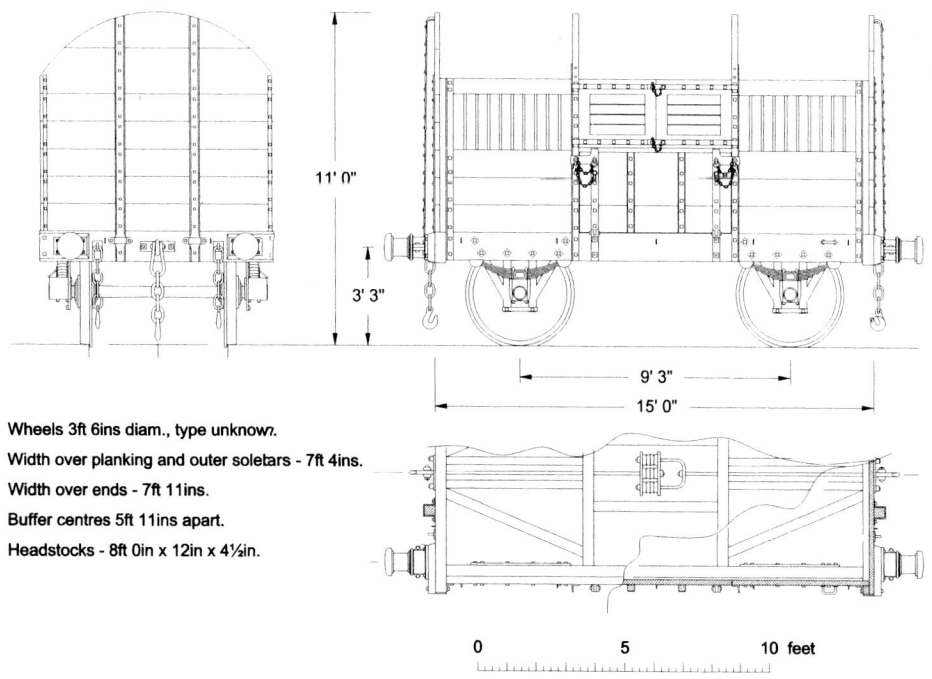

Figure 1.18. 15ft SCR high-sided goods and cattle wagon of 1862.

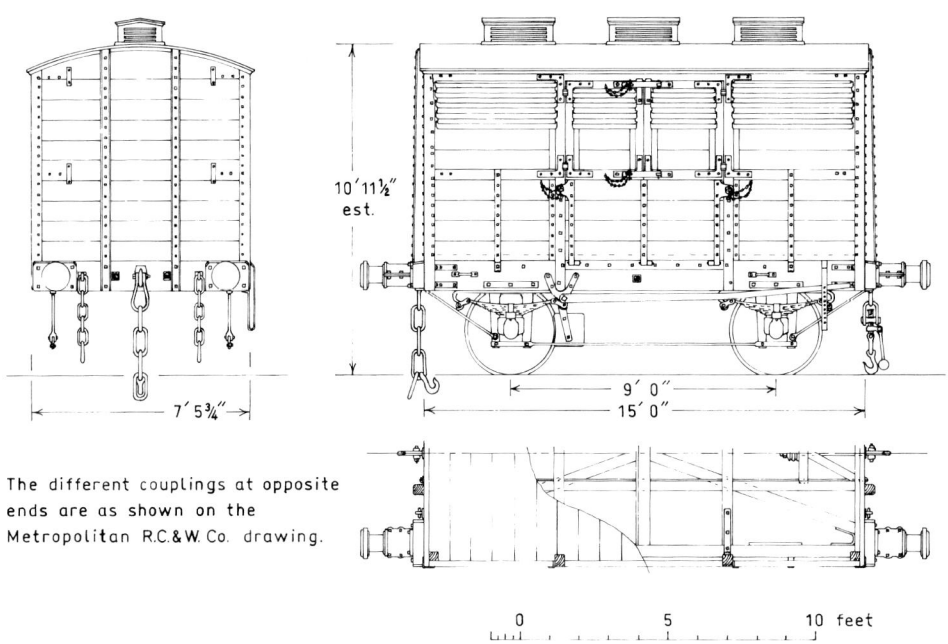

Figure 1.19. 15ft cattle wagon of 1863.

with his louvres and roof ventilators. As an aside, it is interesting to note that the Somerset and Dorset Railway, as it had then become, had a revised version in 1863, titled "covered goods waggon", that was almost identical to the 1862 wagon except that it had full-height wooden corner pillars, a top rail and a roof, making it look much more like a latter-day cattle wagon.

In November 1863, presumably after satisfactory trials, and following a recommendation from Mr Verrinder, station agent at Barnstaple, Mr Beattie was told to get tenders for 30. A month later, the number was increased to 50, and the tender of the Railway Carriage Co of Oldbury at the price of £82 10s each was accepted.

A circulated notice from the Goods Manager, James Haddow, dated 10th August 1865, drew attention to the spread of contagion among cattle, and instructed that any wagon used for the carriage of cattle or sheep was to be thoroughly cleaned and sprinkled with chloride of lime. This referred to the rapid spread of the cattle plague or "Rinderpest", which had originated in Asiatic cattle imported via Revel and Hull, and led to the Board of Trade closing inland markets and requiring that cattle should not be transported on the hoof. In particular, the LSWR was required to kill all imported cattle at Southampton. It was probably because of this that in April 1866, the Locomotive Committee instructed that six of the covered cattle wagons should be made available for use as meat vans. Shortly afterwards, in August, they ordered that bars should be put on the floors of the covered cattle wagons to prevent the cattle from slipping, although there is no obvious connection.

In the same month, Mr Scott recommended to the Traffic Committee that a deputation should wait on either the Board of Trade or the Privy Council to seek relaxation of the order so as to permit imports at Southampton to be carried live direct to the London cattle market in the same way that imports to the Port of London were allowed to be driven through the streets to the market. However, a letter from Col Harness of the BoT a fortnight later confirmed that foreign cattle must still be slaughtered at Southampton. The LSWR decided to continue to press the matter in conjunction with the dock company, with the result that in January 1867, Mr Scott was able to report that the Port of Southampton had been licensed for the importation of cattle, and that by a special order in Council, foreign fat cattle could once again be conveyed by rail from there to the London cattle market. The cattle wagons used for this traffic had a red band painted round them, and they were not allowed to be used for any other purpose.

The order (circular 6 of 1867) stipulated that the cattle had to be loaded directly at the loading bank in Southampton Docks and taken without stopping (except if necessary for water and fodder) to the cattle market (Maiden Lane station, Copenhagen Fields), via Nine Elms. The wagons had to be returned again via Nine Elms for cleaning and disinfecting.

However, a Contagious Diseases (Animals) Act was passed in August 1867 requiring all foreign cattle to be slaughtered at the docks. Quite clearly, the LSWR tried to gain an exemption because the Traffic Committee, in September 1867, recorded a letter from the Secretary to the Lords of the Privy Council declining to continue the order after the 30th September.

Presumably because of the reservation of several vehicles during the short-lived relaxation, the Officers Committee in July 1867 stressed the shortage of cattle trucks, and Mr Beattie was asked to consider how to convert some round-ended wagons temporarily. Unfortunately there is no further information on this project.

Mr Beattie stated in his January 1868 Annual Report that 55 wagons had been rebuilt, many of them large covered goods and cattle vehicles. At the end of December 1869, it was suggested that, of 100 wagons it agreed to buy from Metropolitan, 25 should be cattle wagons, but nothing more is recorded about this. A year later the Oldbury company again got an order for 30 cattle wagons, but by April 1871, they were having to explain away the delay in delivering them.

The description of goods stock given in the LSWR Correspondence Book as at October 1870 has only a single entry for cattle wagons, describing them as 13ft 3in long by 7ft wide inside, with an overall length of 17ft 9in. The height of sides is given as 6ft 2in and the inside capacity as 571cu ft. These dimensions appear to indicate that they were uncovered. No quantities are given.

The half-year report for January 1872, given by Mr Beattie, gives more details in Table 3.

Without any illustrations it must be admitted that these figures do not mean a lot! The picture of cattle wagons only really starts to emerge with the decision of the Traffic and Locomotive Committee to order 50 in April 1876. Despite a delay in delivery, a further 50 were ordered from Metropolitan in October 1877 at a price of £48 10s each; this order was increased to 75 a month later. They were 16ft 9in long over the headstocks to LSWR drawing 2164, the later ones being to drawing 2404. The only obvious difference is the omission in the second batch of the large wooden blocks between the buffers and headstocks. Both the Nine Elms and the Metropolitan versions of the drawings for both batches have survived, and are represented here as figure 1.20. Rather curiously, the Nine Elms drawings are dated a few weeks later than the Metropolitan ones in each case.

A year later, in October 1878, the Craven company got an order to build another 60 for £69 each, presumably to the same drawing 2404.

In *Southern Wagons, Volume 1* there is a very similar 16ft 9in wagon shown as figure 22. The authors say that this illustration was based on the diagram book, which quotes it to be to LSWR drawing 255. This drawing has not survived, but would logically be dated 1894 when Eastleigh Works was producing updated versions of some older vehicles. Most of the body details are identical to drawing 2404, but external single diagonal bracing has been applied in the opposite direction to the internal iron braces in the earlier wagons, the axle guards and buffers have been replaced by the then current type, the wooden brake block has been replaced by an iron one, and of course it has been vacuum piped. Moveable partitions are also shown, which were not present in the 1877 version, having been introduced as a result of a general agreement between railway companies in 1892 to provide them in all possible cattle trucks from January 1893. The diagram book records 161 in service at the end of 1909, 57 of them with AVB. By the end of 1911 there were still 110, but intriguingly it mentions another thirteen at 16ft long, of which no information is available. Two of these latter were still there at the end of 1914, when the quantity of 16ft 9in ones had reduced to 58.

The General Manager reported to the Traffic and Locomotive Committee in January 1880 that the company was hiring 480 goods vehicles, and recommended that the practice should cease at the end of June, with the company then buying all its stock. It was agreed to get tenders for, among other things, 75 covered cattle wagons. The Metropolitan drawing for these is dated February 1880, but the Nine Elms one (No 2696) was done in February 1879. This drawing was reproduced in *The Railway Engineer, Volume 1* for 1880 with the title "Descriptions and Plans of LSWR 18ft Cattle

Table 3: Half year report for January 1872			
50 covered	14ft x 7ft	height 5ft 10in	doors 5ft 10in x 5ft 4in
50 covered	16ft 6in x 7ft 6in	height unknown	doors 6ft x 5ft 6in
176 uncovered	14ft 2in x 7ft	height unknown	doors 5ft 11in x 4ft 11in

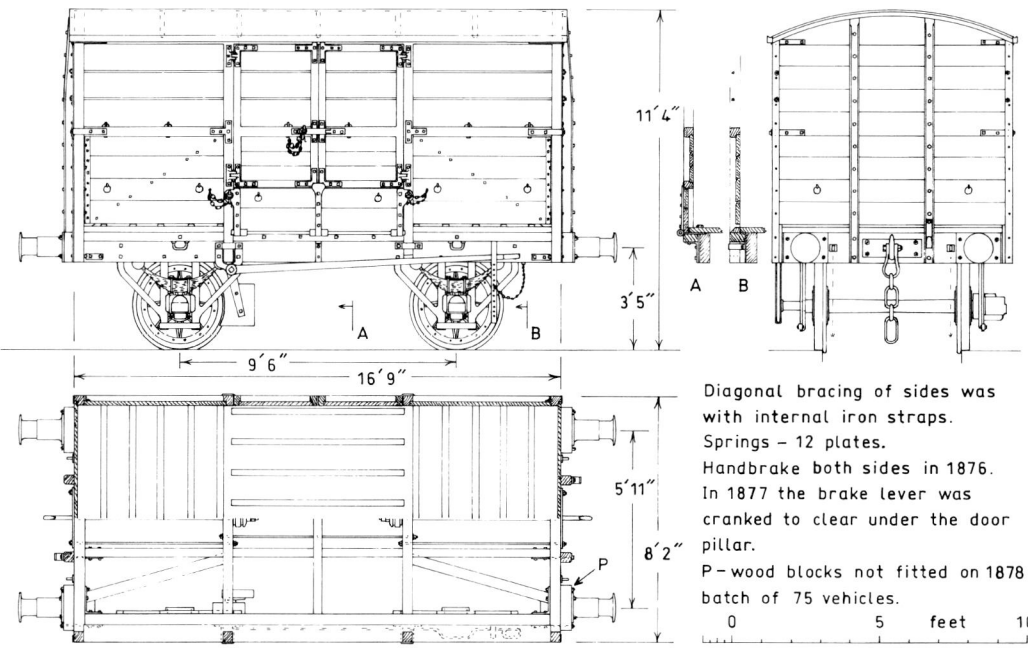

Figure 1.20. 16ft 9in cattle wagon of 1876/78.

Wagon designed by William Adams". It is represented here by figure 1.21. As with the covered wagon of 1881 (illustrated as Appendix 2 in *Southern Wagons, Volume 1*) and the open wagon of 1881 (figure 1.7), the corner pillars were outside the end planking. Both the original drawings scaled the wheelbase at 10ft, but with the dimension stated as 10ft 6in. The drawing in *The Railway Engineer* shows it scaled and dimensioned as 10ft 6in so it is shown thus here.

The article states that the underframe was built of Dantzic oak with the solebars plated outside with 12in x ⅜in steel. The flooring was of larch fir with oak battens. Underframe bolts were mainly ¾in and ⅞in diameter with nuts outside. Most of the body fixings were ⅝in bolts or coach screws.

Most of the further developments are covered in *Southern Wagons, Volume 1*, but a few more comments are worthwhile. Mr Adams wrote to the Locomotive and Stores Committee in August 1885 with a specification and plans for 50 cattle wagons. It was approved that these should be built at Nine Elms on the capital account at an estimated cost of £93 11s each. Then, a further 200 were ordered in November 1887. There is no record of any new drawing around these times, so one can only conjecture as to whether they were simply a variant of the 18ft ones of the 1880 pattern. Certainly the next surviving drawing, No 257 in the Eastleigh series (dated July 1894) was generally similar, although with more usual corner pillars and a slightly narrower door opening, also just ½in less in internal height. It appears to be this version that is illustrated in *Southern Wagons, Volume 1* as figure 23. It includes the movable partitions mentioned above as being required from 1893, although these are not shown on drawing 257. The LSWR diagram book notes 102 of this length still in service at December 1909, falling to 45 at the end of 1913 and six at the end of 1923, but there is no distinction between the variants.

The next design is illustrated in *Southern Wagons, Volume 1* as figure 24, but only in one version, so it is being dealt with again here. There is possibly a little confusion in dating it. The surviving drawing numbers are appropriate to 1895, but notes in the wagon register record some of them as being built in 1894. This design increased the length to 18ft 8½in, and 50 were ordered in May 1895. Before they were completed, it was decided that they should be fitted with AVB. Another 50 were ordered in March 1896, again with AVB. From SR records it is evident that some of the 1895 wagons were not fitted with AVB, but had the usual goods single-side brakes, as shown on LSWR drawing 588 of 1895. Later on some of these were vacuum piped. From a photograph it is evident that some (or at least one) of the earliest batch had AVB using the skew brake rigging as for the 18ft milk and meat vans of 1887. At the end of 1895, drawing 648 was

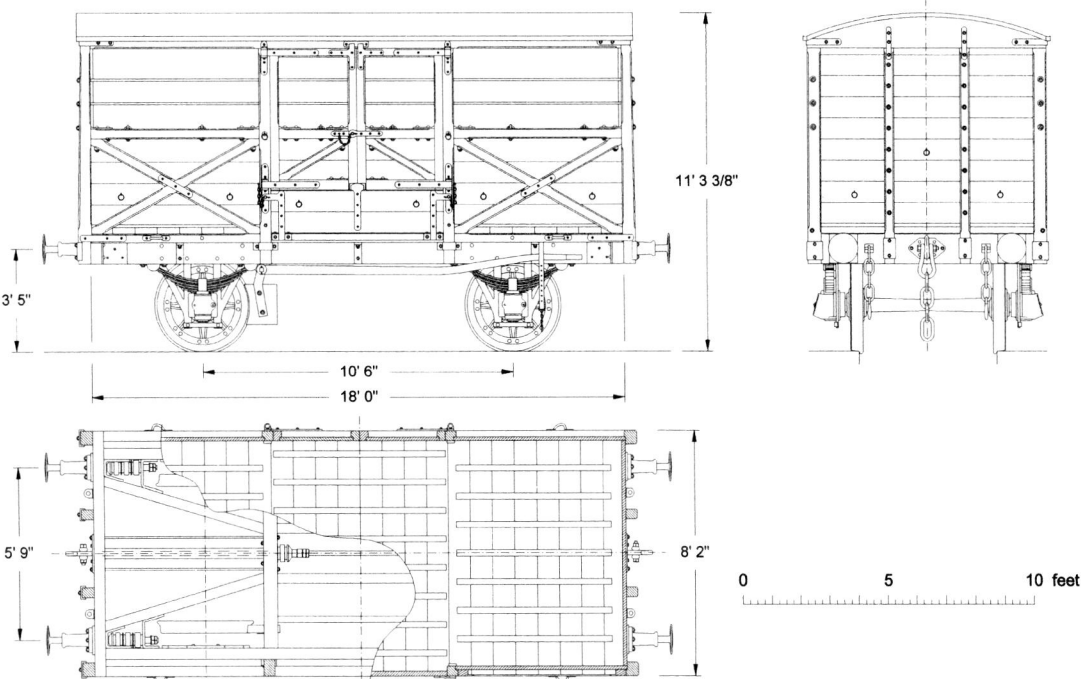

Figure 1.21. 18ft cattle wagon of 1880.

prepared showing just the underframe for the AVB version, using the vertical form of brake rigging. All of these had basically the same body, apart from some small variations in such things as the corner plates at the bottom of the door pillars to allow bolt holes to take account of the different wheelbases, and different coupling backplates. With the exception of the skew brake version, they are all covered here by figure 1.22.

There was later what one might describe as a degree of "mix and match" regarding the combinations of brake arrangements, but substantially they remained the standard type of LSWR cattle wagon until 1923, with many being built both as replacements and additions to stock. Some of these batches were 10 in 1908, 50 in 1910/11, another 50 in 1911, 18 in 1913/14, 30 in 1915, 20 in 1917 and 25 in 1922. By the end of 1902, there was a total of 818 cattle wagons of all types in service.

A wartime notice to railways in August 1917 stated that military horses, including officers' chargers, were to go in cattle trucks, not in horseboxes, except those of Generals commanding Divisions, which were allowed to go in horseboxes if desired. The cattle trucks were to be sheeted to protect the horses from the weather.

One little point of interest here – study of the various LSWR drawings shows there to have been no consistency over the placing of the vacuum pipes.

In most, but not all, cases the main pipe ran on the opposite side of the underframe to the brake cylinder. In many cases it ran right through on that side, so appearing to the right of the coupling hook at one end and to the left at the other, but in other cases it crossed over so as to appear to the right at both ends.

Going back to 1888, presumably under the November 1887 authority for 400 cattle wagons, five special ones were built. Later, the General Manager got approval for three additional "specially constructed cattle trucks" in October 1890, when the provision of AVB was specified. They were all later referred to more simply as special cattle wagons. Their size was 18ft 3in long by 8ft 6in wide and the recorded cost was £147 10s 5d in all cases.

Judging from the photograph of one of the first batch at Barnstaple in or after 1906, it is probable that the first five were only through-piped at some time after they were built, possibly when the next batch was ordered, and never fully AVB fitted. The other three, which were actually built in 1891, were fitted with AVB and the "skew" type of brake rigging. This need for AVB, or at least piping, was because they were intended for the carriage of valuable bulls or prize cattle, and to enable them to be run in fast fitted goods trains. They were included in the wagon stock list with numbers 8377 to 8381 and 8833 to 8835 respectively. The main difference from ordinary cattle wagons was that the

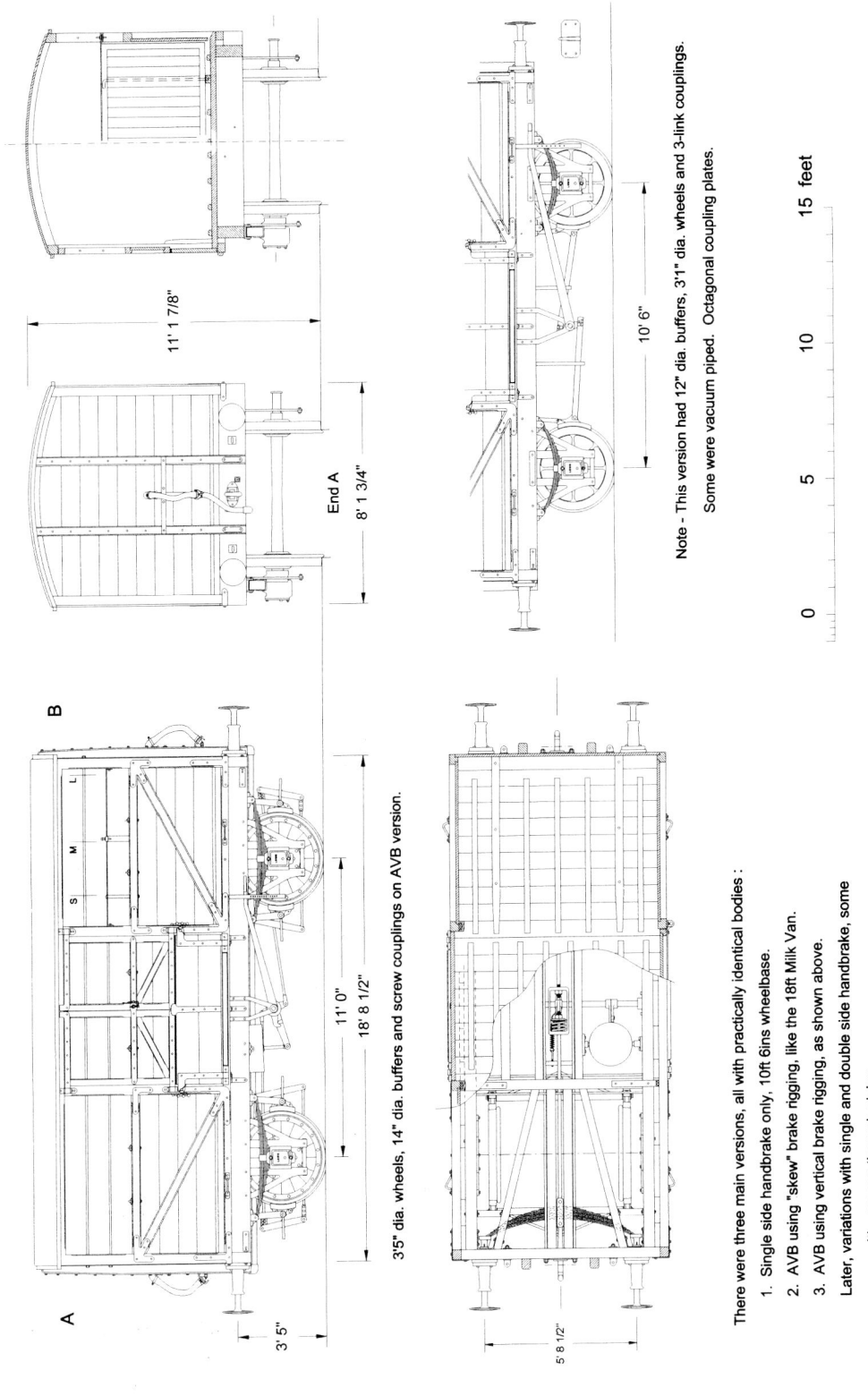

Figure 1.22. 18ft 8½in cattle wagon of c.1895.

Plate 1.22. Exeter cattle dock. Note the travelling crane in the background, a good variety of open wagons, and sheets over some of the cattle wagons. (J Tatchell collection)

upper sections of the sides, instead of being open, were closed with louvres.

Additional ventilation was provided by large openings in the ends, protected by bars and, when necessary, by vertically sliding hatches. Unfortunately, the official drawings and profile diagrams have not survived. The accompanying drawings, figures 1.23 and 1.24 respectively, are therefore based only on the sparse outline dimensions from the diagram books, and on the only two known, and rather distant, photographs together with reference to details of other vehicles of the period. Although they give a reasonably fair representation their accuracy in detail cannot be guaranteed!

Twenty more were approved in November 1898, and built during 1899. These were 18ft 8½in long, again with AVB, and similar to the ordinary cattle wagons of that length except that, like the earlier ones, there were louvres in the upper sections. Also, like the earlier ones they were classed as wagons with numbers 12464 to 12483. In their post-1906 form they were illustrated in *Southern Wagons, Volume 1* and are not repeated here, although their original appearance can easily be deduced.

In January 1906, on the General Manager's recommendation to the Traffic Committee, it was agreed that twelve of the cattle vans used in passenger trains should be altered as soon as possible to give accommodation for the men travelling with the cattle, with the remaining 28 to be altered during their normal visits to workshops. The estimated cost was £10 each vehicle; this was confirmed by the Locomotive, Carriage and Stores Committee at their next meeting. The curious thing is the quantities mentioned in both minutes, since there were only 28 in total at that time!

The alteration consisted of installing a partition to create a very cramped passenger compartment with a sideways sliding hatch into the cattle compartment. As much as possible of the materials were to be recovered from scrapped old carriages, which accounts for the very low estimated cost, though even so one might wonder how they accounted for the fairly substantial amount of labour involved. A roof lamp fitting was also installed, and an instruction states that a properly trimmed lamp was to be provided if the man travelling in charge of cattle being taken to or from a show needed it. With these changes it was considered that the vans now became passenger-rated and they were given a new series of numbers from 1 to 5, 6 to 8 and 9 to 28 respectively. They were also written into the Carriage Register and the Carriage Diagram Book, but with another oddity – although both the LSWR

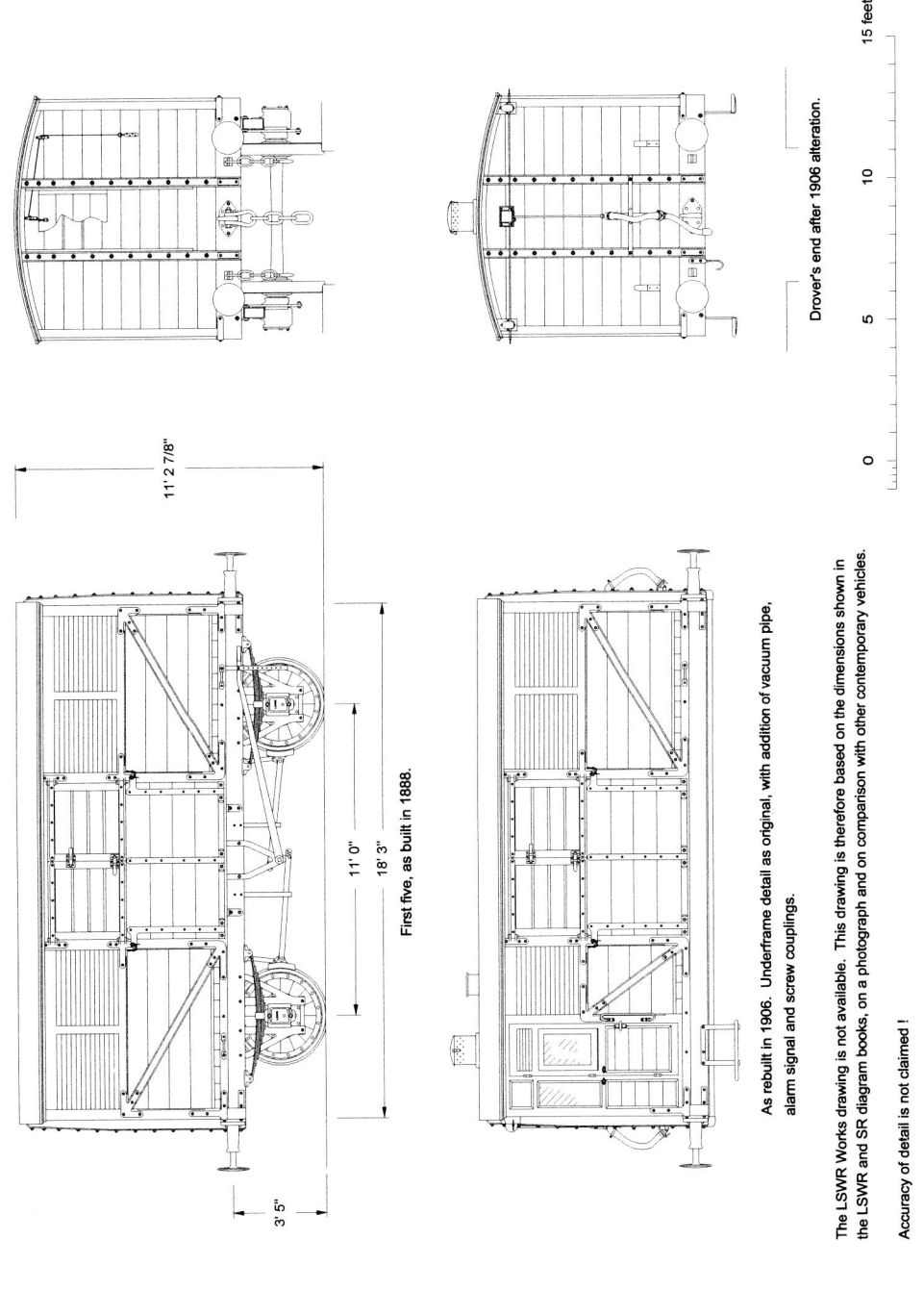

Figure 1.23. 18ft 3in special cattle wagon of 1888.

GOODS VEHICLES

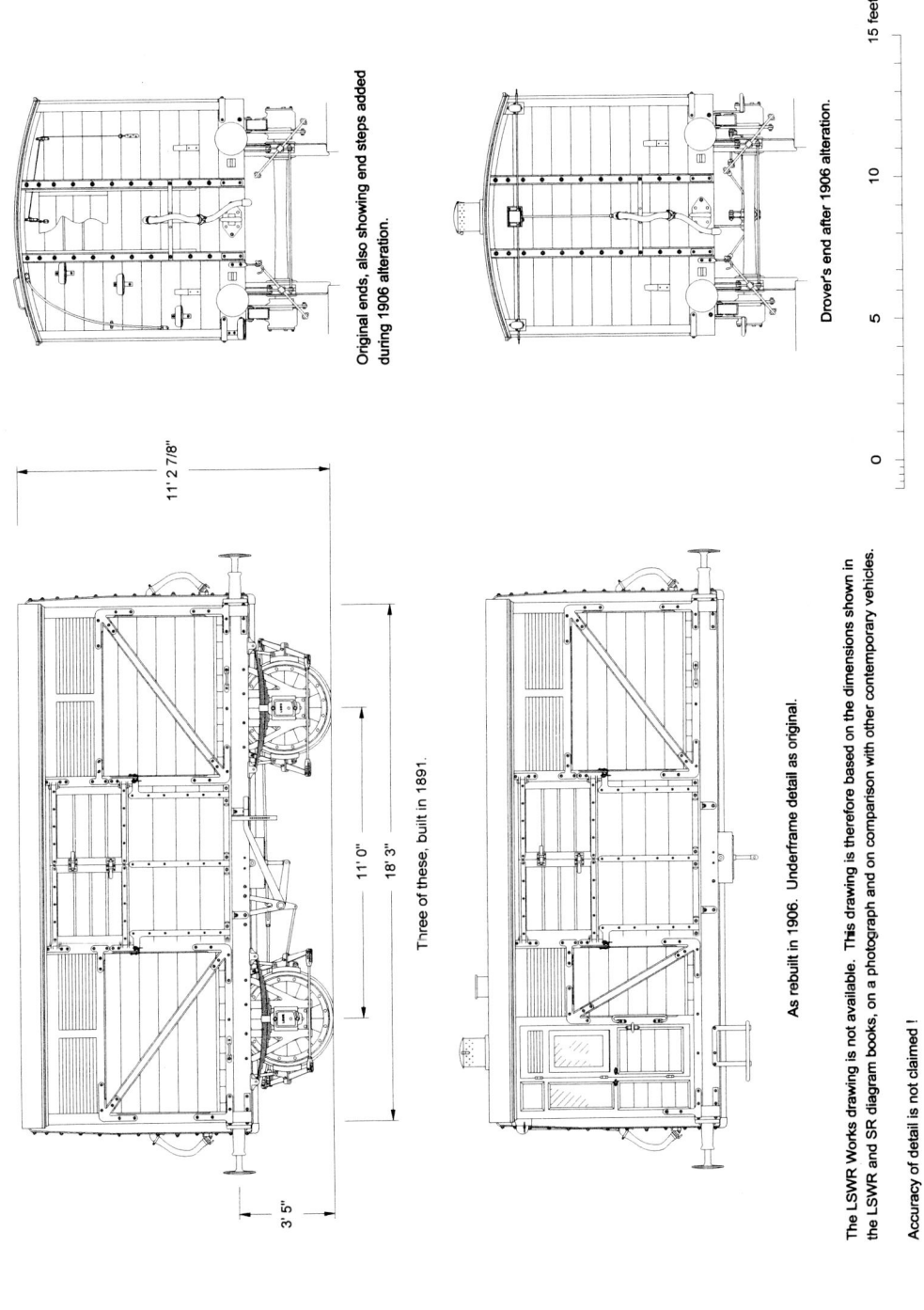

Figure 1.24. 18ft 3in special cattle wagon of 1891.

Plate 1.23. 18ft 3in special cattle wagon No 8381, as altered to No 5 in 1906, at Barnstaple. (Loco and General)

Plate 1.24. Weybridge, July 1923. 18ft 3in special cattle wagon no 8833 of 1891, also an L&BSCR 30ft passenger brake van. At left are the steps of the junction signal box. (F Foote)

GOODS VEHICLES

and the SR diagram books showed the first eight as 18ft 3in long, the Carriage Register recorded them as 18ft 2in.

The oldest three 18ft 3in ones, numbers 1 to 3, were cyphered in 1910 (although number 2 remained in use until about 1928) and replaced by three new ones, 22ft long, that had been authorised in April 1909 as part of the renewals programme. These had both AVB and Westinghouse brakes, together with steam heating through pipes. Two more of these were built in 1914 following withdrawal of the remaining two oldest ones. From the outset, they had drovers' compartments of slightly more comfortable dimensions than the earlier conversions. They are illustrated here as figure 1.25.

With the introduction of the complete renumbering of the carriage stock after 1912, it was decided that all these vans should once again be regarded as wagon stock, so all the pre-1910 ones reverted to their original wagon numbers between 1913 and 1916, except No 23, which was either allocated to the S&DJR in 1914 or was sold to Messrs Edmund and Radley for the Brecon & Merthyr Railway in 1909/10. Its original number, 12478, was then taken in the renumbering by the first of the 22ft ones, the others becoming 8378 to 8380 and 8835. Most of them were withdrawn by the Southern Railway in the late 1920s; the last to go was former 12478 in August 1931.

In an Appendix to Rules of 1911, and probably in many other such notices, it was stated that, between 1st November and the following 30th April, any vehicle carrying sheep that had been shorn within the previous 60 days had to be covered and enclosed to protect them, but without obstructing ventilation. This note is included here because sheep as well as cattle were normally carried in cattle trucks.

Meat Vans

The first specific reference to vehicles specially adapted for the carriage of meat in 1861, has already been noted in the section on covered wagons. Later, on 10th April 1866, the Officers' Committee decided that six of the covered cattle wagons should be made available for use as meat vans. There is no indication of whether this simply meant that they were reserved and marked for this purpose or whether they were altered in any way.

The next mention is on 22nd September 1870, when Mr Ming of the Goods Department obtained the approval of the Directors for the construction at Nine Elms of twelve new meat vans on the capital account. This was carried out, since it was mentioned in the July 1871 half-year report. Another twelve were ordered similarly on 23rd October 1873. Whether they were identical to the previous ones is not known, but Nine Elms drawing No 1922 was dated 29th November 1873, and shows a 15ft 4in wagon with ventilation louvres in the upper parts of the sides and double sliding doors. This is illustrated here as figure 1.26. The ends were internally braced with double diagonal iron strips, and the sides with single diagonal angle irons. The outer face of the planking, framing and louvres of the doors was completely flush. A total of 120 meat hooks were fastened to the roof sticks. The drawing gives the impression that a handbrake was provided on each side.

Another twenty were authorised on 22nd October 1874, probably to the same drawing, but there is no proof of this.

There are no more clear references to vehicles for meat traffic until March 1887 when the Traffic Committee approved the construction of thirty new meat vans, fitted for running in passenger trains. These and the various versions of covered and refrigerated vans fitted for meat traffic from then on have all been illustrated in *Southern Wagons, Volume 1* so will not be repeated here, but it is interesting to note that at many stations, particularly in the West Country, there were LSWR-owned slaughterhouses, although the running of them was doubtless leased out to local butchers. During World War I, these were all taken under the control of the Ministry of Food, and remained so until 1920 when they were released. The LSWR's estate agent was then instructed to find new tenants. Among those listed were Barnstaple, Copplestone, Crediton, Eggesford, Holsworthy, Halwill Junction, Lapford and Sampford Courtenay.

A rather odd note in the Working Time Table for 1892 records the allocation of three open goods trucks for meat to and from Dorchester as numbers 2396, 2734 and 2945, which leaves several questions unanswered. Another puzzling note in the same document gives the numbers of thirty "new meat vans" as 8140 to 8169 inclusive, but these were the numbers of the meat vans of 1887 mentioned in the last paragraph, so "new" seems to have been a rather elastic word in the LSWR.

Refrigerator Vans

There is a complete chapter on the subject of insulated and refrigerator vans in *Southern Wagons,*

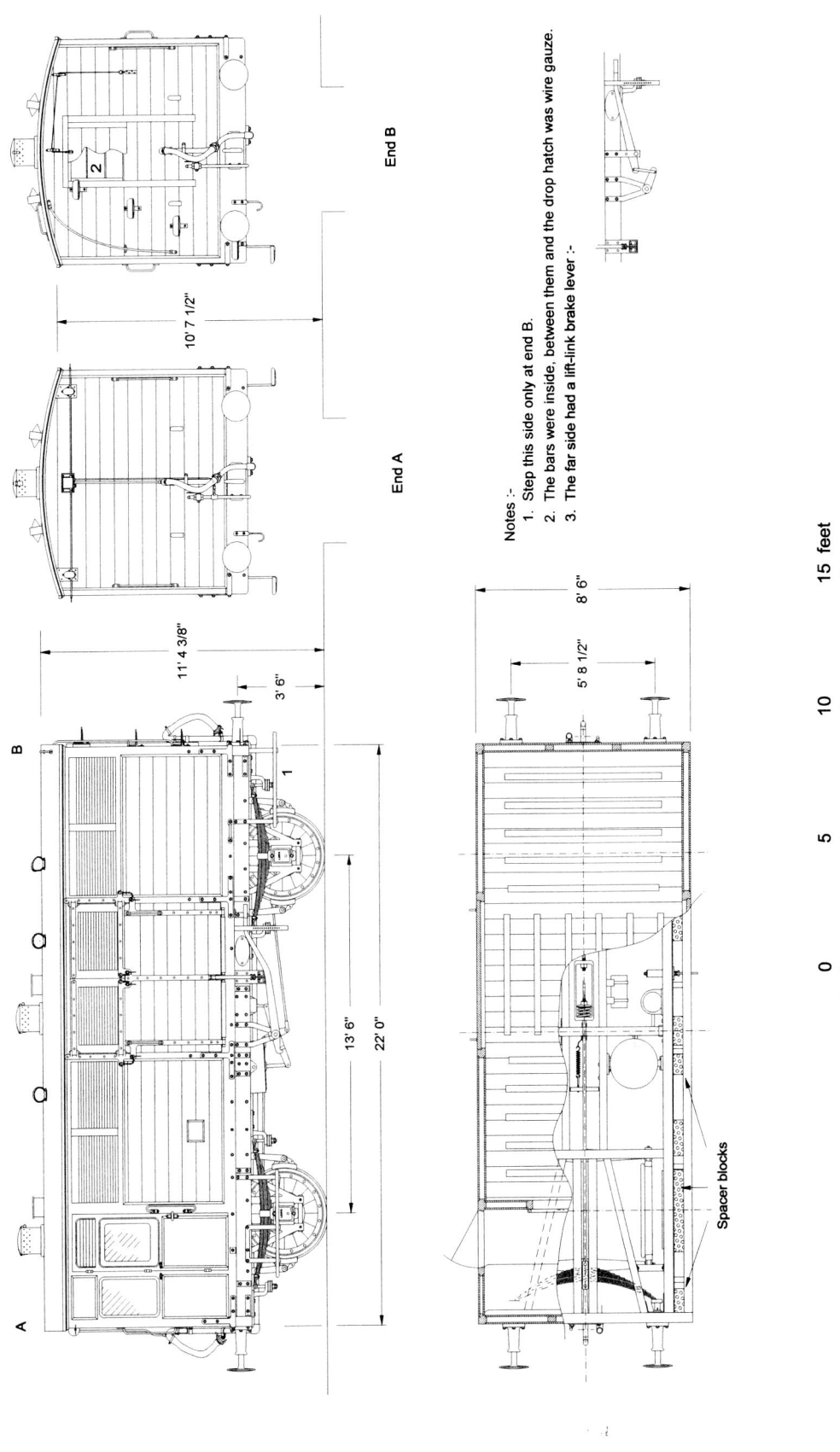

Figure 1.25. 22ft special cattle van of 1910.

GOODS VEHICLES

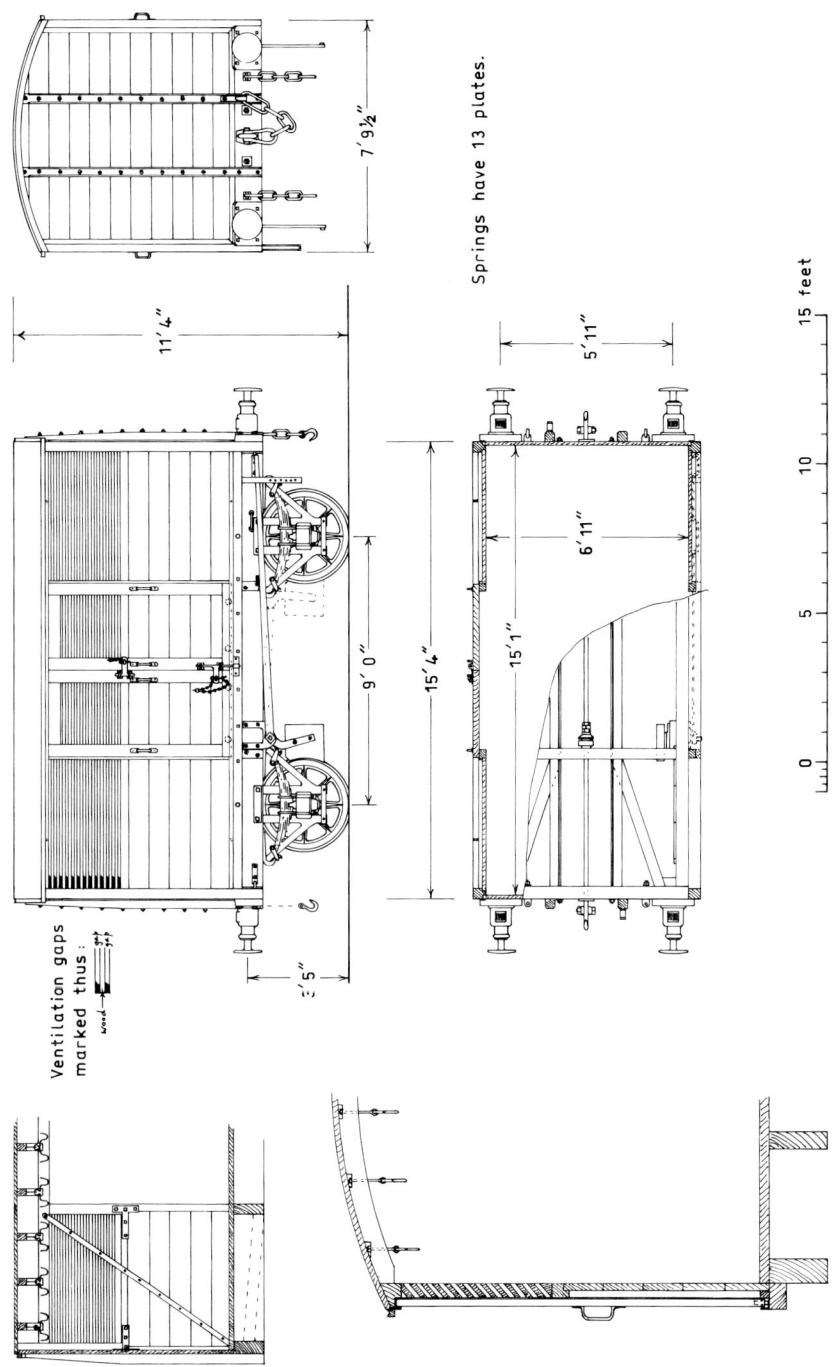

Figure 1.26. 15ft 4in meat van of 1873.

Volume 1 so none of the illustrations will be repeated here. However, a few notes might be of interest.

The LSWR took over the Southampton Docks in 1892. In April 1893 the General Manager reported to the Traffic Committee that a meat importer had urged that the company should build twenty refrigerator vans to convey meat traffic from Southampton to country stations during the summer months. This was approved, and drawing 302 was signed by Mr Panter a fortnight later. This was for a 16ft by 7ft 11½in van described in the above book as SR diagram 1461. The brake cylinder was at the centre with the V-hangers offset, and a handbrake lever on one side only, operating on one wheel. The brake rigging was Mr Panter's "skew" arrangement.

Some fresh drawings were prepared in 1899, one showing a similar body to the earlier one (drawing 830) and two versions of underframe. One (drawing 817) shows full AVB with vertical brake rigging and a hand lever on one side only, the other (drawing 825) with neither AVB nor through pipe, but with wagon style two block brakes and Mr Panter's cross lever handbrake. These drawings were in advance of the General Manager's recommendation to the Traffic Committee in April 1900 that another twenty-five refrigerator trucks should be built, which was approved.

That approval was repeated for another 25 in August 1900, when there was a body drawing showing the width reduced to 7ft 9in (drawing 971), and again in October when the approval was for fifty more "in view of the requirements in connection with the cold storage accommodation to be provided at Southampton Docks early next year". An underframe drawing (drawing 983, probably of 1901), which might relate to either or both batches, shows full AVB with handbrake lever on one side together with a Westinghouse through pipe.

In the following July, the General Manager recommended another 25, but this time the Traffic Committee disagreed and the matter rested there until November 1903, when the GM again recommended the provision of fifty more, together with 25 long van trucks and fifty (road) meat carts, in consequence of the opening of a new cold store at Southampton Docks. This was approved.

There was a drawing of an 18ft steel underframe for a refrigerator van in 1903 (drawing 1262), but there is no evidence that any such vans were built. It seems most likely that the fifty were to the previous drawings, as also were the next thirty, which were authorised in August 1905, "as additions to the present stock of one hundred and ninety-five".

The next approval was in January 1907 after the Goods Manager repeated the 1903 request for fifty refrigerator cars plus 25 long van trucks and fifty meat carts. These refrigerator vans (cars!) had the same 7ft 9in bodies but the underframes were fully fitted with both automatic vacuum and Westinghouse brakes. Handbrakes were fitted on both sides, the lever on the side away from the brake cylinders being left-handed (underframe drawing 1572, body drawing 1579). Fourteen of them,

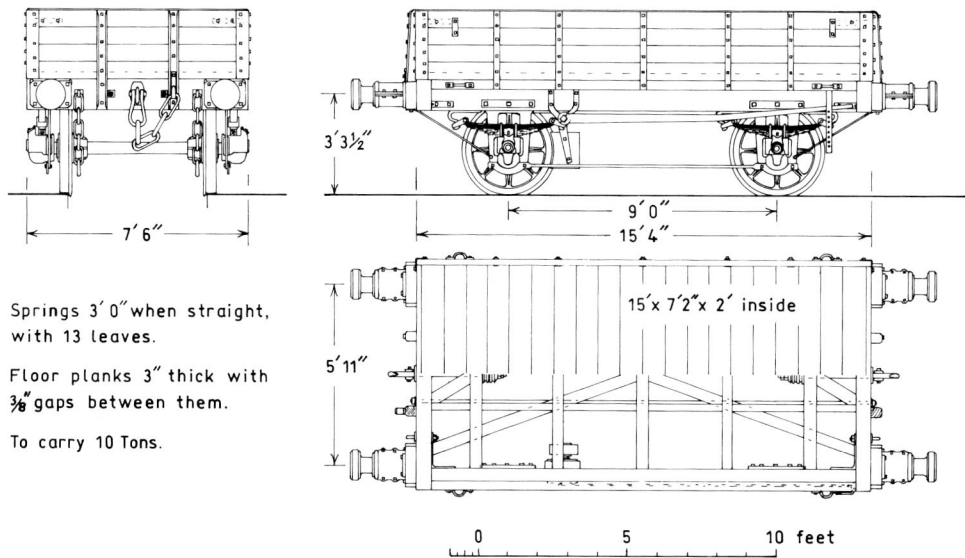

Figure 1.27. 15ft 4in stone wagon of 1870.

GOODS VEHICLES

numbers 13824, 13826-8, 13830 and 13834-42, had the left-handed lever replace by a right-handed one operating through "snail" cams in, or after, 1909 (drawing 1788).

25 of the earlier vans had clearly not been fitted with AVB because in June 1907 the General Manager got approval that they should be fitted with AVB at an estimated cost of £25 each "in order that they may run in fast trains".

Another 75 of the 1907 type, presumably with the modified handbrake, were built in 1908/9, (although the matter appears to have escaped record in the minutes!) followed by fifty more that were authorised in May 1911. These still had the same bodies, but only had vacuum through pipes and goods brake gear on one side with long handles, the one on the brake side being "lift-link", (drawing 2018). Another six were authorised in May 1922, but were not actually built until 1928, when they appeared to a Southern Railway design (diagram 1476) 17ft 6in long on a 9ft wheelbase and numbered 50494 to 50499, but that is outside our scope.

Stone Wagons

Another rather specialised traffic was the carriage of stone, generally as medium to large blocks, as distinct from the smaller stuff used for ballast. The first records of this trade on the LSWR were in 1870, although clearly stone was already being carried because in March, Mr Scott reported to the Traffic Committee that in order to maintain and extend the traffic in Portland stone, it would be necessary to erect, at Nine Elms station, a gantry with a crane to travel on top of it for the purpose of transferring stone into a stone depot and thence into barges; it was then agreed to provide a gantry with a 10-ton crane.

A couple of weeks later, it was decided that 25 of the goods wagons that had been authorised in December 1869 should be built as stone wagons with sides 2ft high, a door on each side and capable of carrying 10 tons. The result was the wagon shown here as figure 1.27, from which it can be seen that the structure was broadly similar to the open wagons but with some of the frame members, including the headstocks, thicker and stronger. The springs had 13 plates instead of the 11 on the ordinary wagons. Floor planks were 3in thick instead of 2in or 2½in, separated by ⅜in gaps for drainage. However side doors were not provided.

Shortly after that, in July 1870, Mr Scott reported that additional accommodation was required at Portland station for handling the stone traffic. The estimated cost was £844, of which the GWR was willing to pay half. This was approved.

In October 1874, the matter came up again when it was agreed that fifty of the wagons that had recently been authorised should be low-sided for stone traffic. And they certainly were low-sided, one fixed plank to be precise. Once more they were 15ft 4in long on a 9ft wheelbase. Rather unusually, they had Mansell style wheels of 3ft diameter and a handbrake on each side. They are shown here as figure 1.28.

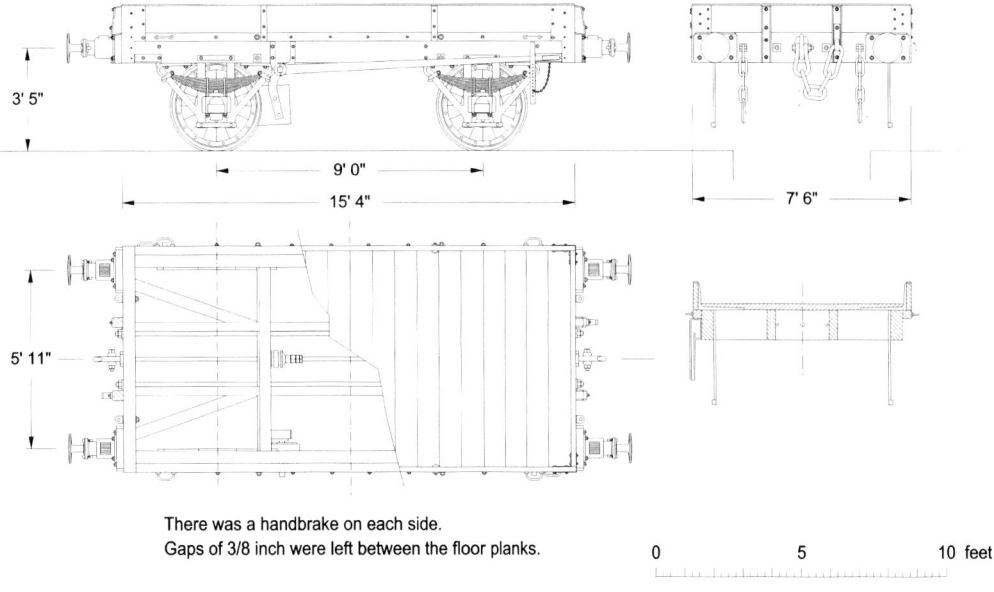

Figure 1.28. 15ft 4in stone wagon of 1875.

Under the heading "Eddystone Granite Quarries, Cornwall" the General Manager told the Traffic Committee in July 1889 that he had received an application by the Marble, Granite and Stone Co for the LSWR to work their line between the Bodmin & Wadebridge Railway and the De Lank quarries. This was agreed, subject to a proper agreement.

No further items about stone wagons appear in the minutes until May 1915, when the renewals programme included two 15-ton stone wagons. However there were more varieties, and these can be seen in *Southern Wagons, Volume 1*. They were probably included in authorisations of renewals under the quite common heading of "... (quantity) wagons to be withdrawn and replaced by the same type".

Ballast Wagons

The first note about ballast wagons in the minutes was in July 1839, when it was reported that engines had been damaged by "running against ballast wagons", and a survey of the wagons was ordered. There is no indication as to whether they belonged to the Company or were those of the line construction contractors.

In March 1847, the Court of Directors endorsed a recommendation of the Traffic Committee to order 100 goods wagons, 200 coal wagons and 50 ballast wagons to the designs of Joseph Beattie. Tenders were invited from several firms: Williams (Bristol), W Beattie (Liverpool), Woolferston (Salisbury), Tiges (Salisbury), Lloyd Foster (Wednesbury), Haigh Foundry (Wigan) and Mr Pace (no town stated). Those of William Beattie were accepted at £85 15s each for the goods wagons, £98 for the long coal wagons, £86 10s for the short coal wagons and £79 for the ballast wagons. Rather strangely, and without any explanation, they also accepted the tender of Mr Woolferston to supply a further 25 ballast wagons for £116 each. However, as already stated, the stock return for mid-1848 shows fifty existing at that time.

The Engineering Department applied to the Locomotive, Carriage and Stores Committee in December 1859 for more ballast wagons, and it was decided to transfer a number of coal wagons for the purpose. Whether this was done, or whether still more were needed, is not recorded, but there is a Joseph Wright & Sons drawing, clearly dating it to before 1863, marked "L&SWR" and with a note that some slightly amended measurements were to be worked to. This is the basis of figure 1.29. It is interesting that very wide single planks were used for the ends and falling sides, and that the floor planks, which again were rather wide, were laid longitudinally.

There was a useful item in the minutes for April 1869 when the Locomotive and Traffic Committee agreed that 25 "old small goods wagons" should be painted red and used as ballast wagons. This seems

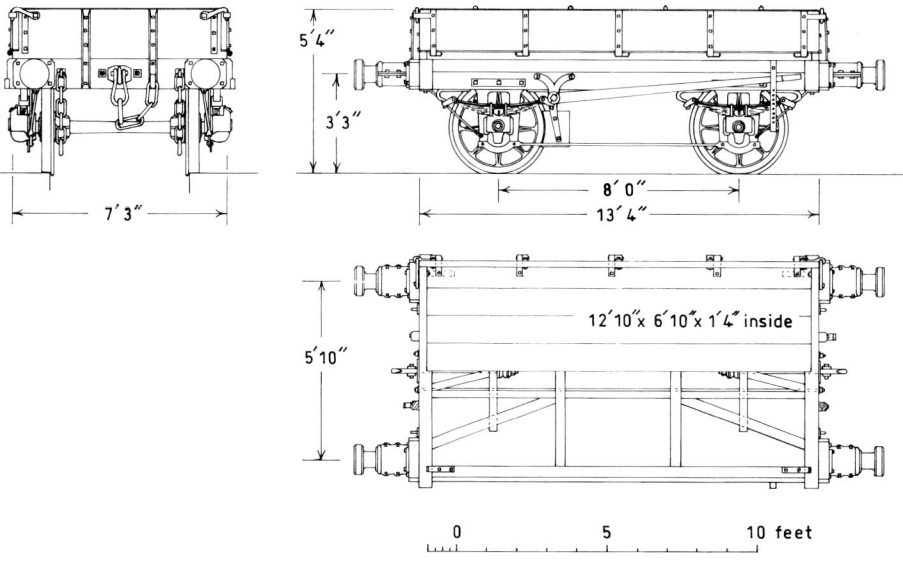

Figure 1.29. Ballast wagon, pre-1863.

GOODS VEHICLES

to be the only mention of the livery for Engineering Department vehicles and probably means red oxide, which quite rapidly weathered to a kind of pink.

Again in January 1877, the same committee agreed to transfer 47 old goods wagons to the Permanent Way Department for use as ballast wagons. The subject is not mentioned again until July 1897, but it seems certain that more were built or transferred in the meantime. In fact *Southern Wagons, Volume 1* records and illustrates 15ft 4in two- and three-plank dropside wagons that were built from 1887, if not earlier, for both ordinary goods and for ballast use. It might be noted that some of the two-plank ones that were built about 1909 had ordinary wagon buffers rather than those shown. Those illustrations and those of the later steel hopper wagons, which are all in that book, are not repeated here, but the following notes might be of interest.

The Engineering and Estates Committee noted a letter from the Engineer on 26th May 1897 recommending the construction of fifty 8-ton drop side wagons to "enable ballast trains to be worked to greater advantage". This was approved, and referred to the Locomotive and Stores Committee, who instructed Mr Panter to report on the details. In the following July, presumably following his report, they agreed to order twelve patent hopper ballast wagons and two brake vans with spreading ploughs from the Ballasting Plant Co at a total cost of £1850, with an additional statement that 36 more ballast wagons were to be built at Eastleigh. A year later, they recorded that 22 additional ballast wagons and three brakes were to be built, but without stating where.

Between then and September 1899, seventy more were built somewhere "to replace those hired from TJ Firbank for conveyance of ballast between Southampton Docks and Basingstoke". A year later, in October 1900, 25 additional ballast wagons were to be built.

Six more ballast hopper wagons were ordered from the Ballasting Plant Co in August 1901 at the cost of £115 each. In December 1903, tenders were accepted from GR Turner Ltd of Langley Mill, Nottinghamshire, for sixteen 40-ton ballast hoppers and from Hurst Nelson for three plough vans and two small hopper wagons. The sixteen large hoppers were to be fitted with AVB at Eastleigh for an additional charge of £50.

Another four of the 40-ton hoppers were ordered from GR Turner in July 1910 "in connection with the working of Meldon quarry" for £299 each, and they also were to be fitted with AVB at Eastleigh.

Timber Trucks

One would imagine that timber was a commodity carried from very early days, and we have already seen that the June 1848 stock return showed 56 timber trucks then in use, but the first clear reference to orders was in a minute of August 1851, when the Locomotive Committee accepted a recommendation from the Commercial Committee to order thirty timber trucks from William Beattie at the price of £30 each.

Not long after this, in 1854, the Traffic Manager reported "a great scarcity of timber wagons and recommended that a dozen pairs should be made at Nine Elms as soon as possible". A fortnight later Joseph Beattie stated that they could not be built in time at Nine Elms, and recommended the acceptance of Mr Worsdell's offer to supply them at the cost of £44 each, delivered on rails at Birmingham, the LSWR supplying the wheels and axles. This was agreed.

A request for a further twelve pairs was approved in April 1860 and in May, the tender from Brown Marshall at £39 17s 6d each was accepted. Only two days later, the Traffic Committee was calling for 24 more pairs, and this was approved by the Court of Directors on 17th May. A few days later, the Goods Superintendent at Nine Elms, Mr Ming, was urging the speedy provision of these and other wagons because of the delays caused by shortages. Whether they were ordered at that stage is not certain, but again in September 1860, there was a call from the Traffic Committee for a further twenty pairs. This brought a query from the Directors as to whether the timber trade paid its way. On being satisfied, they confirmed the order. The order was extended by another twelve pairs, still from Brown Marshall, in the following November.

The next order seems to have started from direct discussions between the Board and Joseph Wright, because the first note is in the Locomotive Committee minutes of 22nd August 1861, stating that they had been advised that Wright could offer timber trucks at £45 10s each for the bodies, plus the cost of wheels, axleboxes, springs, bearings, painting, etc, for £36 17s 4d (a total of £82 7s 4d per wagon). There is no indication of how many were ordered but the Joseph Wright drawing on which figure 1.30 is based is very clearly marked "L&SWR 1861". The dimensions do not agree precisely with those in the October 1870 list already quoted, which might indicate variations between batches, but those listed dimensions are a little suspect anyway. However, from that list it can be seen that these timber trucks were allowed an authorised load up to 6 tons each

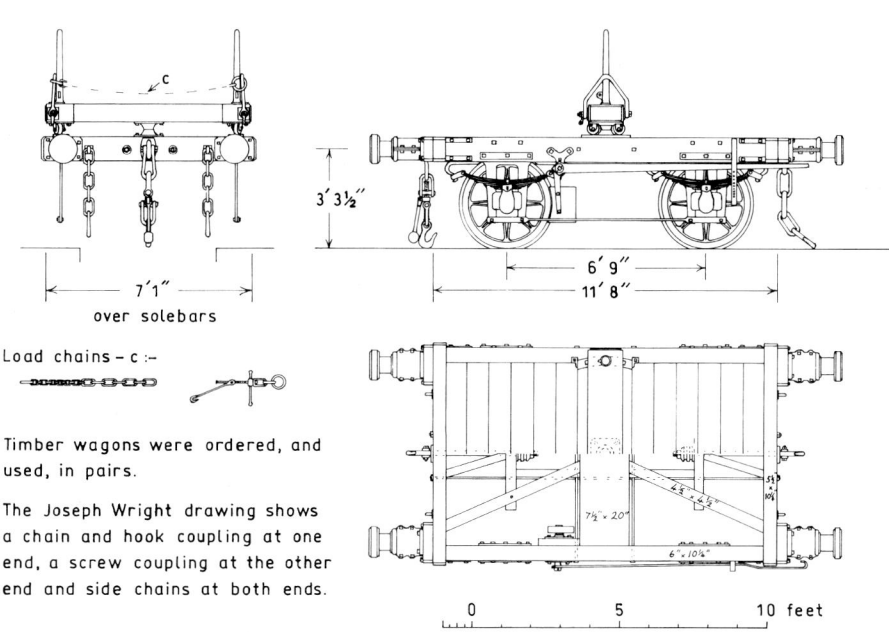

Figure 1.30. 11ft 8in timber wagon of 1861.

and, in common with other types, a maximum speed of 20mph.

In October 1864, the Locomotive Committee recorded that Metropolitan had submitted a tender for twenty pairs of timber trucks at £48 2s each, including delivery. There is no mention of the wheels, etc, but they must have been additional, and probably to be provided by the LSWR; the order was approved. They were doubtless to the 1861 design. Tenders were called for a year later to provide another twenty pairs, and something about this upset someone, because when the Traffic Committee referred the tenders from Metropolitan at £48 12s and from Oldbury at £41 15s (bodies only) to the Locomotive Committee, the latter recorded, "In future no tender is to be opened except in the presence of the Committee", and then instructed that the Oldbury tender was to be accepted.

A notice to staff dated 15th September 1865 stated "When timber is loaded in three timber trucks the stanchions of the centre one ought to be laid down securely on the floor." Drawings show that the stanchions were free to be lifted out of the pivoting bolster, but were attached to it by short lengths of chain.

In December 1873, another 25 pairs were ordered from Oldbury, but the price is not recorded. Again, it is most likely that they were still to the 1861 design, and they were delivered during the second half of 1874. It also looks as though Metropolitan got another order for 25 pairs, because there is a correspondence file dated 22nd November 1876 that lists seven types of vehicle on order from them, but in delayed delivery. Included are fifty timber trucks ordered on 20th June, half to be delivered by 14th November and the rest by 12th December.

In the meantime, in September 1876, the Traffic and Locomotive Committee accepted Metropolitan's tender for fifty trucks to a fresh design, initialled by Mr J Rawlings of Metropolitan on 12th October 1876. Shown here as figure 1.31, it was a few inches longer at 12ft over headstocks, and with separate single shoe handbrakes on each side. As with one or two other types around this time, rather surprisingly, Mansell type wheels were fitted.

The same committee authorised an order with Craven in October 1878 for, among other vehicles, ten timber batten wagons (LSWR drawing 2658) for £56 each. They were described on the drawing as "rail and batten" wagons, and are illustrated here as figure 1.32. Some more were built in about 1888, but then and later, they were only described as batten wagons. For this batch, the main differences were the provision of an iron brake shoe and a longer lever, the later pattern of open spoke wheels, Panter type axleboxes, and transverse leaf buffer springs. Several more were built in the 1890s and later, all looking very similar, and they are described in *Southern Wagons, Volume 1*.

The next mention of ordinary timber trucks was in December 1884 when the Traffic Committee had

GOODS VEHICLES

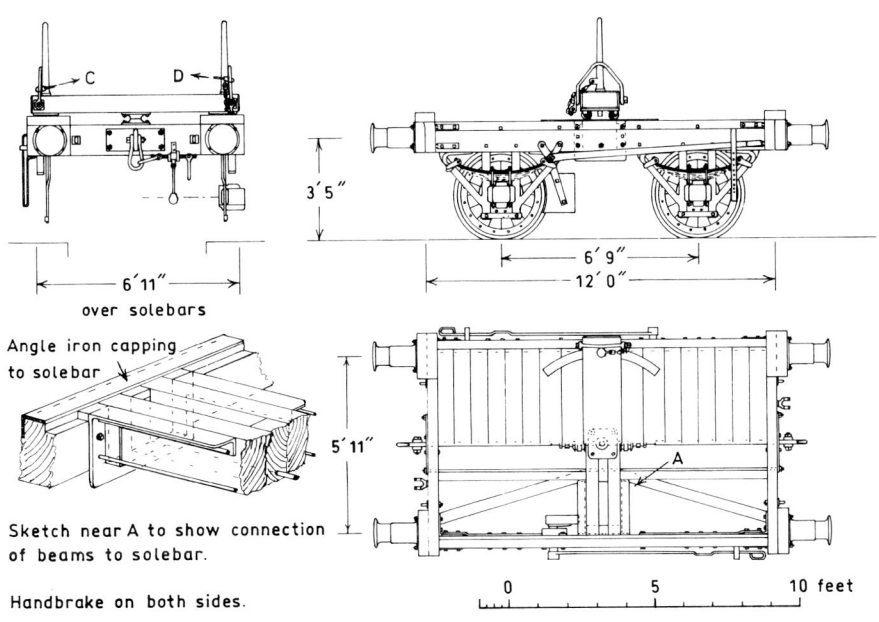

Figure 1.31. 12ft timber wagon of 1876.

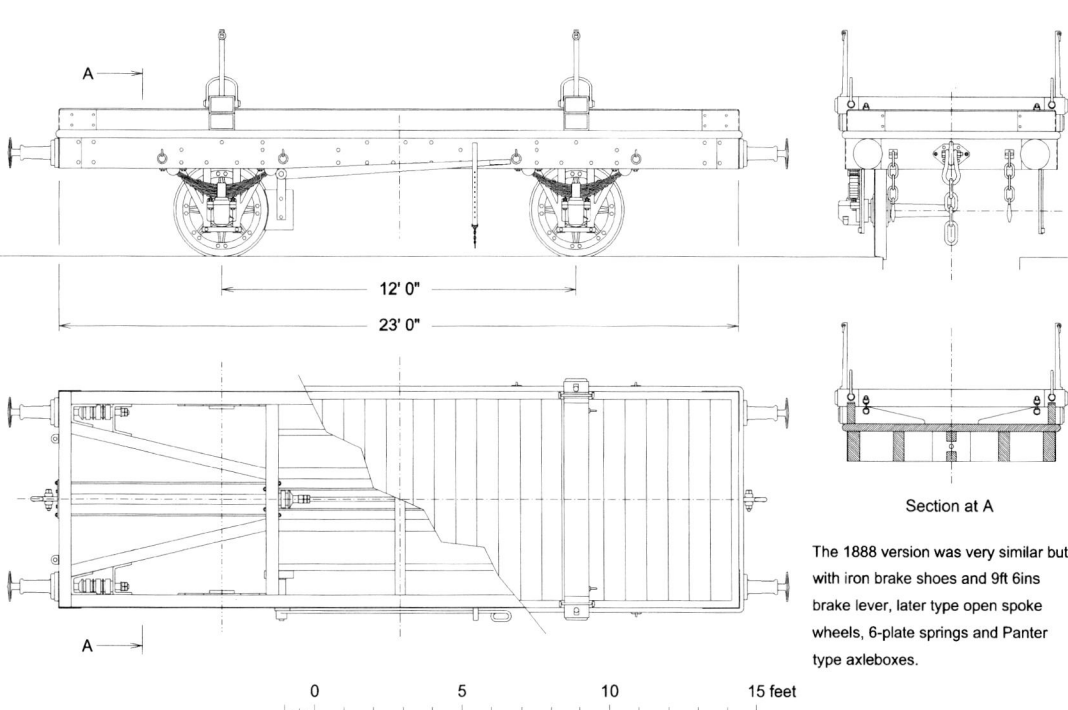

Figure 1.32. 23ft "rail and batten" wagon of 1878.

Plate 1.32. 23ft rail and timber wagon of 1878 at extreme right, the late version of 1900 (No 11716) shows how logs were secured. (J Tatchell collection)

a request from Inspector Leigh, Wagon Master, that the stock of timber and rail wagons should be increased by thirty pairs of timber trucks. This was approved, and in January, the Engineering and Stores Committee agreed that they should be built at Nine Elms. These were to LSWR drawing 4925, and the main difference from most of those before and after was that they had ordinary wagon buffers with rubber springs (like the preceding 23ft batten wagons) instead of the self-contained variety. They were so similar that they are not illustrated here.

Two fresh and very similar LSWR drawings for 13ft timber trucks were prepared. Number 1080 in February 1892, and the other (apparently number 259, amendment 1) dated April 1894. There was also a simplified drawing, number 258, dated July 1894 – a sequence of numbers and dates that is distinctly confusing. The only obvious difference between them is that on the 1892 drawing the central beams were connected to the solebars by simple vertical angle irons, in addition of course to being housed into the solebars. The 1894 drawing shows reversion to the shaped and extended angle iron support as in the 1876 version. Both variants are covered here by figure 1.33.

In 1893, the Locomotive and Stores Committee ordered the construction of fifty pairs. The main differences from the 1876 version were that the floor planks rested on top of the solebars instead of resting in rebates, and the provision of side rails rising 3in above the floor, presumably to prevent the chains or unshipped stanchions from slipping over the sides when unloaded. Quadrant plates and wheels on the bolster ends were dispensed with, the bolster ends sliding metal to metal on the side capping. The pivot pin for the bolster extended through a slot in the continuous drawbar and through a bearing plate underneath the cross beams, where it was retained with a key. A handbrake was only provided on one side, but with an iron brake shoe instead of the former wooden block.

After this order, there are no more references to orders for timber trucks other than for 23ft timber batten trucks in 1893 and 1900 and, in 1913 and subsequently, for bogie timber trucks, which are all illustrated in *Southern Wagons, Volume 1*. However very many of the authorisations for renewals after 1894 state simply that a quantity (anything from fifty to two hundred at a time) of wagons was to be withdrawn and replaced by vehicles of the same description.

A fresh drawing was produced in 1911; the body was similar to the previous ones. Either-side handbrake levers were fitted, operating two shoes on one side with dog and lift-link clutches. From the previous paragraph, it is not certain whether any

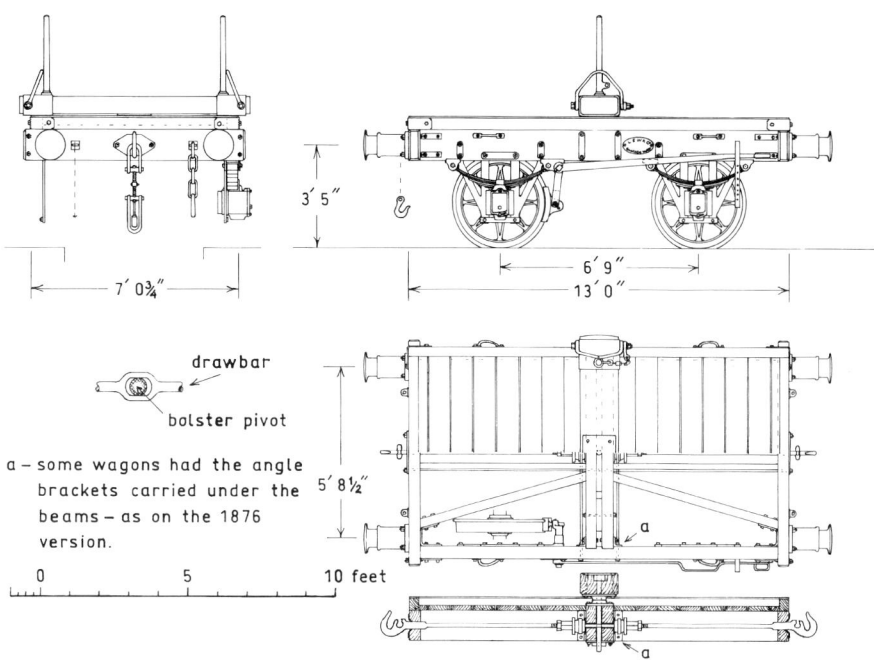

Figure 1.33. 13ft timber wagon of 1892.

were actually built new to this design or whether it was used for upgrading some of the older ones. This version is illustrated in *Southern Wagons, Volume 1*.

Goods Brake Vans

The earliest references to the means for braking goods trains have been mentioned earlier in this chapter. The first serious attention to the matter was in February 1848, when Mr Beattie provided a plan for converting some existing wagons to guards brake vans. He also reported on a proposal to fit a screw brake and a lookout on "road boxes". Later in the same month, he submitted a letter on the "adaptation of the present wagons to the purpose of brake wagons". Unfortunately, the minutes are no more informative than this, but a stock report of 19th July 1848 listed four "Goods Guards Vans, in good order having been lately fitted up". In June 1849, it was agreed that twelve more goods wagons should be altered to guards brake vans. The term "road boxes" is assumed to mean covered vans used for the carriage of relatively small or light items between stations, such that they could be loaded or unloaded during a pause at the station without the train necessarily being shunted into the yard. The term was later superseded by "road vans", which will be mentioned again at the end of this section.

In October 1854 and December 1855, two batches, each of six, were to be "constructed as early as possible". It is not clear from this whether it means they were more conversions or that they were to be built to a new design. Further authorisations were for twelve in February 1857 (later reported as built at Nine Elms) another twelve ordered to be built at Nine Elms in August 1859 and a repeat in February 1860, but this time it was specified that they were to be built by contract. A month later, it was mentioned that the 1859 order was then in hand at Nine Elms, and Mr Beattie reported their completion in July. Thus, the photo of a brake van behind the locomotive *Vesta* at Dorchester in mid-1860 (plate 1.34a) could have been one of the newer designs or a conversion, though it does not look very old. The sketch shown as part A of figure 1.34 is based on this. It is much like the next version, though apparently rather shorter. An interesting feature is that the end was fully planked, including end stanchions, right up to the roof of the lookout, with only one window beside the Guard's seat, although the other end and the two sides appear to have been fully glazed. For a Guard sitting on his seat, the end planking would have caused very little restriction of his view. Another point of note is that it is painted a dark colour, distinguishing it from the light grey of the general goods wagons.

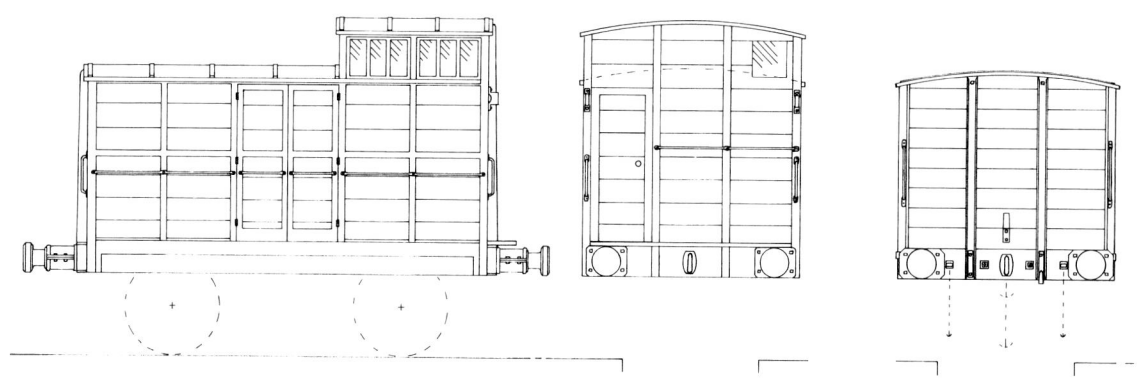

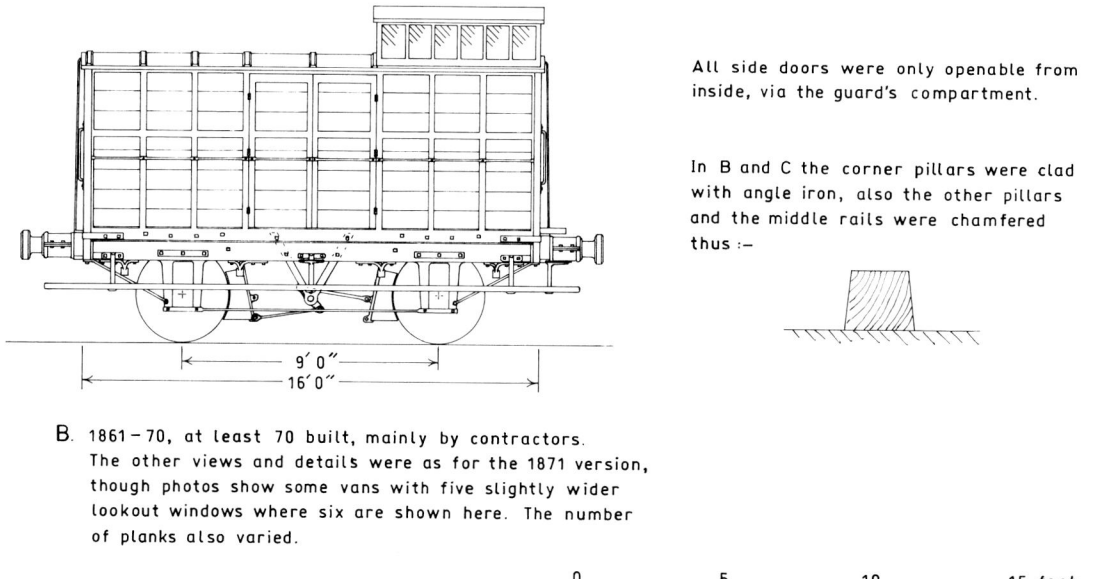

Figure 1.34. Goods guard's vans before 1875 (1 of 2)

Despite these references to quantities, it is not possible to verify the actual number of these vans in use at any one time before December 1868. Until then, all goods vehicles, with the occasional exception of coal and ballast wagons, were lumped together in the rolling stock returns. At that date there were reported to be 98 in existence.

We begin to get a better view of what these vans looked like after Mr Godson, the Goods Manager, asked for twelve more in July 1861. An order was then placed with Joseph Wright at his tender price of £120 each, the vehicles being to a plan by the LSWR. The Joseph Wright drawing for this still exists, though with several illegible measurements; it is illustrated here in figure 1.34 part B. The twelve were delivered before January 1862, and a total of a further 44 were supplied by the Railway Carriage Co of Oldbury and by Joseph Wright & Sons, by then the Metropolitan Co, in 1864 and 1865. Photographs taken at Chard Joint station and at Yeovil Town show vans almost identical to the present drawing, but with only seven panes of glass in the ends of the lookouts. The one at Chard Joint has five in the side but those at Yeovil are too indistinct to count. One can only speculate on where all these were built. Like the earlier ones, they had a pair of hinged doors on each side, but with no external door handles, so access to open them was only through the Guard's compartment. The door to this was on the end of the vehicle,

GOODS VEHICLES

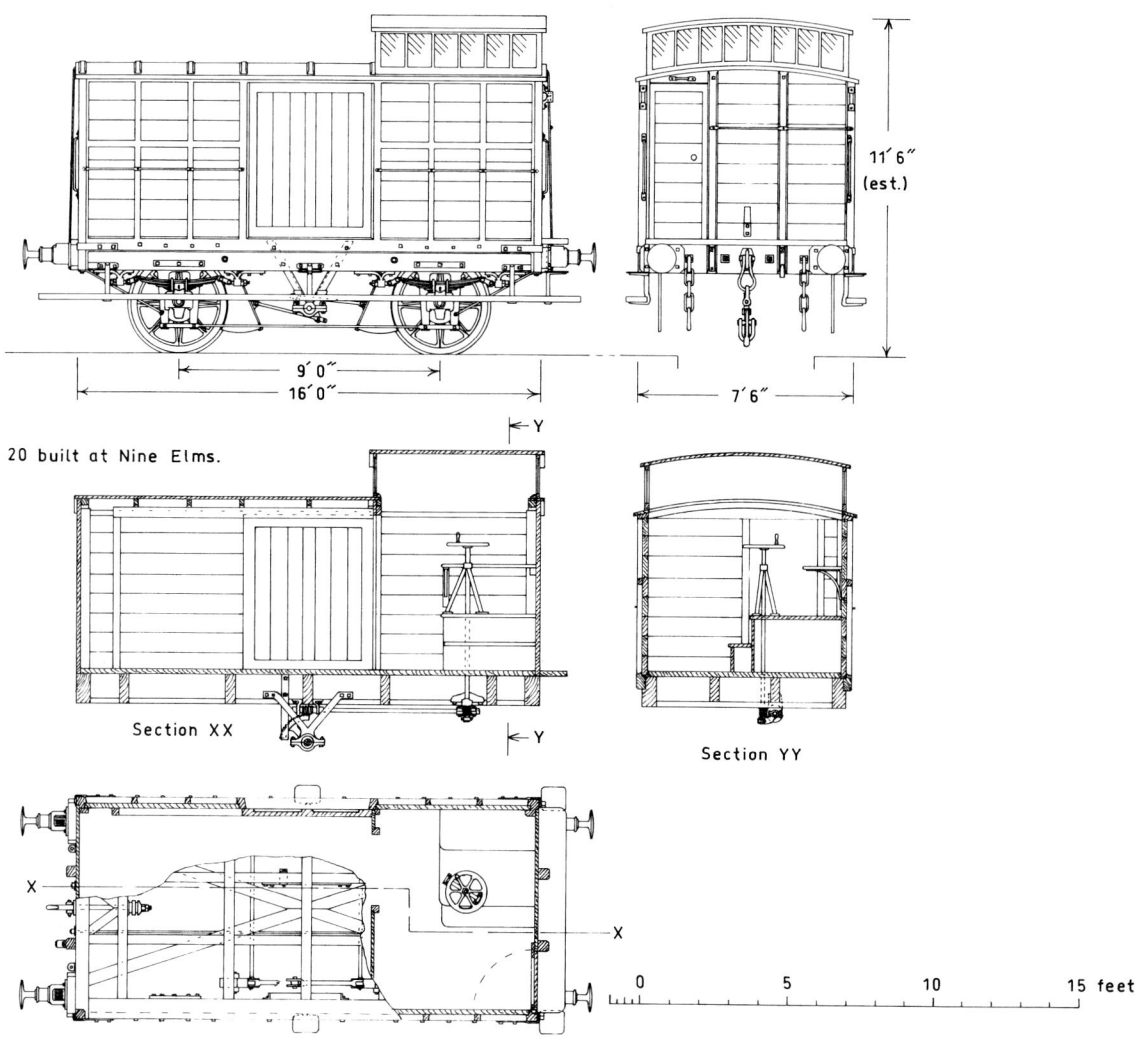

Figure 1.34. Goods guard's vans before 1875 (2 of 2)

reached by way of a narrow plank over the buffer castings.

The small fittings that look rather like odd grab handles high up on the guard's end of versions A and C (and were probably fitted on version B) appear on most brake van drawings, but on some there are dotted lines that indicate a vertical hole down through the casting. We will come to this matter again later.

Just before Christmas 1864, the Locomotive Committee approved a recommendation from the Officers Committee that the ends of all of the company's brake vans should be painted red. It was also agreed that each ballast train should have a brake van at each end, and Mr Beattie was told to arrange for eight vans to be used for this purpose. A month later, it was decided that ten of the "old" guards vans should be transferred for use with ballast trains, and that ten new ones should be built. A couple of months later, Mr Beattie reported that ten of the goods brake vans could be made fit for passenger trains on short branch lines, and that ten would be reconstructed at Nine Elms without delay. The Chard Joint photo is presumably of one of these. Unfortunately, there is no indication of what this alteration involved, though it is fairly certain that they had to be fitted with fairleads, cord reels and a gong for the communication cord.

At the same time there was discussion of the difficulty of getting sufficient brake power for the

Plate 1.34a. Early goods guard's van and corrugated iron hatch roof covered van at Dorchester in 1860.

trains and it was agreed to order another twenty. Whether this indicates that the vans themselves lacked braking power, possibly by not being heavy enough, or whether it just means that more were then needed for the increase in the number of goods trains, is not at all clear. In any case, the next annual rolling stock report in January 1866 recorded that ten had been built by contractors and ten transferred to the Permanent Way Department.

Shortly after this, at the end of March 1866, there was a proposal to convert twelve old second-class carriages into specie wagons. This hung over until July, when it was decided to build twelve new specie wagons, but to make them available as guards brake vans. As so often, there is no indication as to whether these were passenger or goods class, although from the general context the former seems more likely.

So far, apart from the generalised reference above, there had been no mention, either on drawings or in minutes, of the actual weight of the brake vans. Thus, a question arises from the approval by the Locomotive Committee in July 1868 for the construction of a 10-ton brake van for use between Exeter Queen Street and St David's. This is still a notoriously steep incline, and must always have justified more than normal brake power. The implication might be that the earlier ones were less than this weight, which is a little surprising, or that one was just to be reserved and kept always at Exeter for this purpose. We shall probably never know!

The next identifiable reference was the decision in October 1870 to build twenty new goods brakes at Nine Elms, the side doors to slide. LSWR drawing 1662 was issued for these, and showed another 16ft van, very similar to the earlier ones, except that the hinged side doors were now replaced by sliding ones, again with no external handles, access being from the guard's compartment as before. These are also shown in figure 1.34 at part C. Of particular note is the brake system, where a worm at the bottom of the vertical shaft drives a horizontal shaft. This shaft has another worm at the other end engaging in a quadrant pinion attached to the cross-shaft, which has cranks to operate the brake shoes. One can well imagine that this would introduce quite significant friction resistance. The twenty were delivered in the latter part of 1871.

In December 1872, the goods guards and breaksmen submitted a memorandum to the Traffic and Locomotive Committee concerning dangers in brake vans, but the minutes do not give any details, although to modern eyes there could have been

Plate 1.34b. Chard joint LSWR and GWR station. The leading vehicle is a 16ft goods brake van of c.1861. (K Hastie collection)

several possibilities. It was agreed that one van should be altered as suggested. A year later, the same committee decided to have twelve new vans built at Nine Elms. It seems likely that discussions ensued, and resulted in a new and larger van, 18ft 6in long and 7ft 9½in wide, to drawing 1927 dated 27th January 1874. A fortnight later, the Traffic and Locomotive Committee agreed to order two of them, described as heavy brake vans, for the Ilfracombe line. Unfortunately there is nothing on the drawing to indicate what and where the necessary weights were packed.

They are not fully illustrated here, because a revised drawing 1979 was issued in July, followed by a decision in November to buy twelve of these. The only obvious differences were that the two based on drawing 1927 had ordinary arc roofs on the lookout compared with slightly flattened ones on the remainder. Also, the drive to the brakes was by the same system as in the 1871 batch (figure 1.34).

The later ones are shown here as the main part of figure 1.35, from which it is obvious that at least some danger was overcome by providing a small enclosed veranda to give access to the guard's entrance door. The rather weak looking sides were in fact reinforced inside with double diagonal half round iron bars.

It is intriguing that the brake arrangement adopted required four different patterns of carrier for the brake shoes.

Twenty more, presumably still to drawing 1979, were ordered from Brown Marshall in December 1875 at a cost of £153 each. In fact, from the wording of the minutes of two committees, it might be deduced that there were two orders for twenty in each of November and December 1875. A slightly revised drawing 2249 was issued in October 1876, the only apparent differences being in the form of the brake cross-shaft hanger, the alignment of the primary brake rod, the height of the guard's seat, the height of the handrails, a few timber dimensions and a probable change of buffer type. The alterations are indicated in figure 1.35.

There is an oddity in that the width of 7ft 9½in was crossed out on the works drawing and rewritten as 8ft 0in, although no alterations were made to any of the component dimensions. Taken together with some faint sketch marks on the drawing it seems probable that these were notes made of changes to be incorporated in the next drawing.

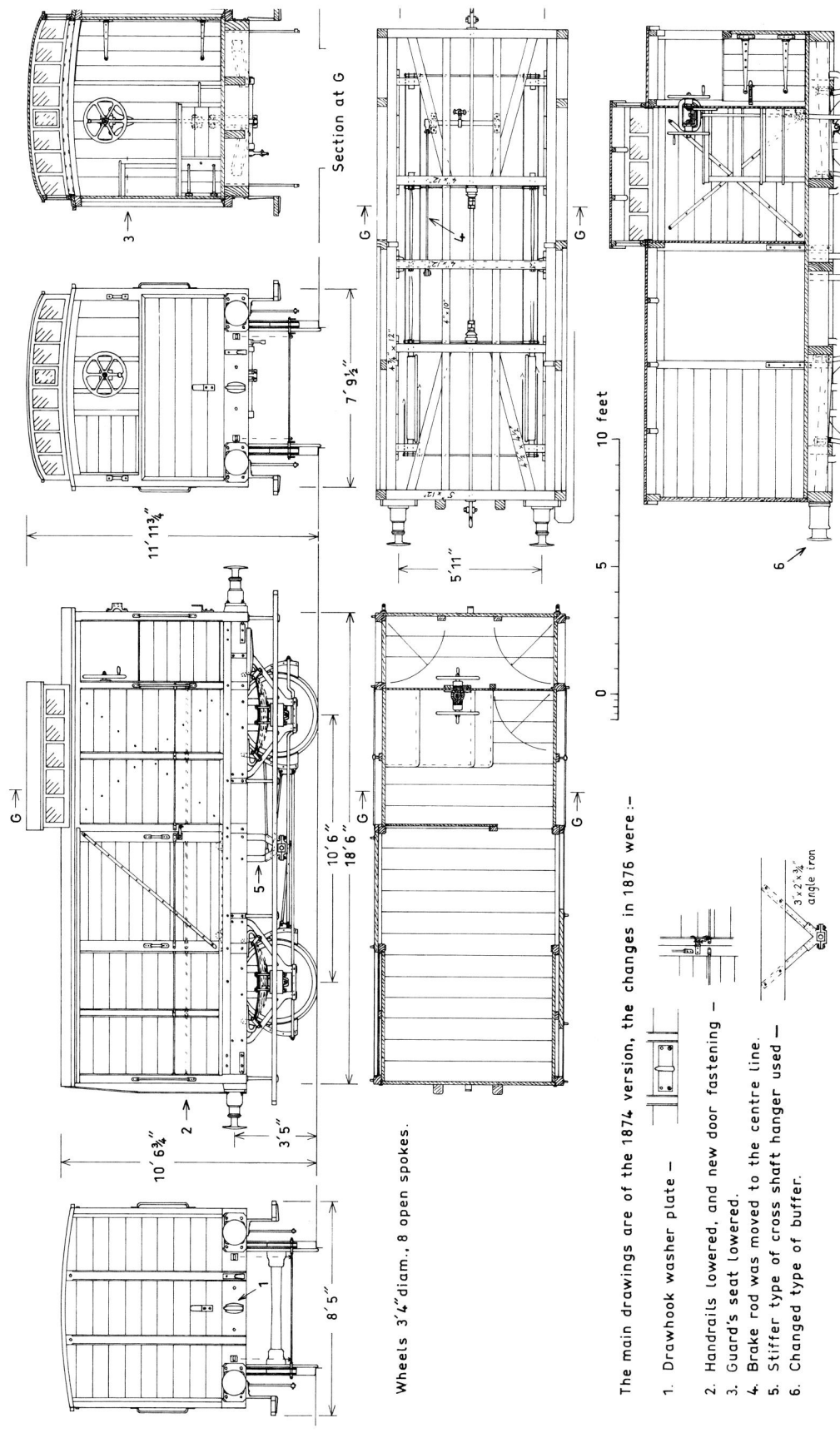

Figure 1.35. 18ft 6in goods guard's vans of 1874 and 1876.

GOODS VEHICLES

An interesting detail of LSWR drawing 2249 is the inclusion of just one elevation of a side light. The brackets appear on several of the goods brake van drawings, but an illustration of the lamp is a rarity. The bracket looks a bit like a small grab handle with a slot down the middle, as mentioned earlier. This lamp has a side fitting with a blade that drops into the bracket slot, an apparently odd arrangement, since these lamps projected 10in beyond the side of the van, bringing the overall width to slightly more than the LSWR loading gauge limit.

The half-year report in January 1877 recorded that 17 goods guards vans had been delivered from contractors.

Two old goods brakes were ordered to be converted to ballast brakes for the Permanent Way Department in December 1876, and another two old goods brakes, together with 53 old wagons, went to the Permanent Way Department in May 1877. Two very old ballast brakes were still in existence in 1923, numbered 018 and 019, and they might have been two of these. In general layout, they were rather like plates 141 and 142 and figure 48 in *Southern Wagons, Volume 1*, although the actual length is unknown. Instead of the outside diagonal frames they had four vertical frames between the end and veranda pillars, and very old-type large wooden brake blocks. There was no close resemblance to any of the vehicles illustrated here, and no other details are known to have survived.

Seventeen more new brakes were authorised to be ordered from Brown Marshall, for £140 each, in August 1878. These were almost certainly built to LSWR drawing 2509, shown here in figure 1.36. The general layout was much the same as the preceding ones, but the body was made 8ft 0in wide, as mentioned above, and there were a few more detail alterations of fractions of an inch; also the semi-elliptical lookout roof was replaced by a simple arc one. The bodies were made stronger with double diagonal outside framing to the side sections and the sliding doors. This compares with the covered goods wagons discussed earlier, where Mr Adams took an existing Beattie design and strengthened it rather than start from scratch with new designs. Rather curiously, the braking system reverted to only one shoe on each wheel, although the shoes were now iron. However, sanding boxes and pipes were provided to deliver sand to the wheels under the veranda end. The two vertical internal and external brake wheels were replaced by a single horizontal wheel on a standard on the top floor of the guard's compartment.

Plate 1.36. 18ft 6in goods brake van, similar to those of 1878 and 1882. The following wagon appears to be a 3-plank stone or ballast wagon. (MS King collection)

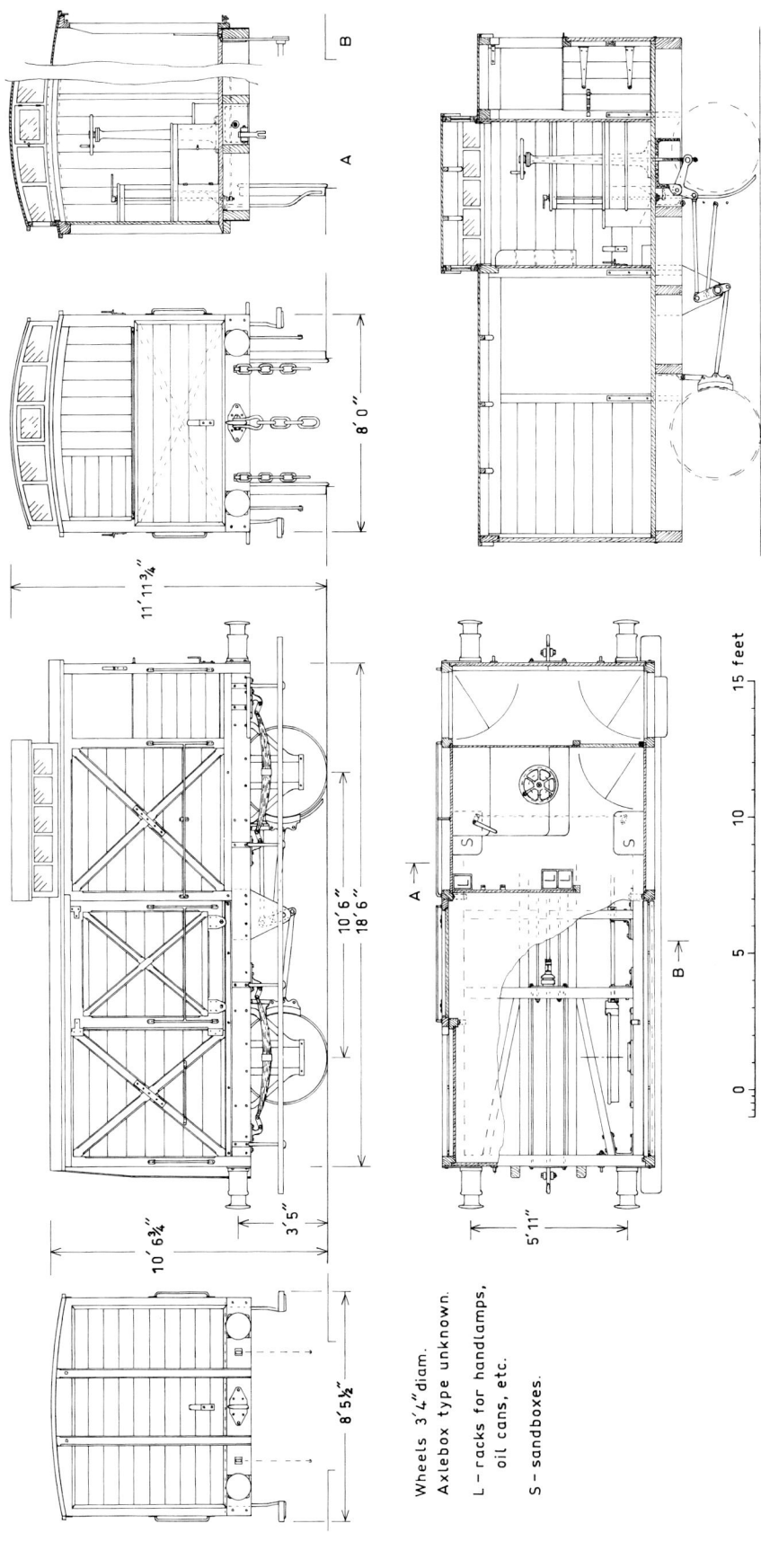

Figure 1.36. 18ft 6in goods guard's van of 1878.

GOODS VEHICLES

Shortly after this, in January 1879, the goods guards asked for stoves in the vans, in a similar manner to those on the LNWR, and it was agreed to fit one as a trial. At the next meeting, in February, Mr Adams objected and recommended that they were too dangerous since the South Western vans carried goods, which he said was not the case with the LNWR, and urged that they should not be fitted. Apparently the guards did not give up, because at the November 1879 meeting of the same Traffic and Locomotive Committee, it was reported that a small stove had been fitted in goods brake van number 3921. It was then agreed that they should be put into other vans as they came in for repair, and that they should be provided in all new vans. No doubt this applied to the twenty that were ordered from Craven after the meeting in January 1880.

A further twenty were approved at the end of November 1881, and an order was placed with Metropolitan early in 1882. The 1878 design of body was largely retained but with a body width of 7ft 9in. The underframe and brakes were upgraded. Compensated brakes were provided, with two iron shoes on each wheel, again with sanding to the wheels under the guard's end, and ballast was loaded into two boxes created between underframe members. This combination gave the vehicle considerably more braking power than its predecessors. A stove was now fitted as standard where part of the partition had previously been. This version appears here as figure 1.37. Twenty more were authorised near the end of 1884.

The last four designs described all appeared in quite a short period. Even so, there are photos that show glimpses of other very similar vehicles, but with further variations such as single diagonal outside framing with a plain boarded sliding door, seemingly different brake arrangements, and so on. Unfortunately, these views are fragmentary, usually just a part at the edge of a loco photo, or in the distance seen between two near vehicles, so no useful conclusions can be drawn other than that this chapter, as already said, does not pretend to be the complete story.

When the Traffic and the Locomotive and Stores Committees approved the construction of twelve more goods brakes in June 1887, they were to a new design under the superintendence of William Panter. The most obvious difference was the elimination of the roof lookout, but the length was also reduced by 6in. Variations of this design continued to be built in large numbers for many years.

At first they had the slotted fittings for side lamps, as mentioned earlier, and then for a time had permanent lamp housings on each side just below roof level, into which lamps could be placed from inside the vehicle. These were later removed and plated over.

These and later brake vans are well described in *Southern Wagons, Volume 1*.

A minute of the Locomotive and Stores Committee of 9th May 1888 records the receipt of a letter from Mr Panter asking for instructions as to discontinuing the use of vermilion paint on the ends of guards brake vans by which, he claimed, a considerable saving would be made. It was then agreed that the practice should be discontinued. The matter does not appear in the minutes again, and has been the subject of some debate. Whether the decision was implemented or rescinded is not known for certain, and of course, photographs give little or no help as red would appear as a dark shade similar to the dark brown.

LSWR goods brake vans are often referred to as road vans, that is, they were designed to be used for the carriage of parcels and small quantities of goods between stations. This was often more convenient than loading, and then trying to find them in one of the other vehicles of the train. These items were in the charge of the guard who was responsible for putting them off at the right destinations. It is not so often realised that they were also used as newspaper and mail vans on many secondary routes where passenger trains were scarce or non-existent during the night hours. In working timetables there were several references to goods trains being required to pass through certain stations at low speed in order for newspaper parcels or mail bags to be dropped off, thus saving several minutes compared with stopping and starting the train. This was also mentioned in Chapter 2 of *LSWR Carriages, Volume 3*.

A rather intriguing goods brake was one described as "Goods Brake with Passenger Compartment". In his *History of the London & South Western Railway, Volume 2*, Mr RA Williams quoted an order of May 1857 stating that the 1.00am goods train from Nine Elms to Southampton was to have a carriage for Customs Officers accompanying bonded goods, thus making it a "mixed" train. It was presumably for the same purpose that drawing 267 was prepared in November 1892 depicting a "Goods Brake with Passenger Compartment". This is shown in *Southern Wagons, Volume 1* as figure 28, where it is noted that two of them were built.

Around 1901, there are entries in the working timetables showing a 1.00am Nine Elms to Southampton goods train and an 11.30pm Southampton to Nine Elms goods train, with the

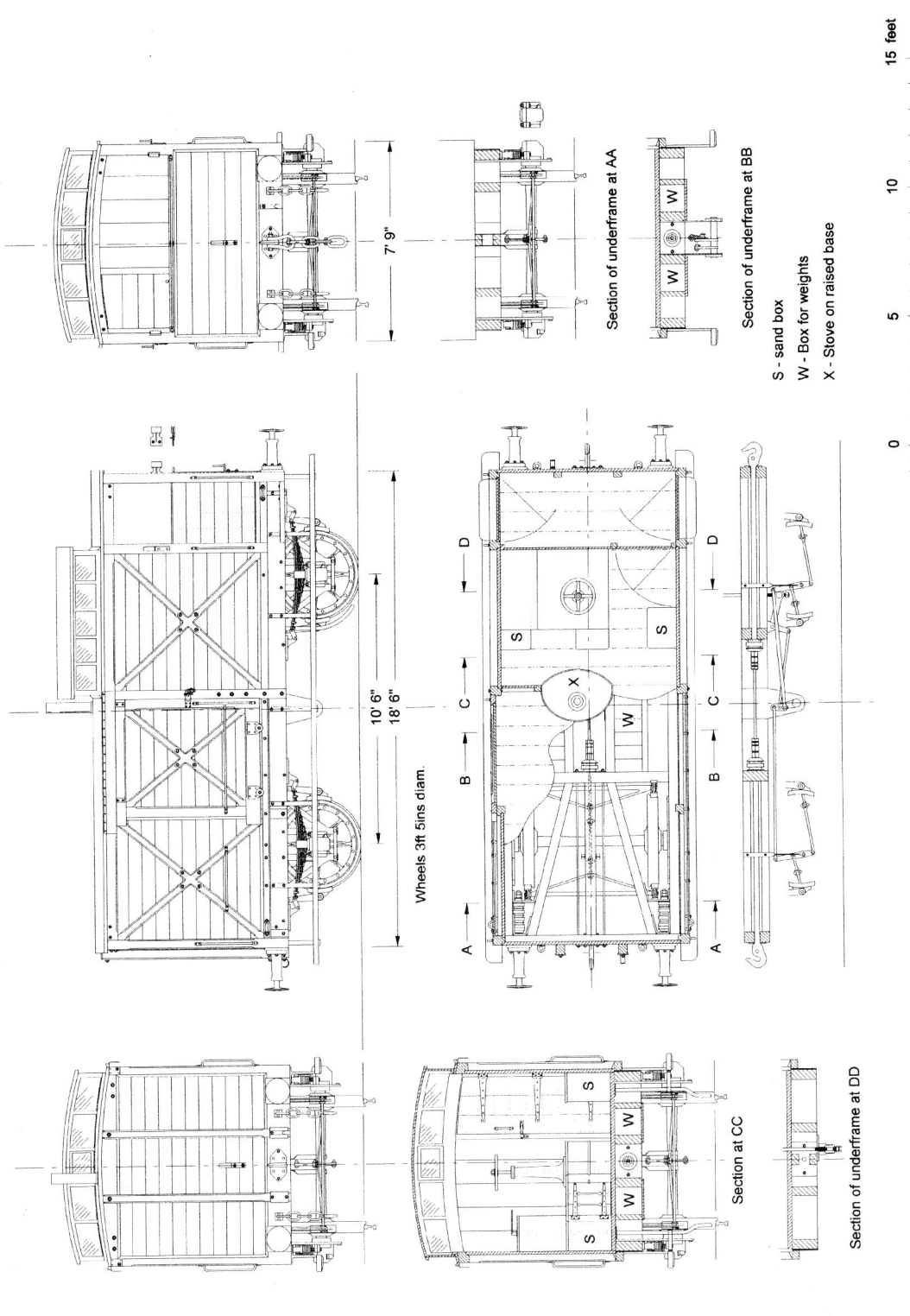

Figure 1.37. 18ft 6in goods guard's van of 1882.

GOODS VEHICLES

note "One of the specially constructed vehicles may be attached for the accommodation of Custom House Officers in charge of bonded goods". In this case the train became a "mixed" train, and thus ran under the appropriate regulations.

The 20-ton heavy brake vans of 1907 are illustrated on page 60 of *Southern Wagons, Volume 1*, but a list of numbers and details of their usage was shown in the Appendix to the WTT for January 1911. The numbers are listed here in the Appendix. After the numbers, it is stated that:

"Any special Goods trains run with a full load on the under-mentioned lines must have a heavy goods brake van, or two ordinary brake vans with a Guard or Brakesman in each, at the rear:

From Woking or stations above to Aldershot.
Cattle Specials, Petersfield to Portsmouth
Meon Valley line
Alton and Winchester line
Amesbury and Bulford line
Salisbury and Dorset line
Swanage line
From Bournemouth West or Bournemouth Central to Wimborne or Hamworthy Junction, and vice versa
Dorchester and Weymouth line
Weymouth and Portland line
Between Wadebridge and Delabole
All Goods trains from Guildford to Tongham which are made up to a double Engine load with coal must have a heavy brake van at the rear."

Miscellaneous

25 china clay wagons were authorised in June 1913, and built in 1914/15 to carry china clay from the North Cornwall China Clay Co works at Wenford to Wadebridge and Padstow. Illustrated here as figure 1.38 and plate 1.38, the wagons were little more than all-steel platform wagons, of mainly riveted construction, with locating brackets formed of angle iron sections to keep the clay containers in place. The maximum load was 8 tons. There were eight containers (described on the LSWR diagram as conveyors) to each wagon, apparently made of pressed steel sheets and designed to be lifted off for emptying direct into ships' holds through hinged side doors. Although the drawing for the wagons has survived, there is minimal information about the conveyors, apart from their internal dimensions and what can be gleaned from the photograph. It is not certain whether the lettering shown on the containers was genuinely painted on, simply marked on for the photograph or added by retouching the photo afterwards.

These wagons had a relatively short life, but the reason why is not recorded. Certainly the clay traffic continued, but apparently mainly in ordinary open wagons, sometimes with tarpaulin covers and sometimes without. Anyway, it was around 1923 that the conveyor location brackets were removed, and new brake van bodies were placed on the underframes, as illustrated in *Southern Wagons, Volume 1*. The LSWR numbers allocated to these brake vans included the number 4133, which is the

Plate 1.38. China clay wagons. (Courtesy of English China Clays Group)

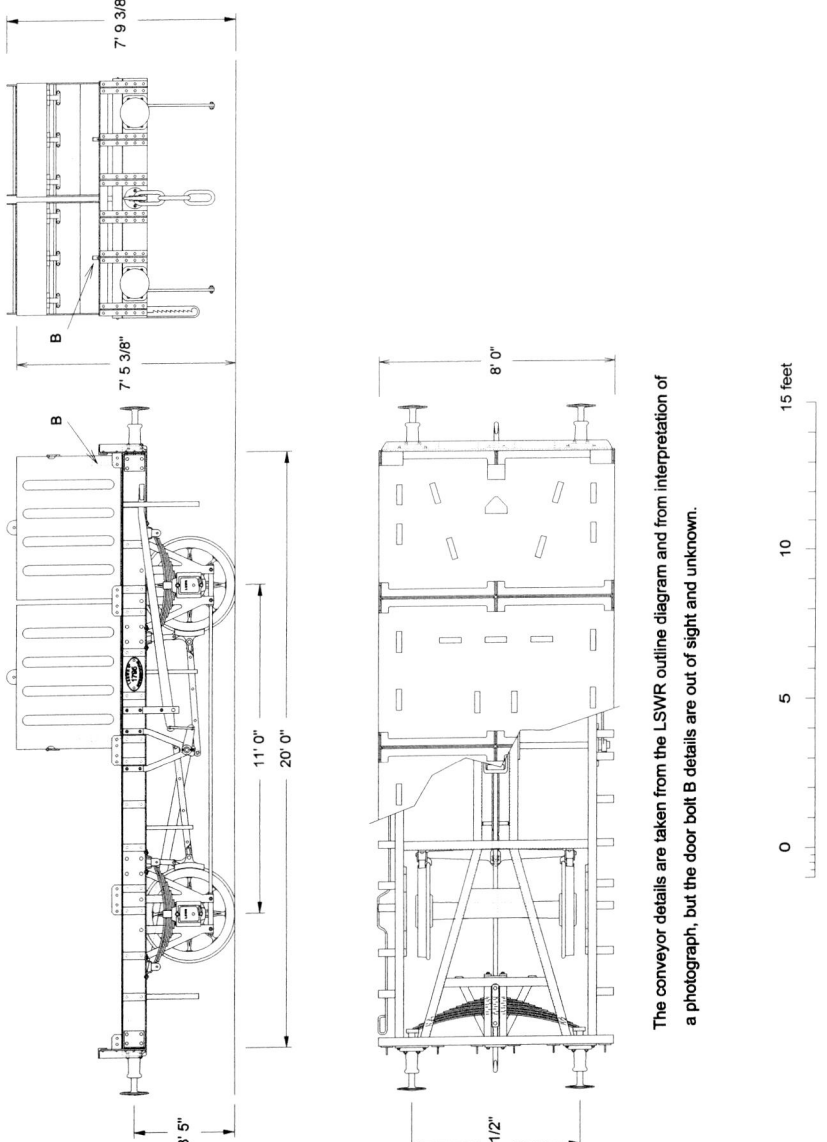

Figure 1.38. China clay wagon of 1913.

GOODS VEHICLES

Plate 1.39. "329" class standard well tank in original condition at Exeter. (Courtesy of Wiltshire County Council Libraries and Heritage)

number retouched in on the photo that was published in 1917. It might be deduced from this that all the other numbers were also the same as those that the clay wagons originally carried. On the assumption that this is correct, they are shown in the Appendix.

This ends the descriptions of particular vehicles, but here follow several photographs, some mentioned earlier, and some already illustrated in *Southern Wagons Volume 1*. They show a few loads or other points of interest.

Plate 1.39 is a photograph of a 2-4-0 well-tank loco at Exeter. At its edge it has another corrugated hatch roof van, seemingly slightly longer than the one in plate 1.34a. The lettering is almost certainly "L&SWRCº" to the left and a four-digit number (possibly 1234) to the right. The long panel over the section that is opposite to the door on the other side has lettering that might read "Doors to be OPENED before" and "opening or closing roof hatch". However, this does not appear to be of a lot of use when the doors were on the other side. A notice could not be put in that position on the door side, but might have been split into two small notices on the doors themselves. Pure conjecture!

Plate 1.39a. Detail from Plate 1.39.

Plate 1.40. Wimbledon, c.1873. See text for details. (Author's collection)

Plate 1.40 is part of a view originally taken to show the LB&SCR station at Wimbledon in about 1874, or slightly later, when the LSWR station was still to the west of the road bridge. The fence behind the platform with the short canopy formed the LB&SCR/LSWR boundary, although at this date the LSWR trains to Epsom were running through this platform. This part of the view shows the LSWR goods siding in the area later built over for the new LSWR station of 1881. Taking the wagons from the left, the first is a dumb-buffered 4-plank wagon from which it looks as though a former top plank has been removed, except for a short section at each end concealing the top few inches of long diagonal bolts (the nuts of which can just be detected). There also appears to be diagonal strapping on the outer sections of the end. The lettering just could be "L&SWRCº" and a number. If so, it is most likely that this is one of the many wagons hired at that period. The second is difficult to be sure about, but is possibly the same as numbers 5 and 7. The next two, numbers 3 and 4, are certainly 8-ton opens of circa 1872, shown earlier at figure 1.5 and in the next photo; the brake lever can just be seen on the further one. Numbers 5 and 7 appear to be 8 tonners of around 1862-65 with tie rods between their axleguards. Number 6 is again difficult. It appears to be shorter than the others, possibly around 13ft 6in compared with the others at 15ft 4in or so. It might just be private owner, but is more likely to be another hired wagon. The low sided wagon at number 6 is another fairly early one with tie-rods between the axleguards, but otherwise unidentifiable. The covered van is another hatch roof one with the door on the far side. This one has planked sides, not corrugated as in the two previous photos of this type, and furthermore, its construction seems to be more in keeping with the covered and meat vans shown at figures 1.16 and 1.26. The final wagon appears to be a dumb buffered coal wagon with a continuous top plank.

Plate 1.41 is a view of Weybridge that can be dated to between the first quarter of 1881 and early 1885, when a third line was laid through the station. I am grateful to Mr M Hutson for several details about the station and signalbox that make this dating possible.

The signalbox and the slotted post signals are beside the original main line, and the signal box appears to be one built by Messrs Saxby & Farmer in 1866 at a cost of £950. The same company provided more signals at the station in the 1866/67, presumably including those seen at the end of the platform. Behind it is the siding running from the Chertsey bay platform, the exit from which to the down main can just be seen in the distance. On the original print, which is not a very good one, it is just possible to detect some parts of the first extension to the station, the footbridge and approach to the down platform, as well as the goods lift and the first increase in the platform heights, all of which were authorised between August and December 1880, and

GOODS VEHICLES

Plate 1.41. Weybridge in the early 1880s. (National Railway Museum 1557/86)

probably carried out in early 1881. The points in the left foreground are those leading towards Chertsey. The line in the immediate foreground continued for some distance and then joined the down main.

Replacement of this signalbox was authorised in September 1880. The crane is probably the 5 ton one authorised by the Traffic Committee in September 1861, and supplied by Lloyds Foster & Co for £100 in June 1862, and fixed by the LSWR Maintenance of Way department for £19 5s.

Taking the group of private owner wagons at the left, the first wagon is No 374 of Stratton Gentry & C° of Kew Bridge, London. The next is probably one of the Midland Railway's dumb-buffered former private owner wagons that they bought up in an attempt to abolish such wagons on their line, but were then thwarted by the private owners who promptly used the compensation money to buy new wagons! It is believed that the large MR lettering was not used before about 1880. The lettering of the next two is not very clear, but from the layout they are both from the Great Northern Railway before that company adopted the large "GN" letters after 1898.

In the next group, the first is one of the 1872 8-ton wagons as seen in plate 1.5. The next is another like the left-hand one in plate 1.40 with the cut away top plank; the nut on the end of the diagonal stay rod is clearer in this view. It can be seen that the brake is pinned hard down. As before, it is not certain whether this belongs to a private owner, to the LSWR or is one hired by the LSWR, though the last seems most likely. Beyond this is a wagon looking rather like an LSWR 10-ton wagon of 1881 (figure 1.7) with its wooden tarpaulin bar rather carelessly stowed. It has been said earlier that this wagon type is the first recorded as having such a bar, but of course, there is no way of being certain of this. In addition, it does appear to have the large letters, "LSWR". Beyond that is another wagon similar to the first with its brake handle pinned well down. The final wagon looks more like a mineral wagon with a through top plank.

Between the second group of wagons and the most distant ones, there is a wagon turntable for which the loading bank was cut back. This feature was common at many stations to permit the turning of vehicles that had doors in one side only.

Plate 1.42. Contractor's train (Lucas & Aird) at temporary River Mole bridge at Leatherhead, probably early 1884. (Railtrack, ref PLRC94)

Plate 1.42 is from the Railtrack infrastructure archive, and shows a scene during the construction of the LSWR viaduct over the River Mole at Leatherhead in early 1884. A diminutive contractor's 0-4-0 locomotive, belonging to Lucas & Aird, heads a dumb-buffered wagon of unknown origin, followed by what looks like an LSWR dropside wagon, then apparently an LBSCR open A and an LSWR 6-ton open dating from before 1865. On the latter, the grey paint appears to have darkened quite a lot, unless it has had a coat of the fairly recently introduced brown paint, but still with the "L&SWRCº" small lettering and number in the door.

Plate 1.43 shows one of the gunpowder vans (No 2134) that were illustrated on page 75 of *Southern Wagons, Volume 1*. The present photograph is understood to be at Dinton, and it looks as though the troops on view are probably railwaymen of a Reserve or Territorial unit, with the possible exception of the Staff Sergeant on the right who looks very stiff and Regular! The notice on the door of the van reads "Notice No unauthorised person is allowed to open these doors".

Plate 1.44 is an enlargement of a portion of the well-known view of the sidings at Yeovil Town, and shows an interesting variety of stock. At the left, in front of the locomotive, is a short passenger train. The next two tracks are occupied by goods vehicles, with the exception of a passenger brake at the far end of the second road. The first vehicle in that road is a goods brake of 1874 (figure 1.35), as is the one in the third road. Both of these appear to have acquired stoves, as approved in 1879. The second one in the second road is a goods brake of 1861-1870 (figure 1.34, part B), then one of 1871-1874 (figure 1.34, part C), on which the side door is open and the end platform for access to the guard's door is just discernable. There then follow a couple of private owner wagons.

Plate 1.45 was illustrated on pages 84 and 85 of *Southern Wagons, Volume 1*, but here it is seen with a slightly unusual load. It is a 40-ton bogie bolster wagon, No 2940, and the load was illustrated and described in *The South Western Railway Magazine* for 1922. It is an anchor and chain, weighing in all 36 tons, for the newly completed White Star liner *SS Homeric*. It had been transferred from Messrs Page and East's barge at Nine Elms wharf for conveyance to Southampton Docks. The wharf had to be strengthened to ensure safe passage of the wagon and load. *SS Homeric* had been launched in

GOODS VEHICLES

Plate 1.43. 16ft gunpowder van No 2134. (Lens of Sutton)

Plate 1.44. Yeovil Town c.1880. (Loco and General)

Plate 1.45. 47ft 6in 40-ton bolster wagon with anchor and chain for SS Homeric, February 1922. (J Tatchell collection)

Germany as *Columbus* in 1913, but was laid up during the war. In 1920, she was one of those handed over to Britain as part of war reparations, was purchased by the White Star Line, completed in Germany and sailed to Southampton to prepare for her maiden voyage to New York. This she made starting on 15th February 1922, complete with the anchor and chain shown here. Before sailing, she was opened to the public with proceeds to various charities, including £20 to the LSWR Orphanage at Woking.

Plate 1.46 is a 12-ton machinery truck No 1196 shown in *Southern Wagons Volume 1* as figure 41, but here we have another unusual load, a marine navigation buoy. Clearly a rather difficult load to secure, it is seen on its side with its base, ballast ring and one of its mooring chains visible.

Plate 1.47 shows how hay was stacked and sheeted in a 5-plank open wagon. By chance this particular wagon, No 921, is recorded on page 23 of *Southern Wagons Volume 1* as having been built in 1901. The sheeting is tied down to the disc clamps on the sides and ends, definitely not to the buffer castings and underframe. This picture also shows why a loading gauge was provided at the exit from sidings so that wagons should not be allowed out on to the running lines with loads that could foul any structures. An illustration of the loading limits and gauges will be shown later in Chapter 4.

Plate 1.48 is of a "700" class locomotive, No 694, near Mortlake with a special goods to Alton. Following a refrigerator van and a covered van, there is a furniture van on a road vehicle truck, then another furniture van on a machinery truck, four road meat wagons on two of the 28ft road vehicle trucks (illustrated on page 72 of *Southern Wagons Volume 1*), a covered van and then a variety of open wagons.

An unfortunately incomplete view of a hatch roof van is seen in plate 1.49 which was taken by William Cunningham Hume, a visitor to England in about 1880. This was brought to my attention by Mr D Marden who is preparing a book on various railway matters to do with Southampton docks. It appears to be very similar to the one seen in the distance in plate 1.40. This one raises more questions than it answers. The company title and "P L" are very clear, but much of the other lettering is not entirely legible. The formal lettering (bottom left) appears to indicate some restriction to running, possibly between London and Southampton, the last word is almost certainly "only", but there are chalk markings routing it to Poole and other places! The colour appears to be darker than the early grey used for goods vehicles, but the earliest mention of zinc brown was in January 1887, so is it a very dark grey or was brown already in use? Then the letters "P L" have not so far seen in any other LSWR picture.

GOODS VEHICLES

Plate 1.46. 12-ton machinery wagon No 1196, drawing 1107, loaded with a marine buoy. (J Tatchell collection)

Plate 1.47. 8-ton wagon loaded with hay or straw.

Plate 1.48. Goods train near Mortlake – see text. (J Tatchell collection)

Plate 1.49. Royal Pier, Southampton c.1880. (Fryer Library, University of Queensland, Hume family papers, image 251)

GOODS VEHICLES

Now for some pure conjecture. Hatch roof vans were originally ordinary goods vehicles, requiring the use of small turntables at goods yards and some stations. It is not recorded when this practice became so inconvenient as to lead to the abandonment of single-sided vans and wagons for ordinary use. However, it is probable that many such vehicles were still serviceable, so may have gone into departmental service. In the case of hatch roof vans, giving weather protection, it would be reasonable to reserve some for passenger luggage strictly between specific points, such as London and the docks, clearly distinguishing them from goods vehicles by painting them differently and marking them with "P L".

The location is the Royal Pier at Southampton at the end of the tramway from Southampton terminus. This pier was used primarily by ferry services to Cowes in the Isle of Wight. The tramway opened in 1871 using a train consisting of a first and a second class carriage together with a van for the passengers' luggage, hauled by three horses. It was not until July 1881 that the use of a small steam loco was authorised by the Board of Trade "as an experiment".

The engines were to be those built by Shanks & Son, *Southampton*, *Cowes* and *Ritzebuttle* as long as they had an efficient brake, a conspicuous nameplate, suitable lifeguards to push aside obstructions, had a whistle, the driver to have the fullest possible view ahead, to be free from noise by blast as far as practicable, and all fire to be concealed from view.

Speed was not to exceed 5mph, they must whistle from time to time, must not produce smoke nor hot air to annoy passengers, must stop when necessary to avoid danger, the speed along Canute Road not to exceed 4mph. A copy of the licence was to be displayed in obvious places at the Terminus and at the Pier. Breaches of the conditions would lead to a penalty not exceeding £10.

In this picture there are signs in the track that suggest that horses were still in use.

The steamer behind the van is probably one of the early Red Funnel steamers used on the Southampton to Cowes service, but it cannot be positively identified. Another similar one can just be seen in the background.

Readers might have noticed that, apart from the references in the general part of this chapter and the dimensions in the wagon returns of 1870 and 1872, there has been no description or illustration of coal wagons. It might be that the LSWR merely marked some ordinary open wagons for coal traffic, but there is no evidence of this apart from a decision in June 1897, by the Locomotive & Stores Committee, that sixty 10-ton wagons were to be set aside for exclusive use as coal wagons by the Locomotive Department.

No official drawings of wagons for this purpose seem to have survived, except for one, LSWR diagram 1182, dated 1903, for a 9-plank 18ft 17-ton coal wagon, but there is no positive evidence that any were built. It is probable, however, that it was the basis of the design described and illustrated in *Southern wagons, Volume 1* at page 24, where the authors state that in 1904, Mr Panter had fifty 8-plank 15-ton coal wagons built. They go on to say that the design was so successful that between 1904 and 1925, 1,300 were built, although after 1913 most were rated from new at 12 tons.

As an indication of the nature of coal traffic on the line, a letter from Stephenson Clarke & Co was placed before the Locomotive & Stores Committee in June 1894 proposing the renewal of the existing contract for coal for the next 12 months, consisting of:

- Aberdare Loco Steam Coal at 14/6d per ton delivered at Southampton,
- Aberdare Loco Steam Coal at 12/6d per ton delivered at Fremington,
- Inland Loco Hard Steam Coal, from Annesley, Blackwell, Barber Walker, at 13/10d per ton delivered at Nine Elms,
- House coal from Annesley at 13/2d per ton delivered at Nine Elms.

All to be delivered as usual with use of Stephenson Clarke & Co wagons over the LSWR system.

This was accepted on 18th June 1894, and it was further noted later that month that Stephenson Clarke would continue the supply of house coal to suburban stations a 20/9d per ton.

Southern Wagons Volume 1 has been mentioned very many times here. It will therefore be no surprise to readers that it is strongly recommended for details of the later vehicles, and particularly for several very good illustrations of details such as lettering, axleboxes, brakes and other fittings, many of which apply to vehicles in this chapter.

It only remains to remind readers of the opening two paragraphs of this chapter. This has not been the whole story, but is probably as much as is now available given how little material survives concerning LSWR goods vehicles and traffic in the 19th and early 20th centuries.

Plate 2.1a. M7 class No 32 with SR gas tank 015S, originally LSWR No 16 built on a 22ft underframe, seen here at Clapham Junction in 1931, apparently on a 24ft frame. (RW Kidner)

Plate 2.1b. SR gas tank 2095S, originally LSWR No 6, later SR 05S. Built on a 22ft underframe, seen here at Newhaven in 1947 on an underframe from LSWR 24ft PLV No 76. (RW Kidner)

CHAPTER 2
TRAVELLING GASHOLDERS

Travelling gasholders belonged to the Traffic Department, but were not normally revenue earning so it seems justifiable to give them a chapter to themselves.

In February 1880, Mr Adams reported on the success of a trial of Pintsch's oil gas lighting in twelve carriages on the Waterloo to Richmond service, and recommended that the company should set up its own gas plant at Clapham Junction; this was approved. A separate letter listed 100 vehicles that had, in fact, been fitted up by the previous December, so it may be that the "twelve carriages" should have read "twelve trains". The cost saving was estimated to be £241 in a half year.

Seven years later, it was stated that a carriage gasworks would be built at Bishopstoke (Eastleigh) as the Clapham plant was by then unequal to the demand. Then, in March 1891, it was decided to prepare plans and estimates for plants at Exeter and Kingston Stations for the same reason. In July, the Resident Engineer submitted his plans for the gasworks at Exmouth Junction, instead of Exeter Station, with a capacity for filling 500 carriages per week. The building could be of timber and corrugated iron construction for an estimated £3,200, or of brick for £3,600. A decision was deferred! In February 1893, revised plans for the Kingston gasworks were considered and approved in principle at an estimated cost of £3,523, but again, site details were to be reviewed. It was not until March 1895 that fresh plans for the gasworks at Exmouth Junction were finally approved at the much-reduced cost of £2,350.

The restriction of only being able to replenish carriage gas tanks at Clapham, and later at Bishopstoke, had to be overcome more quickly and flexibly than by building more gasworks. So in January 1896 the Locomotive and Stores Committee agreed that two portable gasholders should be bought, one for Exeter and one for Salisbury "as required by the Traffic Department", and that they should be mounted on old underframes. One year later, it was similarly agreed to buy two more portable gasholders for use at Woking, again to be mounted on old underframes. This was repeated in January 1898 for two "travelling gasholders" for use at Salisbury and Bournemouth at an estimated cost of £145 each.

One of the Southern Railway records shows some travelling gasholder trucks as built about 1883 and 1887, but these dates clearly relate to the origin of these old underframes.

Plate 2.1c. LSWR gas tank No 12 at Guildford in May 1931. Originally on a 22ft underframe but seen here on a 24ft one. (HC Casserley)

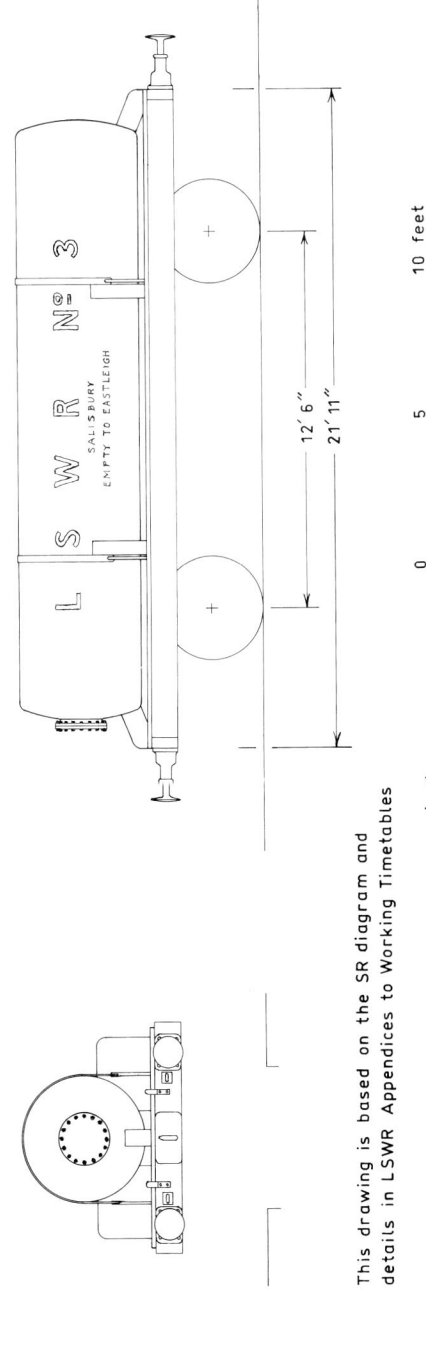

Figure 2.1. Travelling gasholders numbers 1, 2, 3, etc of 1896.

TRAVELLING GASHOLDERS

Plate 2.1d. LSWR gas tank No 7, on underframe from 31ft third No 61, seen as SR 06S at Southampton Docks. (F Foote)

Travelling gasholders were not enough for the needs and *The South Western Gazette* for July 1899 carried a description of the recently completed compressed oil gasworks at Wimbledon, "one of the largest in the kingdom", capable of producing 45,000 cubic feet of compressed oil gas in every 24 hours. The raw material was heavy petroleum oil, with a specific gravity of about 0.8. This was piped from tanks to the retorts where it was heated to 1750°F converting it to a thick vapour. At this temperature, the tar products partially separated out, and the still-impure gas passed to condensing tanks where the rest of the tar was collected. The gas then passed through a washing process, and was filtered through sawdust and lime, after which it could be compressed at the rate of 4000cu ft per hour into eight storage holders at 150psi. The description then went on to mention the gas cylinders under the carriages, and said that the quantity for one carriage would last for about 36 hours of lighting. The Wimbledon plant produced an average 80cu ft of gas from one gallon of oil, giving a light intensity of about 45 candle power at a cost of between 5/- and 8/- (25p and 40p) for 1000 cu ft.

Another eight portable gasholders were authorised in March 1898 for use at Richmond, Twickenham, Windsor and Hampton Court at a total cost of £1160. In the following November, one more was approved for use at Andover Junction, again costing £145. More must have been agreed, or were not referred to the main committees (unless I have missed the references) because a list of carriage and wagon stock dated December 1902 shows twenty "gas tanks" and the *Appendices to Working Timetables* for 1st January 1911 and 25th July 1921 both show twenty. At the latter date, the filling plants were at Clapham Junction, Wimbledon, Wimbledon Park Sidings, Eastleigh and Exeter, with the gasholder vehicles being stationed at various places listed at the end of this chapter. Originally numbered simply 1 to 20, by August 1917 most of them had acquired the suffix "S" with a few locations altered. All had the "S" suffix by 1921, then, in or shortly after 1924, the Southern Railway added the cyphering prefix "0", before completely renumbering the survivors around 1945.

Works drawings exist only for numbers 10 and 11 of 1898, for an alteration to number 5 in 1915, and for numbers 118S and 119S of 1921. Except for the last, the underframes are not in sufficient detail to be positively identified, although the layout and bolt holes for numbers 10 and 11 coincide almost exactly with the underframes for the various 24ft luggage vans of the 1890s, whilst that for number 5 is just in outline, but has buffers like the 22ft luggage vans of 1883. Since all of those vans can be accounted for, and no others of the right length and wheelbase descriptions appear in the surviving

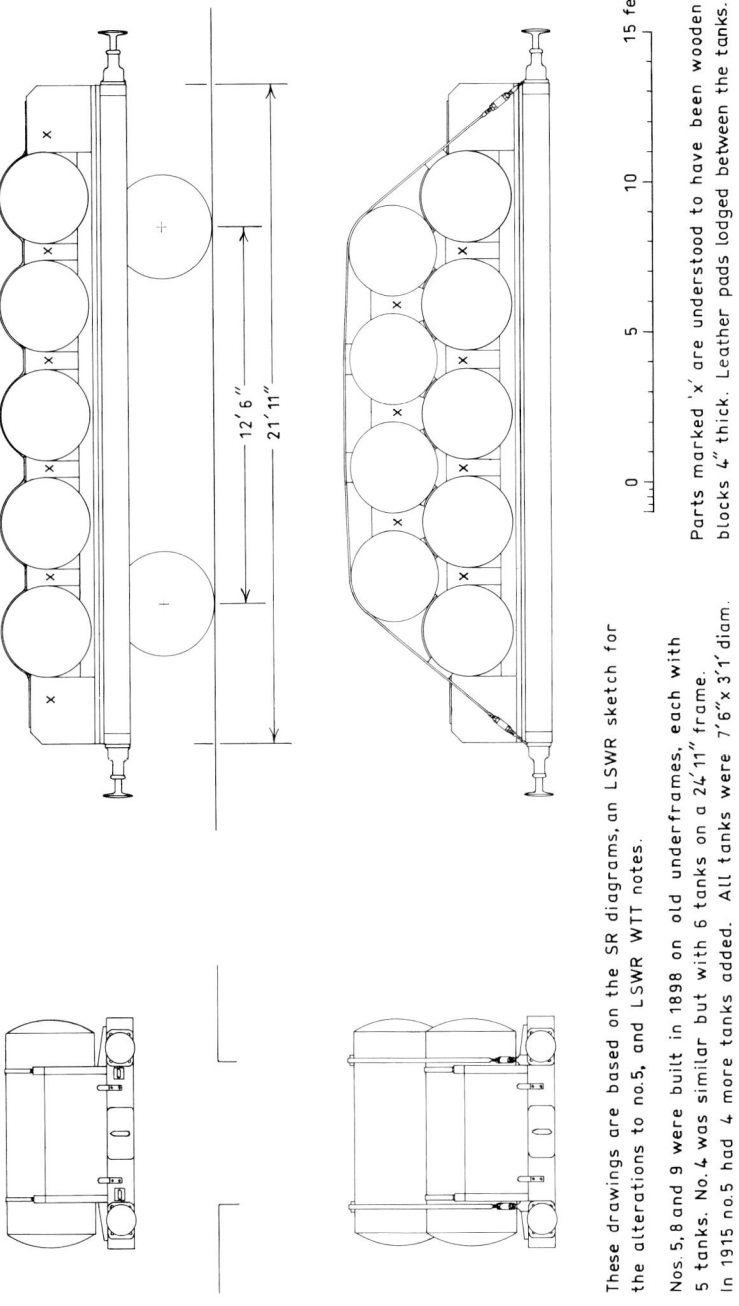

Figure 2.2. *Travelling gasholders numbers 5, 8, and 9 of 1896.*

TRAVELLING GASHOLDERS

Plate 2.2a. Portland. To the left is gasholder No 9, next two GWR open wagons, then two trains, each headed by an 02 class loco. The nearer train has a 48ft third, 32ft brake third c.1891, 34ft third c.1882, 32ft compo c.1881, 32ft compo of 1880, 34ft third c.1882, and 34ft brake third c.1882. (Author's collection)

Plate 2.2b. Travelling gasholder LSWR No 5, as altered in 1915. (J Tatchell collection)

Plate 2.2c. Travelling gasholder No 5, as altered in 1915, at Woking in May 1934. (HC Casserley)

records, it might be inferred that the works sometimes decided that it would be easier to build new underframes to existing designs rather than look around for and convert old ones.

In some cases it seems more likely that genuine old frames were used. Number 4 could well have had the frame from one of the various 25ft carriages of the mid 1870s. Similarly, a very likely source for number 20 is one of the 28ft block set or similar carriages of the late 1870s, most of which were being withdrawn around 1900. The SR diagrams of 1924 confirm the dimensions, but do not help with identification. Between 1921 and the end of 1923, four more were built, but there are old underframe numbers for two of them. Rather curiously, these last were given the numbers 118S, 119S, 123S and 124S. The underframes for the first two were from 30ft thirds numbers 1015 and 813, of April 1890 and Sept 1886 respectively. The other two were also on frames from 30ft thirds, but cannot be identified; many of these vehicles were being scrapped at that time.

In about 1918, there was a proposal to build a gasholder, using 21 gas tanks from old carriages fastened transversely on the underframe of a former 22ft carriage, but there is no evidence that this was carried out. However, there is a Southern diagram showing a larger gasholder wagon on the same principle. Mounted on the underframe from a 30ft carriage, there was a bottom layer of twelve 6ft 3in by 2ft 10in tanks, on top of that a layer of eleven 5ft 3in by 1ft 9in tanks, and another layer of 10 of the same size on top of that. This vehicle was given the number 0499S, so presumably it was built just after the Grouping, and so is not illustrated here (apart from the fact that no photographs or detail drawings have so far come to light!)

The actual gasholder tanks carried the numbers, and these outlasted the original underframes by a long time. Certainly numbers 6, 7 and 8 were reframed before the Grouping, number 7 being the only one identified as transferred to the underframe from 22ft passenger luggage van number 19 of 1883 in October 1914. Number 6 went onto a 24ft 5in frame, and number 8 to a 23ft 11in frame before 1921 and then to another of the same size from luggage van number 283 in February 1937. All nineteen survivors from the original twenty (number 3S was withdrawn sometime between 1921 and 1924 so when the SR added a zero in front, all the numbers from 4 to 20 shifted down one) were transferred to other second-hand 4-wheel or 6-wheel frames, sometimes twice. Some of these can be traced in the Appendix lists for thirds and luggage

TRAVELLING GASHOLDERS

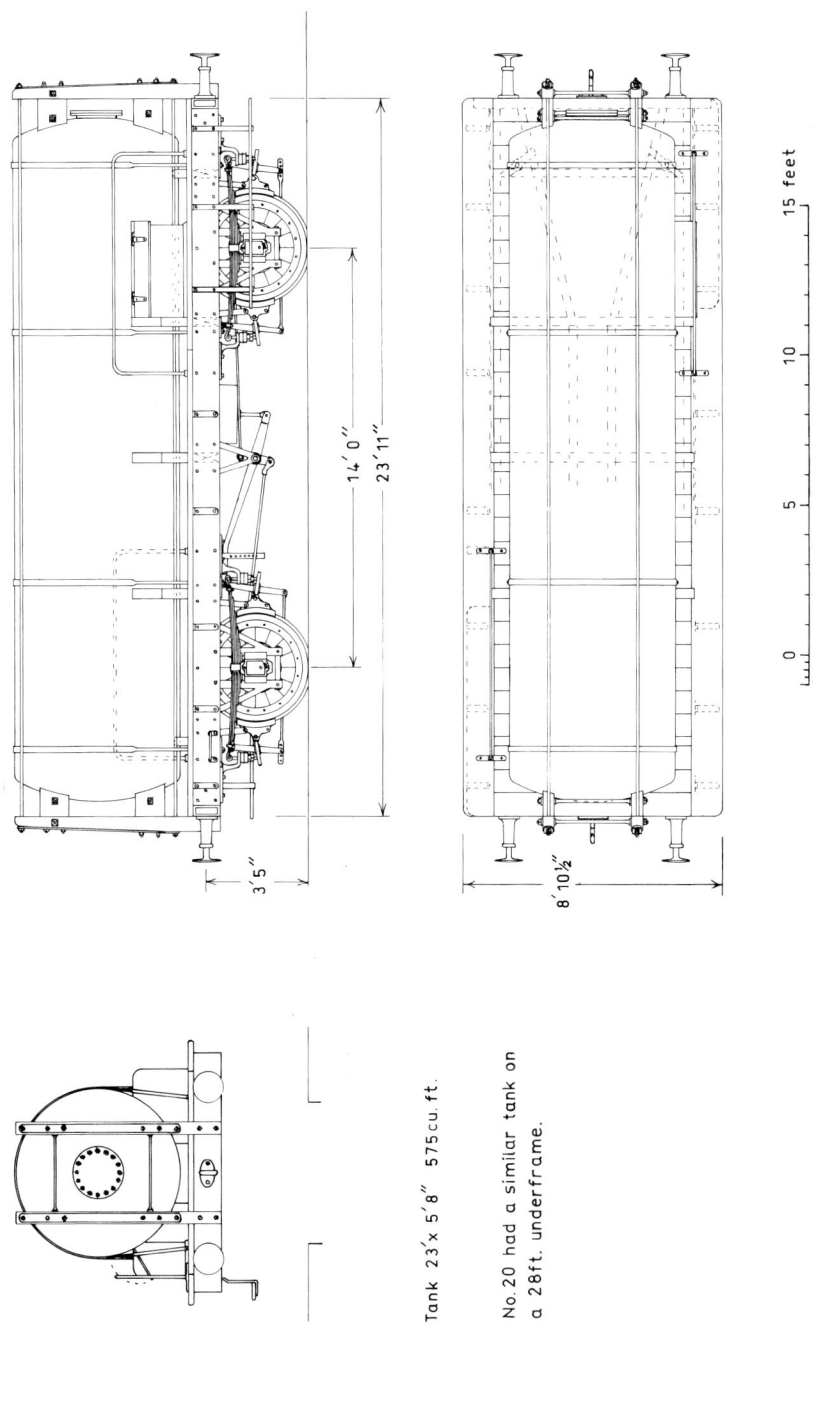

Figure 2.3. *Travelling gasholders numbers 10 and 11 of 1898.*

Plate 2.3. Gas tank No 20, 23ft x 5ft 8in tank on 28ft underframe. (J Tatchell collection)

vans. In the process, some had the tank arrangement altered so the whole subject is rather confusing!

There are several different records of gasholders in the Southern period, and of course, they include those from the LSWR, the LB&SCR and the SE&CR, as well as some built by the SR. Given that many tanks were transferred to fresh, but still second-hand, underframes (which were not necessarily from the same original company), that sometimes two old tanks replaced one, and that there was one partial, and one major, renumbering scheme, it is hardly surprising that it is now virtually impossible to put together a coherent story of what happened to these vehicles after 1923. In any case it is (fortunately) outside the scope of the present work.

In general, tanks were supported on substantial oak blocks bolted through the solebars and framing members. Additional shaped oak blocks were used to separate multiple tanks. Where there were two long tanks, they were strapped to each other, and then the pair strapped down to the frame. The straps were steel strips terminating in tensioning screws or turnbuckles. In some cases, a floor was laid across the underframe, but in others, the frame seems to have been left open except for part at the ends. A toolbox was provided, presumably for spanners, spare pipe couplings and possibly a length of gas hose. A pressure gauge and filling valve was attached to some convenient part of the tank support timbers, although in one indistinct photo it looks as though they might have been actually inside the toolbox. In the case of multiple tanks there were also interconnecting pipes and valves, but these were not shown on the diagrams and are only partially and faintly seen on some photos.

Because there are no fully detailed works drawings, and photos of gasholder trucks in original LSWR condition seem to be almost totally lacking, the present drawings, figures 2.1 to 2.4 inevitably include some assumptions. The numbering and allocation information is shown below.

It is possible that some of these travelling gasholders were used for other purposes than supplying gas for carriages. In February 1905, the General Manager got the approval of the Locomotive, Carriage and Stores Committee to enter into an arrangement with Trinity House to supply 40,000cu ft of oil gas a year for the gas lights on the breakwaters of Portland, for which they agreed to pay 24s (£1.20) per 1000cu ft, in addition to the carriage of the gasholders from Eastleigh.

As to the actual production of the gas, there is a detailed description of this in *The Engineer* for June 1874, where there are details and drawings of both the production plant and the lamps designed by Herr Julius Pintsch of Berlin. It was claimed that whale oil, dead oil, common blue shale oil, coarse petroleum, fat – in fact almost any cheap hydrocarbon, could be used. Using 90psi pressure, a

TRAVELLING GASHOLDERS

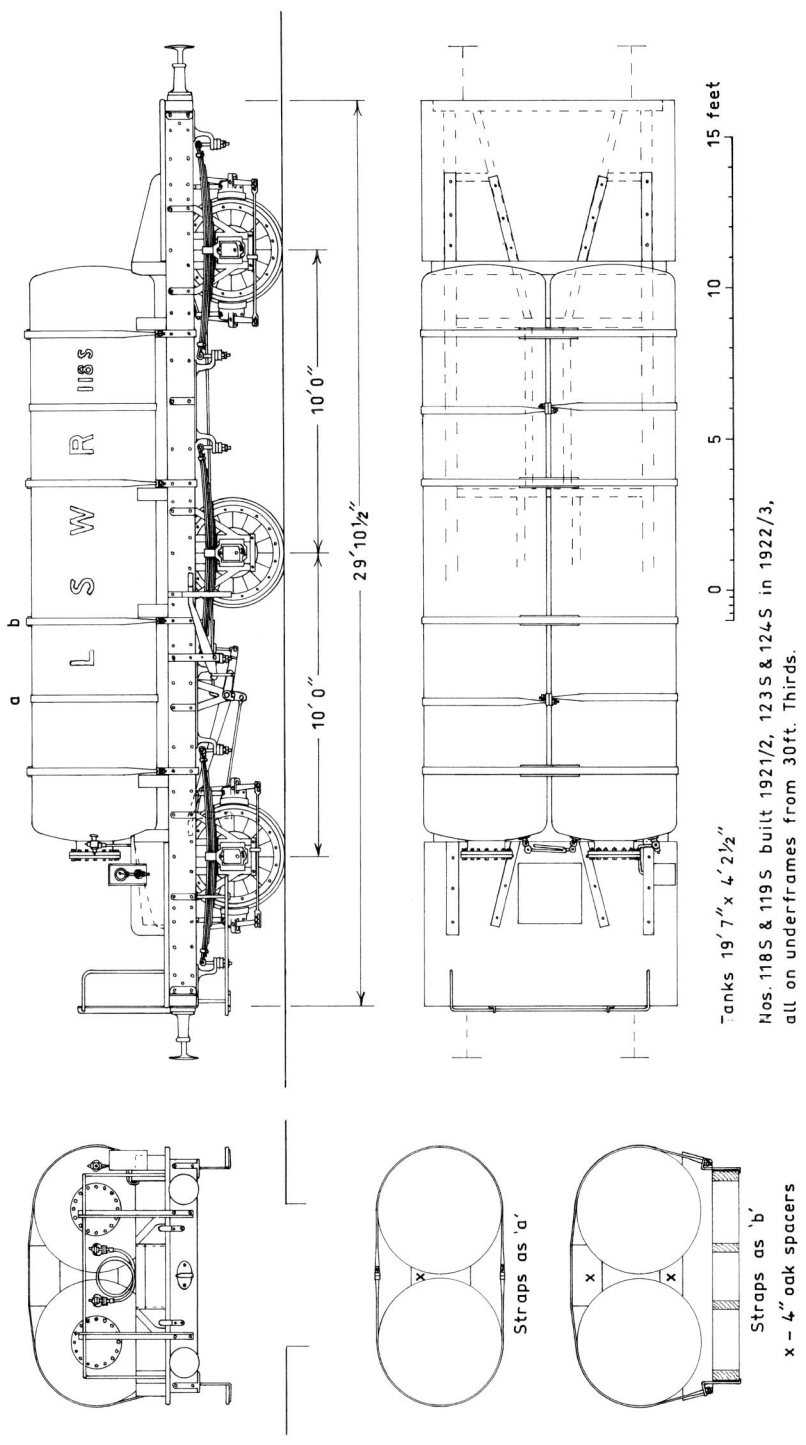

Figure 2.4. Travelling gasholders numbers 118S and 119S of 1921.

Plate 2.4. LSWR gas tank 123S, SR 022S. On underframe from 32ft brake third LSWR No 456.

long train could be charged in about eight minutes. It was already well in use on the Continent, and was then on trial on the LNWR, where a trial carriage with a reservoir measuring 5ft 10in by 1ft 4½in diameter had run over 1000 miles on one charge.

Another description of gas production, with diagrams of a gas production plant on the Great Northern Railway, as well as a very great deal of other information and diagrams on a wide variety of aspects of carriage and wagon construction, was written by Sidney Stone MIMechE between 1892 and 1903. This was reprinted and published under the title *Railway Carriages & Wagons, Part 2* by Peter Kay of Teignmouth, South Devon (ISBN 1899890122).

A more recent description, including details of the actual gas and electric light systems in carriages, was written by Henry Fowler (later Sir Henry) of the Midland Railway, in Volume 6 of *Modern Railway Working*, published in 1911. Incidentally, the chapters on rolling stock from Volume 5, and the chapter on lighting from Volume 6, were reprinted (with a little updating) in 1923 in Volume 2 of *Railway Mechanical Engineering* by the same publishers, The Gresham Publishing Company.

Briefly, the gas was made from oil distilled from Scottish shale oil and later from American or Russian oils, at a stage between burning and lubricating oils. This oil was delivered to the railway companies by rail tank wagon, and was fed into coke-fired retorts, where it was converted to gas, compressed to around 150psi, and then stored in tanks for delivery to the rolling stock sidings or to gasholder trucks as required. By the time the gas reached the carriages, it was at around 100 to 110psi. This was far too high for the burners, so each carriage had a reducing valve within the underframe; pressure gauges were fitted on the solebars to show the cylinder pressure. The filling valve on LSWR vehicles was a small fitting about two or three inches in diameter on a bracket somewhere just under the solebar, probably near to the gauge, but I have not shown it on my drawings, because the location is rarely shown on official drawings and rarely shows up on photographs. However, according to Hamilton Ellis, the small covers were painted red.

In November 1917, the Locomotive and Carriage Committee approved a plan to lay in a gas main to Wimbledon Park Sidings gasworks, and similarly in May 1918 to Eastleigh and Exmouth Junction gasworks in connection with a scheme to mix coal-gas with oil-gas for lighting the carriages. There is nothing further in the minutes to say what became of this.

The lists of gasholder vehicles from surviving records are given in the following tables.

TRAVELLING GASHOLDERS

1. List of gasholder trucks shown in the *Appendix to Working Timetables*, 1st January 1911 (all vacuum braked):

No	Stationed at	Charged at	Length over headstocks	Number and size of cylinders	Capacity (cu ft)	Changes by 1st April 1916	
						Stationed at	Charged at
1	Portsmouth	Eastleigh	22ft	1 20ft x 4ft 2in	270	Portsmouth	Wimbledon
2	Exeter	Exeter	22ft	1 20ft x 4ft 2in	270	Exeter	Exeter
3	Salisbury	Eastleigh	22ft	1 20ft x 4ft 2in	270	Salisbury	Wimbledon
4	Portsmouth	Eastleigh	25ft	6 7ft 6in x 3ft 1in	330	Portsmouth	Wimbledon
5	Andover Junction	Eastleigh	22ft		275	Andover Junction	Wimbledon
6	Farnham	Eastleigh	22ft	1 20ft x 4ft 2in	270	Farnham	Wimbledon
7	Fulwell Loco	Wimbledon	22ft	1 20ft x 4ft 2in	270	Weymouth and Lymington	Eastleigh
8	Exeter	Exeter	22ft	5 7ft 6in x 3ft 1in	275	Exeter	Exeter
9	Portland and Lymington	Eastleigh	22ft	5 7ft 6in x 3ft 1in	275	Portland and Lymington	Eastleigh
10	Weymouth and Lymington	Eastleigh	24ft	1 23ft x 5ft 8in	575	Southampton Docks	Eastleigh
11	Salisbury	Eastleigh	24ft	1 23ft x 5ft 8in	575	Southampton Docks	Eastleigh
12	Woking	Wimbledon	24ft	1 20ft x 4ft 2in	270	Woking	Wimbledon
13	Basingstoke	Wimbledon	22ft	1 20ft x 4ft 2in	270	Basingstoke	Wimbledon
14	Exeter	Exeter	22ft	1 20ft x 4ft 2in	270	Exeter	Exeter
15	Eastleigh	Eastleigh	22ft	1 20ft x 4ft 2in	270	Eastleigh, Botley and Gosport	Wimbledon
16	Woking	Wimbledon	22ft	1 20ft x 4ft 2in	270	Salisbury	Wimbledon
17	Bournemouth West	Eastleigh	22ft	1 20ft x 4ft 2in	270	Bournemouth West	Eastleigh
18	Petersfield	Eastleigh	24ft	1 20ft x 4ft 2in	270	Petersfield	Wimbledon
19	Guildford	Wimbledon	22ft	1 20ft x 4ft 2in	270	Woking	Wimbledon
20	Bournemouth West	Eastleigh	28ft	1 23ft x 5ft 8in	575	Bournemouth West	Eastleigh

The provision of two at Southampton Docks during World War I was to cater for the large number of troop and ambulance trains running from there. The two at Woking were strengthened by a third one borrowed from the Great Eastern Railway, specially marked "Not to be returned to the Great Eastern Railway".

2. The *Appendix to Working Timetables* for 25th July 1921 lists gas-filling plants at Clapham Junction, Wimbledon, Wimbledon Park Sidings, Eastleigh and Exeter. It also lists all of the gasholders (all vacuum braked) at that time:

No	Stationed at	Charged at	Length over headstocks	Number and size of cylinders	Capacity (cu ft)
1S	Portsmouth	Eastleigh	22ft	1 20ft x 4ft 2in	270
2S	Exeter	Exeter	22ft	1 20ft x 4ft 2in	270
3S	Salisbury	Wimbledon	22ft	1 20ft x 4ft 2in	270
4S	Portsmouth	Eastleigh	25ft	6 7ft 6in x 3ft 1in	330
5S	Woking	Wimbledon	22ft	9 7ft 6in x 3ft 1in	495
6S	Farnham	Wimbledon	24ft 6in	1 20ft x 4ft 2in	270
7S	Weymouth/Lymington	Eastleigh	22ft	1 20ft x 4ft 2in	270
8S	Exeter	Exeter	24ft	5 7ft 6in x 3ft 1in	275
9S	Weymouth/Lymington	Eastleigh	22ft	5 7ft 6in x 3ft 1in	275

LSWR CARRIAGES VOLUME 4

2. The *Appendix to Working Timetables* for 25th July 1921 (continued):					
No	Stationed at	Charged at	Length over headstocks	Number and size of cylinders	Capacity (cu ft)
10S	Southampton Docks	Eastleigh	24ft	1 23ft x 5ft 8in	575
11S	Portsmouth	Eastleigh	24ft	1 23ft x 5ft 8in	575
12S	Guildford	Wimbledon	24ft	1 20 ft x4ft 2in	270
13S	Basingstoke	Wimbledon	22ft	1 20 ft x 4ft 2in	270
14S	Exeter	Exeter	22ft	1 20ft x 4ft 2in	270
15S	Eastleigh/Botley/Gosport	Wimbledon	22ft	1 20ft x 4ft 2in	270
16S	Salisbury	Wimbledon	22ft	1 20ft x 4ft 2in	270
17S	Bournemouth West	Eastleigh	22ft	1 20ft x 4ft 2in	270
18S	Farnham	Wimbledon	24ft	1 20ft x 4ft 2in	270
19S	Woking	Wimbledon	22ft	1 20ft x 4ft 2in	270
20S	Bournemouth West	Eastleigh	28ft	1 23ft x 5ft 8in	575

3. The Southern Railway renumbered the tanks after 1923 as follows, and some of the transfers to fresh, but still second-hand underframes are also shown:			
LSWR No	SR No	Transferred to underframe from, and date	1945 Ren
1S	01S	24ft PLV No 66 (SR 1264) 9/1931	
2S	02S	24ft PLV No 55 (SR 5055) 9/1927	2092S
3S		Presumably scrapped between 1921 and 1924	
4S	03S	30ft PBV No 484 (SR 101) 7/1937	
5S	04S	24ft PLV No 292 (SR 1341) 8/1932	
6S	05S	24ft PLV No76 (LSWR/SR 076, ex-Southampton Docks restricted) 7/1930	2095S
7S	06S	22ft PLV No 19, 10/1914, then to 31ft Third No 835 (ex-Second) (SR 61) 5/1933	2071S
8S	07S	24ft PLV pre-1921, then 24ft PLV No 283 (SR 1332) 5/1937	
9S	08S	24ft PLV No 366 (SR 1414) 3/1932	
10S	09S	30ft Fruit van No 5496, ex-Third 1014 (SR 1674) 10/1929	2001S
11S	010S	30ft PBV No 90 (SR 40) 12/1935	2002S
12S	011S	24ft PLV No 82 (SR 5082) 8/1930, then to 24ft PLV No SR 1493 3/1942	2096S
13S	012S	24ft Wireless van 1623s, ex-PLV No 148 (SR 1512) 2/1945	2093S
14S	013S	24ft PLV No 86/5086, 2/1927, then to 31ft Third No 1596 (ex-Second) (SR 9) 10/1933	2006S
15S	014S	24ft PLV No 100 (SR 1290) 8/1931, then to 24ft PLV No 5090 (SR 1481) circa 1942	2097S
16S	015S	32ft Postal Sorting Van No 5 (SR 4901) 1/1935	2072S
17S	016S	24ft PLV No 65/5065, 1926, then to Third No 174 (SR 26) 10/1935	2007S
18S	017S	24ft PLV No 69 (SR 1267) 8/1931, then to 24ft PLV No 5167 (SR 1536) 8/1942	2098S
19S	018S	31ft Third No 1575 (ex-Second) (SR 12) 10/1934	2064S
20S	019S	32ft Brake Third No 331 (SR 2611) 1/1932	2003S
118S	020S	Built on u/f of 30ft Third 1015/593, re-u/f on B/Third 518 (SR 2619) 12/1931	2074S
119S	021S	Built on u/f of 30ft Third 813, not reframed	2075S
123S	022S	Built on u/f of unknown 30ft Third, re-u/f on 32ft B/Third 456 (SR 2615) 9/1934	2076S
124S	023S	Built on u/f of unknown 30ft Third, not reframed	2077S

CHAPTER 3
TRAVELLING CRANES

Cranes rarely came to the notice of the public, and not even to most railway staff, but they were a very important part of the railway scene. Little has been written about them, except perhaps in the context of train accidents, so it is difficult to appreciate their place in railway life. This is particularly so in the case of the LSWR since virtually all the crane records as represented by the Crane Registers were lost during the British Railways clear-out of old material in the 1960s. About the only surviving information was in the Southern Railway Service Stock Registers, which included what had been taken over from the previous companies, and in some LSWR and SR diagrams, which are only side elevation sketches with the length and wheelbase dimensions.

Even some of those SR entries are somewhat suspect, at least in the "built" date, due to the apparent practice by the LSWR of renumbering cranes (or at least the breakdown ones) when replacement ones were bought. For example, the main Nine Elms breakdown crane seems to have been number 1, but when a new one arrived it became number 1, while the previous one was transferred elsewhere with a fresh number, possibly taking the number of the one that it replaced in turn!

On the LSWR, the need for cranes and their replacements appears to have been initiated by the various committees dealing with locomotives, traffic, commercial and stores departments, but the records were the responsibility of the Resident Engineer up to mid-1905, when they were transferred to the Mechanical Engineer. As already said, none of these has survived, and the only information is what little can be picked up in the committee minutes. There are some boiler registers that include a few boilers on cranes, but these can be misleading as in some cases the date of building appears to be the date for the boiler (or in some cases a replacement) rather than of the crane mentioned.

The earliest note is the decision of the Traffic and Locomotive Committee in June 1864 to purchase a travelling crane and its accompanying van from Messrs Bray, Waddington & Co of Leeds, to be delivered complete and erected at Nine Elms. From the inclusion of an accompanying van it may be deduced that it was intended for breakdown purposes. Also, from a later note, it might be concluded that this became Nine Elms number 1, with a lifting capacity of 5 tons, later renumbered as Nine Elms Traffic travelling crane number 4, and declared to be broken down beyond repair at the end of 1900. Long before that, there had been a Locomotive Department number 4 in 1875. The SR register shows number 1 as built in 1880, but the crane described was actually built in 1908, showing the difficulty of presenting an accurate story without the proper records.

Identification is not helped by the apparent separate numbering in the departments, with their match trucks either retaining their former running

Plate 3.1. At the extreme left a crane similar to the early breakdown cranes can just be seen, possibly being used in connection with the ballast train, which appears to be working on the approach to the Wimbledon East carriage sidings. The line to Wimbledon Park and Putney is in the background. X2 class No 582 is leading an Exeter train. The 48ft lav brake third was built in 1899 and looks very new, so this might date the photo. Beyond it are a 48ft lav tri-compo of 1897, a 48ft lav third of 1898, a 48ft lav compo of 1898, and a 44ft brake. (B Curl collection)

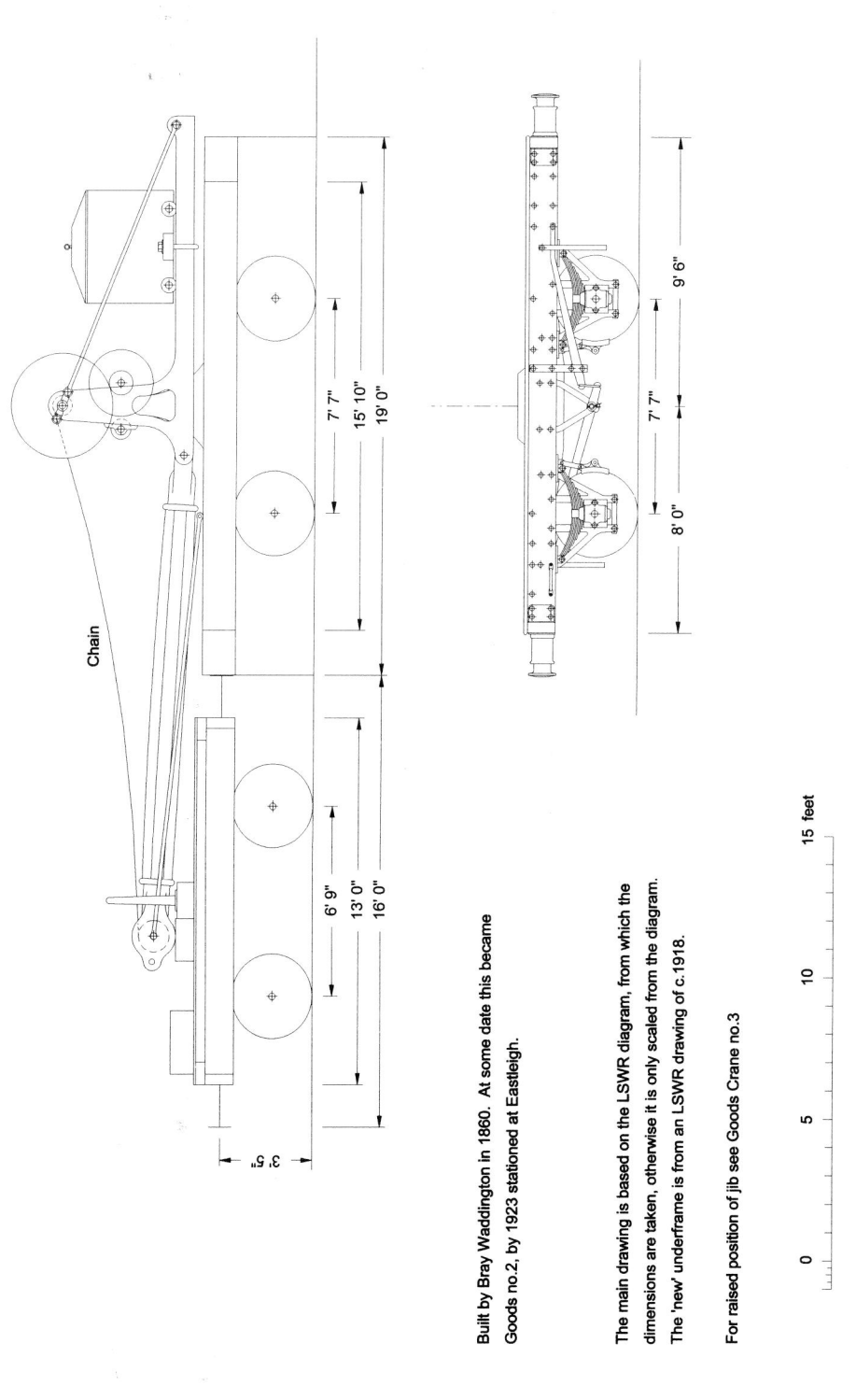

Figure 3.1. 3-ton crane of c.1860 (later goods crane No 2).

numbers if they were conversions, or a new number (followed by a later renumbering at an unknown date) into a service stock list when the letter "S" was added. Later still, and again at an unknown date, the cranes and match trucks were all put into a common list, for example, Locomotive Department breakdown crane number 2 and its match truck number 8809 became 31S and 31SM respectively, but this was not all. Some shops cranes had numbers such as M76 (later 52S), 1 (later 54S) and Y15 (later 56S). What the system was is far from clear!

Although breakdown cranes could obviously be used for other work, this could have caused major problems in the event of an emergency. It was realised quite early that travelling cranes were needed for such things as permanent way construction, the erection of bridges and buildings, and for other work at the main depots. A few of these were similar, or even identical, to the breakdown cranes but others were considerably smaller.

Apart from travelling cranes, there were also gantry cranes, such as one at Nine Elms goods depot and others in the various works, and also numerous dockside cranes at Southampton, Nine Elms wharves and other such places. In addition, the majority of stations had one or more fixed hand cranes in their goods yards, some in the open and others inside the goods sheds.

The gantry crane at Nine Elms was ordered following a minute in March 1870, when it was reported that, in order to enable the LSWR to maintain and extend the traffic in Portland stone, a gantry with a 10-ton crane on top was needed to transfer stone into the stone depot and into barges. Apart from that, and some undetailed approvals of wharf cranes, no information is available of any of them, apart from what can be gleaned from photographs.

Due to the lack of original information, the following pages can only attempt to show some of the cranes used without any pretence of telling the whole story, and the reader will doubtless spot many irritating gaps! Similarly, the drawings are all based on the LSWR and SR diagrams, so lack detail and (in some cases) leave questions as to the true arrangement of the gear trains. In the few cases where photographs exist, it has been possible to add some estimated detail to the drawings, but no great accuracy can be claimed!

Although the earliest minutes reference was in 1864, as mentioned above, two cranes came into Southern ownership that were recorded as supplied by Messrs Bray, Waddington in 1860. By 1924, they were allocated to the Goods Department: number 2 (later 41s) at Eastleigh, and number 3 (later 42s) at Basingstoke. It would not be unreasonable to conjecture that, unless the SR date was incorrect and should have been 1864, they were originally bought for general purposes, including breakdowns, and were probably under the control of the Resident Engineer, but based at Nine Elms and somewhere else down the line – possibly Northam. The SR Register shows number 2 as having a load capacity of 3 tons, and number 3 as 4 tons, which is a little odd in view of the fact that number 2 had one more stage of gearing than number 3. In other respects, they were similar and fairly typical of the period before the introduction of steam cranes in about 1870. They are shown here as figures 3.1 and 3.2, titled as in their later life as goods cranes. One of these, or a very similar one, can be partially seen at the left edge of plate 3.1.

Their carriages were dumb-buffered, and the cranes were pivoted on a full height central column casting; a large balance weight could be moved along the tail rails of the frame. There was no provision for derricking, that is, for raising or lowering the jib when loaded. The single winding gear was used to raise the jib into a position where two stays from the jib end could be connected to the top of the frame, and then the winding gear could be used for a load. The jib was made of wood, almost certainly of octagonal section. There was apparently no means of braking or locking the frame on its pivot, so slewing could be dangerous if on canted track, or if a load started to swing. The SR diagram shows no detail of the underframe, but it was presumably of a heavy-duty wagon style with journals and springs rated for about 20 tons with a wagon style handbrake. The match trucks shown are ex-timber wagons of 1890 and 1911 respectively, but presumably the originals must have been similar.

In November 1875, the Locomotive Committee received a recommendation from the Officers Committee that two travelling cranes should be obtained for use in case of breakdowns, and placed at Salisbury and Exeter. They only approved the purchase of one, from Messrs Appleby Bros, for the price of £750, without stating where it should be based. However, from the records this apparently became number 4, and was assigned to Guildford, as can be seen in the photograph. The drawing, figure 3.3 is based on the LSWR diagram and on the photograph.

It seems possible from the recorded building date of 1875 that Messrs Appleby were able to deliver this one from stock, because when the Traffic and Locomotive Committee agreed, in January 1878, to order another one for use at Exeter, "similar to the one at Nine Elms", they in fact accepted the tender in February from Messrs

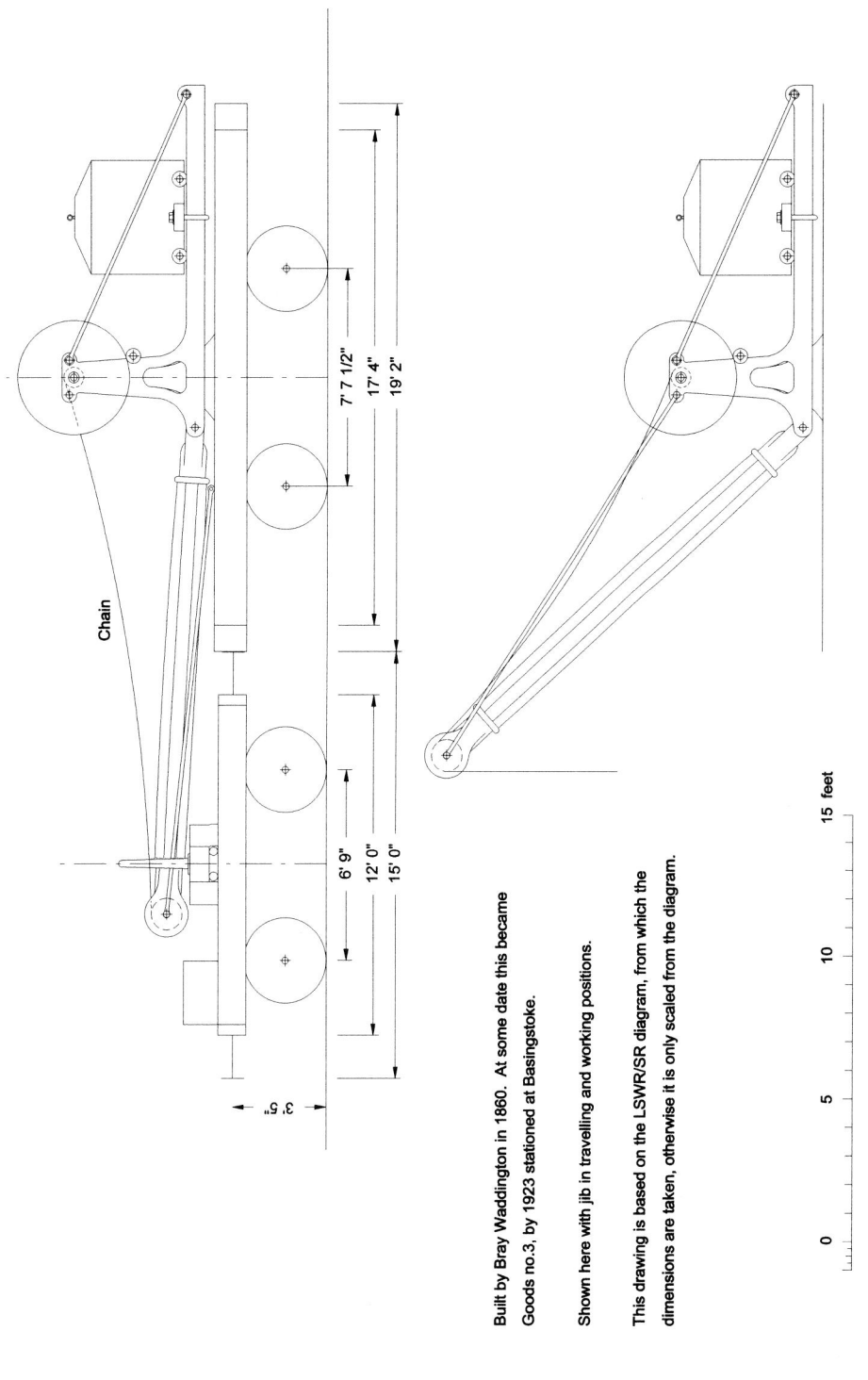

Figure 3.2. 4-ton crane of c.1860 (later goods crane No 3).

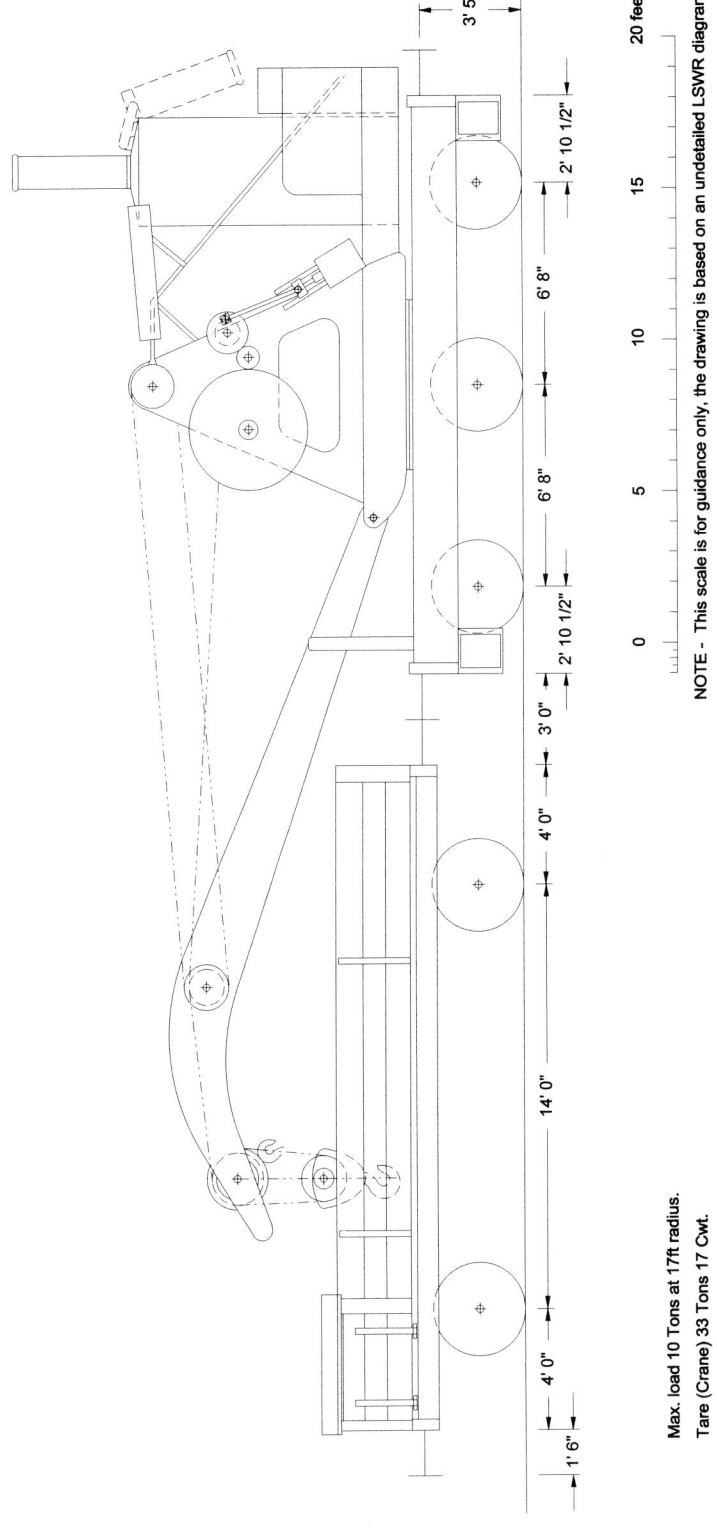

Figure 3.3. Breakdown cranes numbers 2 and 4 of 1875.

Appleby for a 10-ton one at £785. This one was recorded as in service in 1880 as number 2. It is apparently this one that is illustrated on page 111 of *The North Devon Line* by John Nicholas (OPC), where it is seen replacing a bridge on the Exeter and Crediton line. When number 4 was withdrawn from Guildford in 1925, number 2 replaced it there.

Between the orders for these two cranes, orders were placed with Metropolitan Carriage and Wagon Co in November 1877 for a breakdown van, and in December 1877 for a "Wagon for 10 Ton Steam Crane" – clearly number 4. The breakdown van was assigned to the Nine Elms breakdown train number 1 which included crane number 1. Apart from the earlier tool van that was ordered from Bray, Waddington in 1864, and which was also included in the Nine Elms number 1 train, these are the only vans recorded as specifically ordered for breakdown use. All other such vans seem to have been adapted from ordinary carriages or wagons, a practice that continued as long as there were formal breakdown trains.

The 1877 breakdown van is shown here as figure 3.4. Unfortunately, the earlier tool van can only be illustrated by the photographs, as no dimensions are known.

Two 4-ton travelling cranes were bought from Messrs Ellis for £341 each in October 1878, but nothing further is recorded about them. Presumably, at this capacity they were for the Traffic (Goods) Department.

Not mentioned in the minutes was another breakdown crane that entered service in 1885 as Nine Elms number 1. This was a 15-ton 6-wheel crane built by Dunlop & Bell, illustrated here by figure 3.5 based on the SR diagram, but greatly aided by the several good photographs that exist. When a new 20-ton crane (mentioned below) was ordered for Exeter, but diverted to Nine Elms as a replacement number 1, the Dunlop & Bell one was renumbered number 3 and assigned to Northam (referred to in a boiler register as "Eastleigh Red Rover", Northam loco shed having closed in 1903), then Strawberry Hill and then to Bournemouth Central by the time it appeared on the SR Register, being finally withdrawn in about 1946.

In June 1907, the Locomotive, Carriage and Stores Committee received a recommendation from the Mechanical Engineer that a 20-ton steam crane should be ordered for use in the Western District, and that the existing 12-ton one at Exeter should be transferred to the docks at Southampton. This was approved, and tenders were to be invited. However the same committee received a report in April 1909 stating that the new 20-ton crane had, in fact, been put into use at Nine Elms, and that the Exmouth Junction one was by then worn out and past repair. So, for the second time, a new one was approved for the Western District. In the following month, May,

Plate 3.3a. Crane No 4, Locomotive Department. Built in 1875 by Appleby Bros. (J Tatchell collection)

TRAVELLING CRANES

Plate 3.3b. 10-ton crane No 4 at Strawberry Hill, June 1921. (HC Casserley)

Plate 3.3c. Match truck to crane No 4 at Strawberry Hill, June 1921. (HC Casserley)

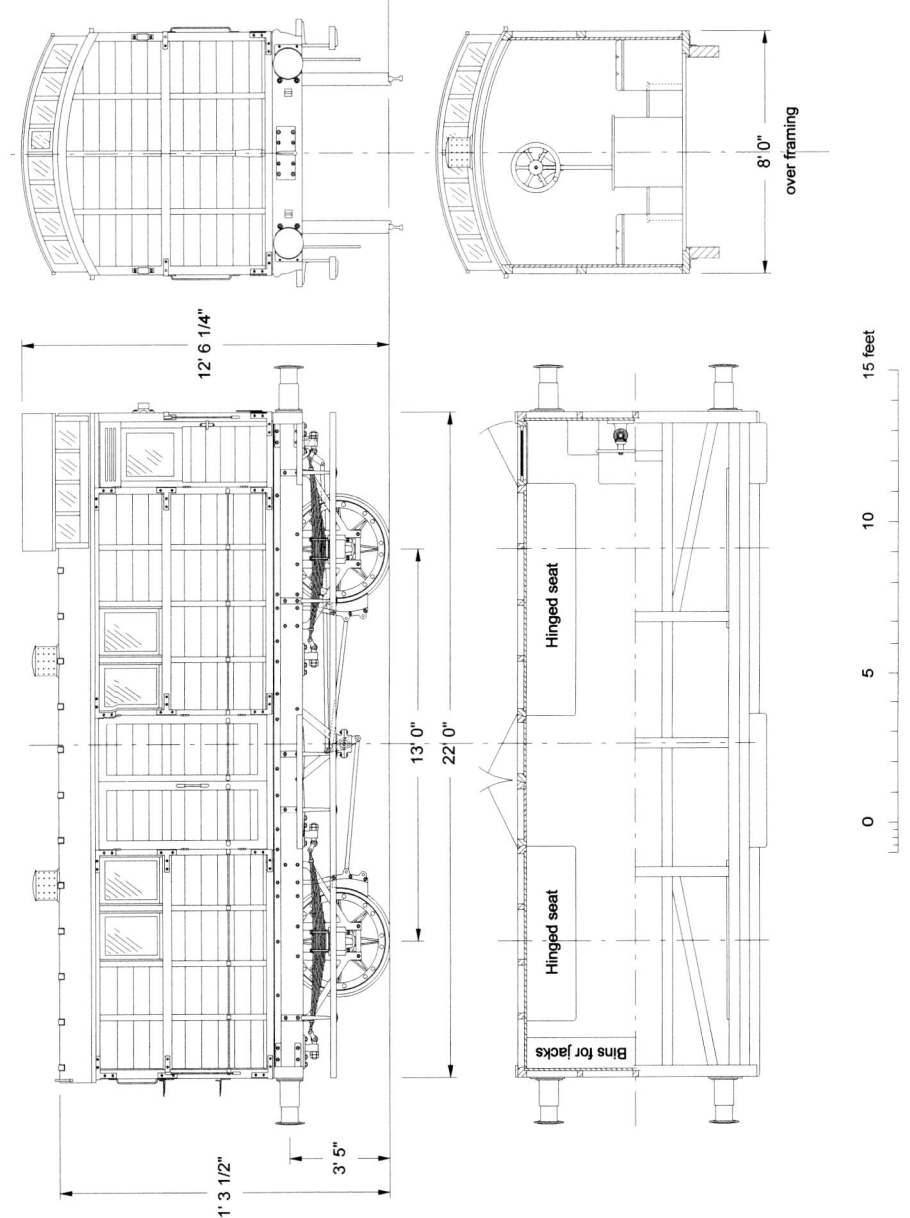

Figure 3.4. 22ft Nine Elms breakdown van of 1878.

TRAVELLING CRANES

Plate 3.4a. 22ft breakdown van in Nine Elms breakdown train, built 1878.

Plate 3.4b. Tool van of Nine Elms breakdown train, built in 1864 by Bray Waddington together with the first breakdown crane.

Plate 3.4c. Possibly the tool van ordered from Bray Waddington in 1864. (J Tatchell collection)

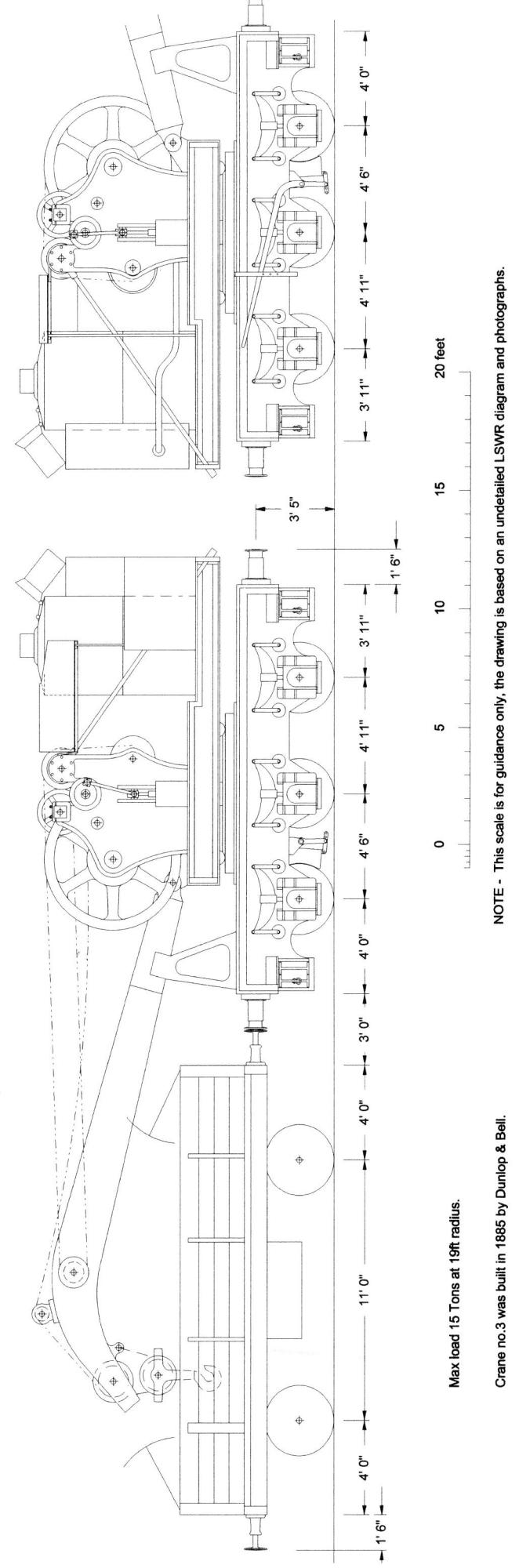

Figure 3.5. Breakdown crane No 3 (formerly No 1) of 1885.

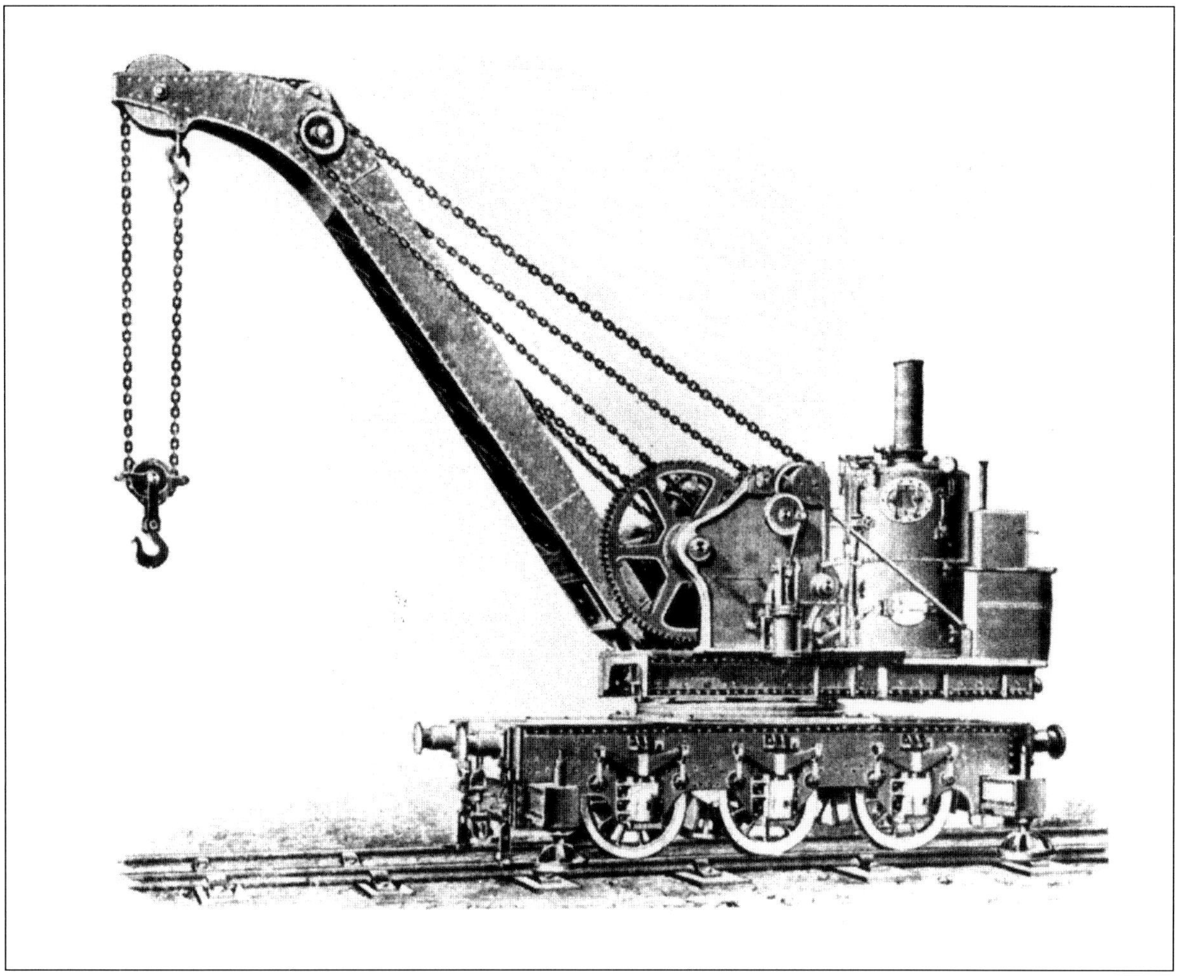

TRAVELLING CRANES

Plate 3.5a. Dunlop and Bell illustration of the 15-ton crane supplied to the LSWR. (Dunlop and Bell catalogue)

Plate 3.5b. B4 class 0-4-0T No 88 with Nine Elms breakdown train c.1896. 15-ton Dunlop and Bell crane of 1885. (HV Tumilty collection)

Plate 3.5c. 15-ton crane No 1 (later No 3) built by Dunlop & Bell in 1885. (HV Tumilty collection)

Plate 3.5d. Nine Elms No 1 of 1885. (HV Tumilty collection)

Plate 3.5e. Nine Elms No1 of 1885. (HV Tumilty collection)

Plate 3.5f. 15-ton crane No 1, seen as SR 32S with replacement match truck. This shows the opposite side of the carriage from the other pictures, with no brake lever. (HV Tumilty collection)

there were details of the tenders, from which the one from Stothert & Pitt of Bath at £1793 was accepted, subject to some alterations required by the Mechanical Engineer. The crane appropriated by Nine Elms became a new number 1 whilst that at Exmouth Junction became number 5.

An article appeared in *The Railway Gazette* for 12th March 1909 describing the new breakdown crane for the LSWR. This was accompanied by a drawing, but although it corresponds with photographs and the LSWR diagrams, in some respects there are marked discrepancies in others. The present drawing, figure 3.6, is therefore based mainly on the diagrams and photographs but with details from the *Railway Gazette* drawing.

From *The Railway Gazette* article, the two cylinders were 10in diameter by 12in stroke, the boiler was 4ft 3in diameter by 8ft high with a working pressure of 80psi. The water tank included a feedwater heater.

The main lifting wire was 4½in circumference, wound on a 2ft diameter barrel and long enough to give a lift of 22ft above rail level. A large brake ring was attached to the barrel, the strap round it was lined with wood and operated by a foot treadle powerful enough to hold a full load at any position; a hand screw backed this up.

The slewing gear operated independently of the lifting, derricking and travelling gear. The latter was driven by a vertical shaft running through the main centre post to gearing under the carriage. This gear could be disconnected from the axles to allow the crane to travel at speed in a train.

The carriage was mounted on four axles, two of them in a bogie (so perhaps it could be considered as a 4-4-0T or a 0-4-4T according to which way it travelled!) As with most such cranes, screw jacks were fitted at the axles to permit the weight to be taken off the springs when working. The usual clamps and screw shackles were shown at each headstock for clamping the crane to the track when lifting, there were also three outriggers with screw jacks on each side.

As can be seen in the photographs, no roof at all was provided initially for number 1, but at some date, probably quite soon, a kind of half-roof was added covering the driving control area (which was later extended to the other side according to a diagram) and finally a full cab was built. The 1909 drawing in *Railway Gazette* shows a full cab of corrugated iron except on either side of the driver's area, but the photographs demonstrate that whilst this may have been on Stothert & Pitt's normal offering it was not adopted by the LSWR.

This number 1 remained at Nine Elms ("Nine Elms Red Rover") until 1918, when it was replaced by a new 36-ton crane, number 6. Number 1 was then allocated to Eastleigh whilst number 5 remained at Exmouth Junction.

Because of the increasing weight and size of locomotives and rolling stock, it was decided in January 1915 to order a new crane with a lifting

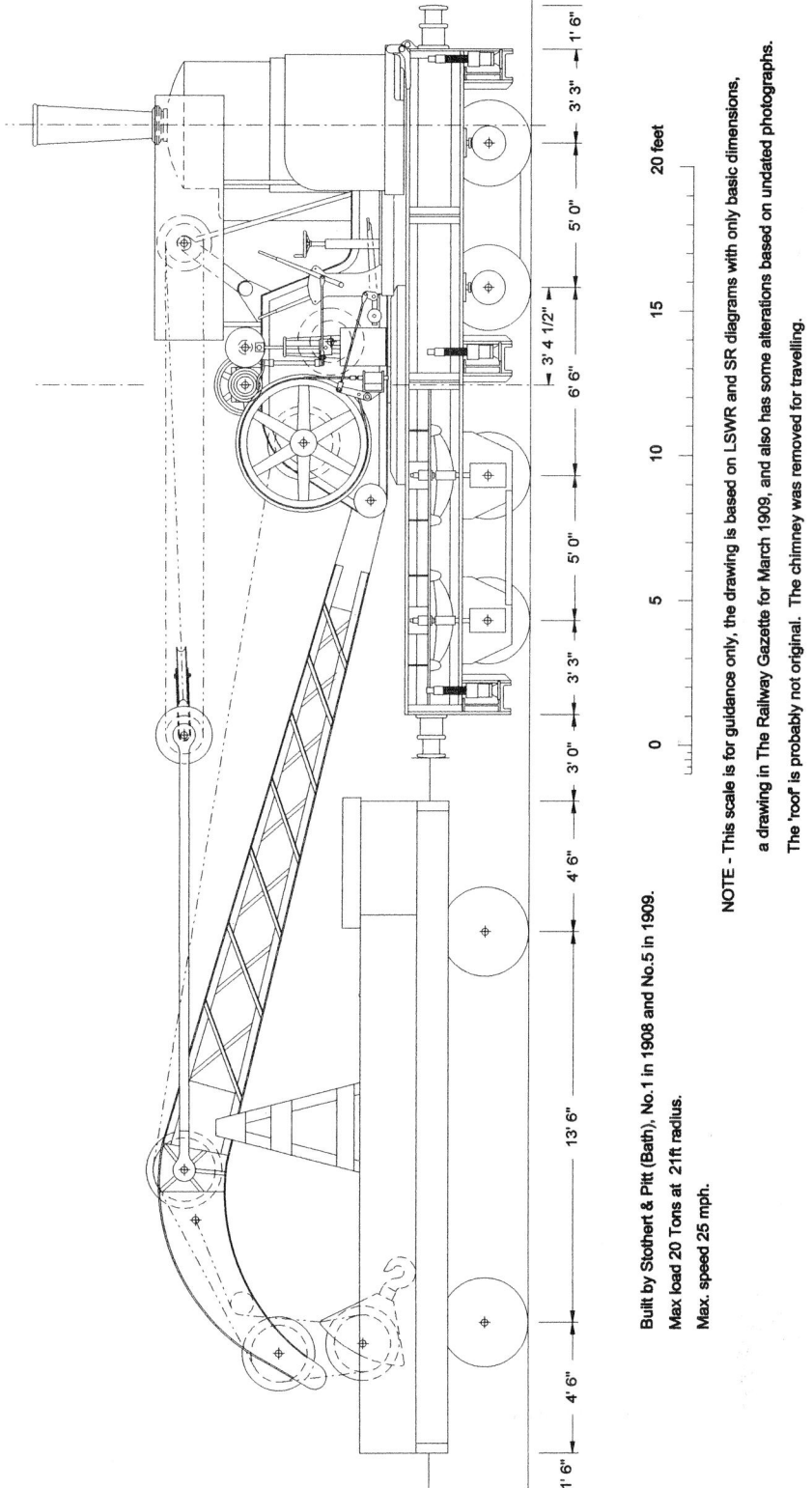

Figure 3.6. 20-ton breakdown cranes numbers 1 and 5 of 1908/9 (1 of 2).

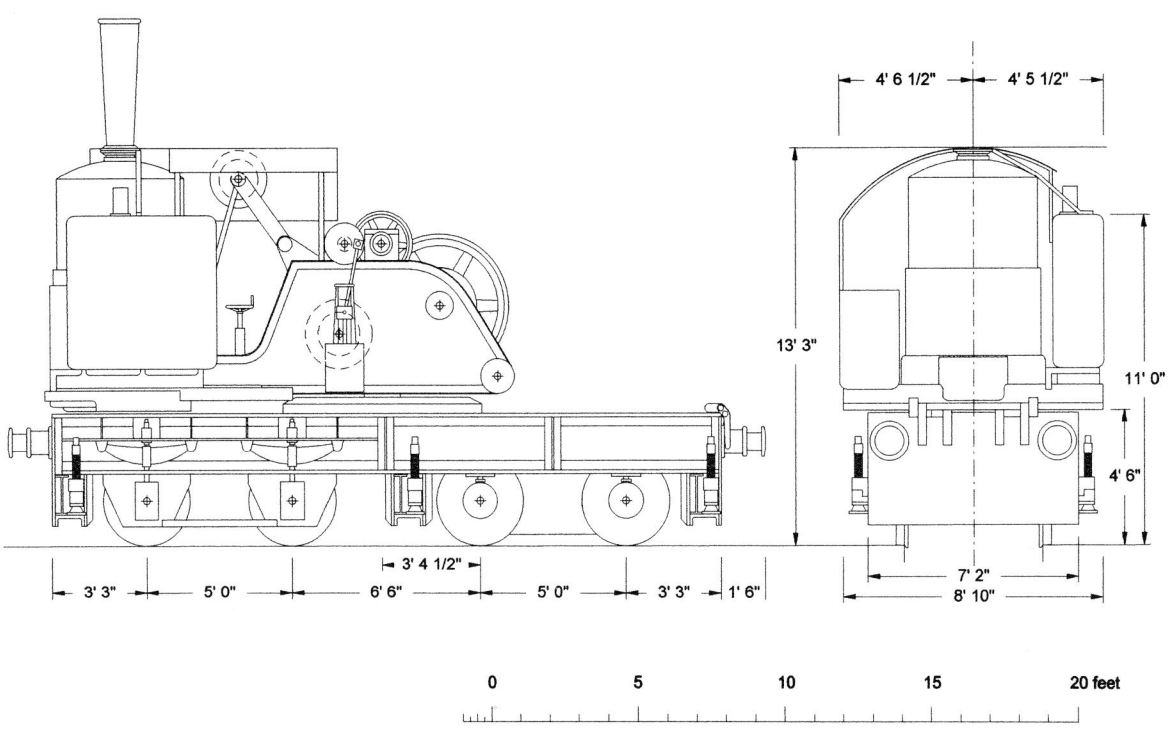

Figure 3.6. 20-ton breakdown cranes numbers 1 and 5 of 1908/9 (2 of 2).

Plate 3.6a. 20-ton crane No 1, as built by Stothert & Pitt in 1908. (J Tatchell collection)

Plate 3.6b. 20-ton crane No 1 of 1908. (Real Photographs Co)

Plate 3.6c. 20-ton crane No 1 of 1908, later No 5, in final condition as SR 34S. Note the lever and cams for locking the crane to the carriage when running, and also the jacks and rail clamps. (F Foote)

capacity of 36 tons for use at Nine Elms. Tenders were invited from Cowans Sheldon, Ransomes & Rapier and from Stothert & Pitt. The replies and prices were not recorded, but it was Ransomes & Rapier who got the order. This crane was delivered in 1918, but it did not become a replacement number 1 as was the earlier practice, but became number 6.

Number 6 was mounted on a 10-wheel carriage, consisting of six wheels in a rigid frame and a 4-wheel bogie. Rather surprisingly for such a large self-propelled machine, it was not provided with vacuum brakes, only hand ones. The match truck, or runner, was constructed at Eastleigh from a pair of old tender frames in the form of permanently coupled 4-wheel trucks numbered 68S. The present drawing, figure 3.7, is based on the SR diagram and photographs.

In July, the General Manager recommended to the Locomotive and Carriage Committee that another 36-ton crane should be obtained. The tender from Cowans Sheldon for delivery in three months for the price of £8950 (the LSWR to provide wheels and axles) was accepted in December 1920. However, the SR Service Register records it as being put into service in 1922 as number 7 (later 37S) and allocated to Salisbury.

Number 7 had similar dimensions and performance to number 6, and the LSWR actually described one diagram as covering both. In fact, the machinery layout was quite different, as can be seen in figure 3.8, and the SR did separate diagrams for them.

Now to cranes for the Traffic, Goods or Commercial Departments, practically all of which were hand powered. On the titles, it appears that the LSWR used Traffic and Goods as meaning the same department, and then the SR changed the title to Commercial Department.

In December 1900, when it was stated that the Nine Elms Traffic travelling crane number 4, to lift 5 tons, was broken down beyond repair, it was agreed to invite tenders. A new number 4 entered service in 1901 (figure 3.9). This was provided by Alex Chaplin & Co of Glasgow. Its capacity was again 5 tons on a 4-wheel carriage with a match truck that appears to have been a cut down open wagon.

Readers might already have noticed the omission of a goods crane number 1. This is because one is not mentioned in the surviving records, although one could guess that it was similar in type and date to those already described as numbers 2 and 3. Anyway, the minutes of the Locomotive, Carriage and Stores Committee recorded that tenders were received in October 1902, from which an order to Ransome & Rapier for a 5-ton crane at £385 was approved, but reduced by £46 on the basis that the wheels and axles would be supplied by the LSWR. This became the new goods crane number 1, shown here as figure 3.10.

Plate 3.7a. 36-ton crane No 6, Locomotive Department, outside Waterloo. (J Tatchell collection)

TRAVELLING CRANES

Plate 3.7b. 35-ton crane No 6, Locomotive Department, SR 35S, near Wimbledon in February 1928. (HC Casserley)

Plate 3.7c. 36-ton crane No 6, Locomotive Department, SR 35S, at Clapham Junction.

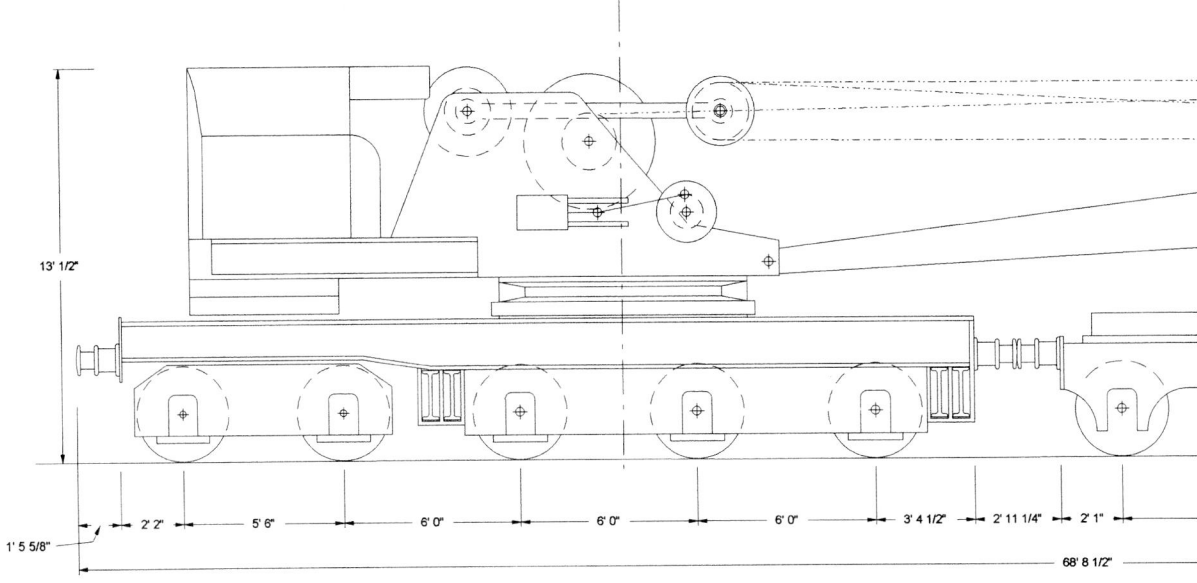

Figure 3.7. 36-ton breakdown crane No 6 of 1918.

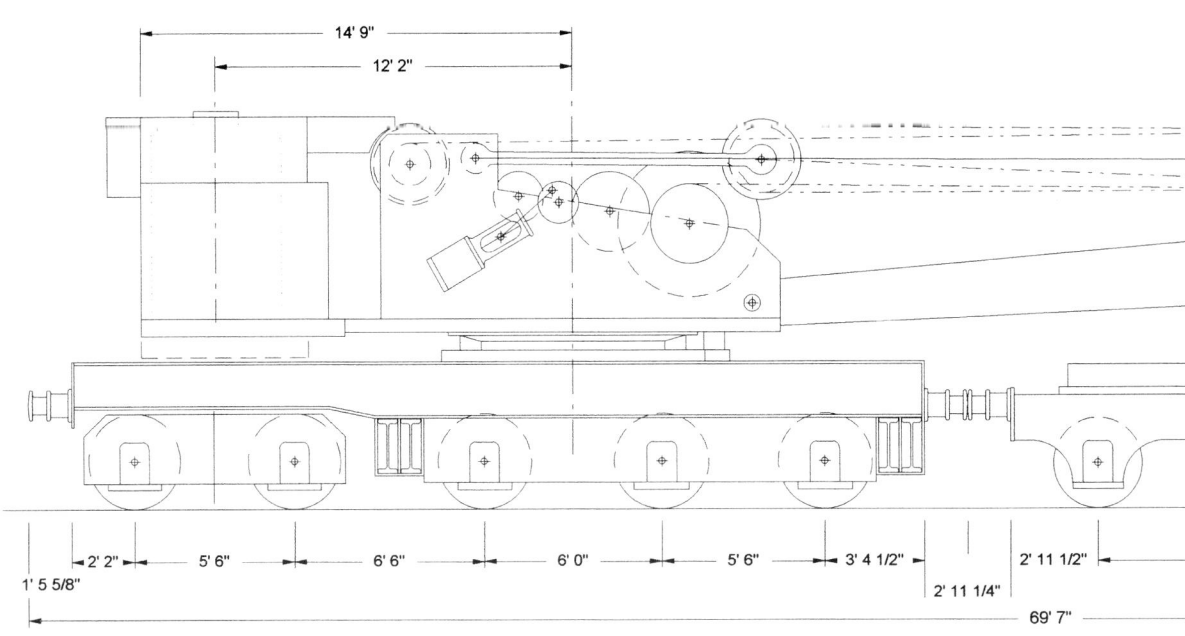

Figure 3.8. 36-ton breakdown crane No 7 of 1922.

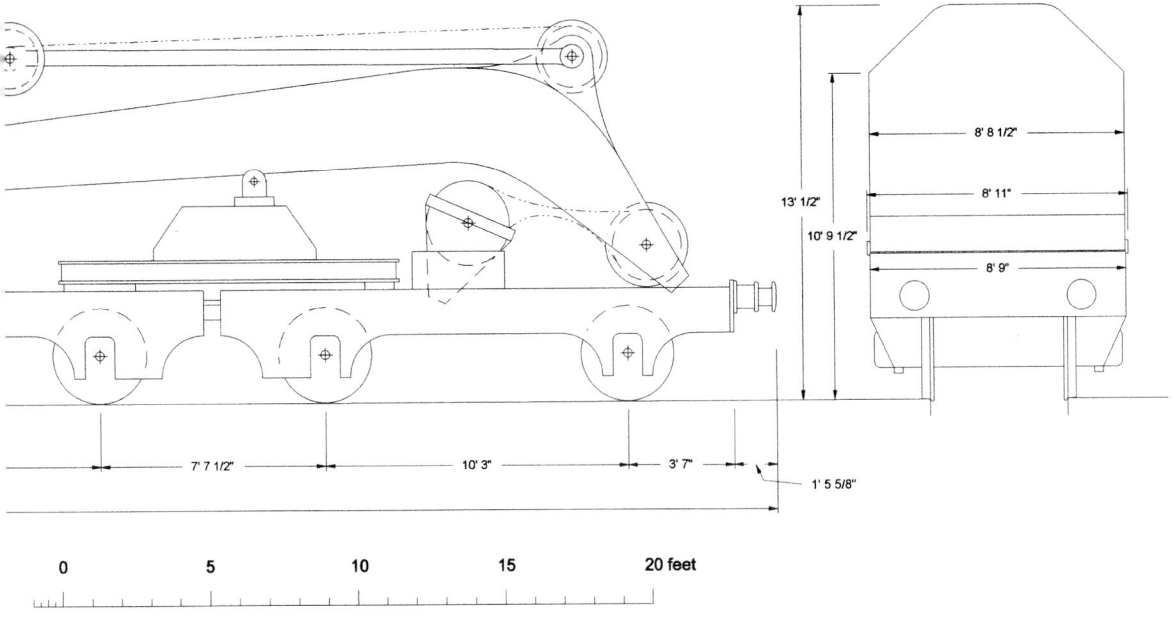

NOTE - This scale is for guidance only. The drawing is based on the Southern Railway diagram W.844.Amd1 (which states the cab has been added) and photographs, there are detail discrepancies!
The length over buffers is stated on the dgm as 69' 7" but by addition and by the scale it appears to be 68' 8½".

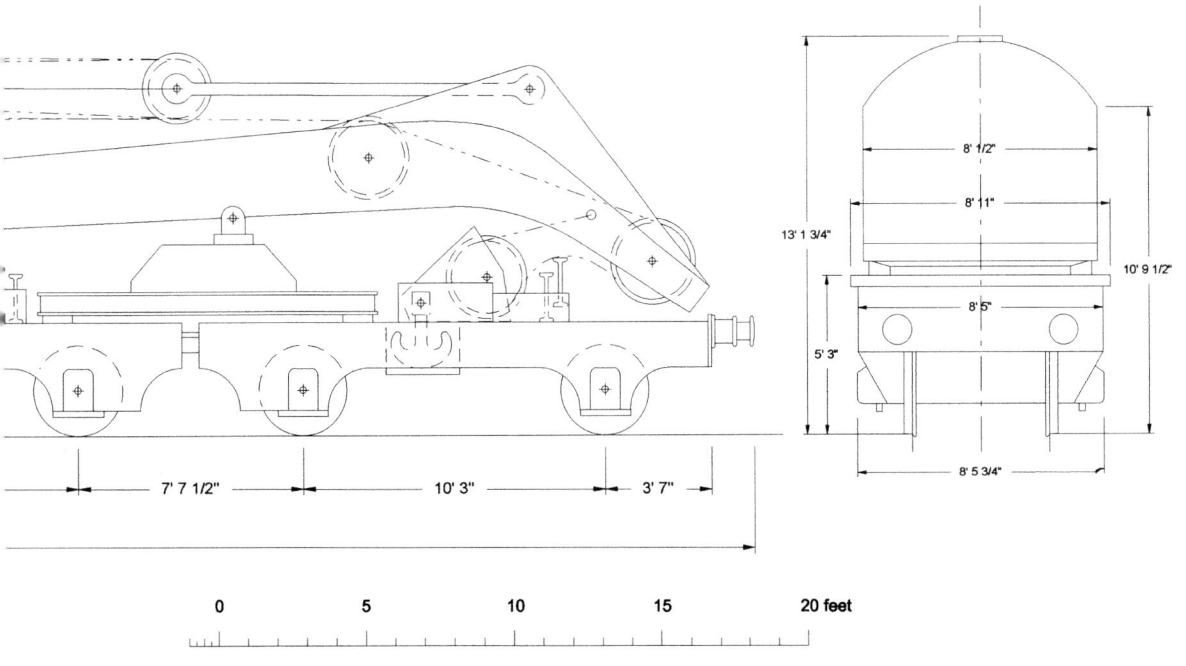

NOTE - This scale is for guidance only. The drawing is based on the Southern Railway diagram W.845

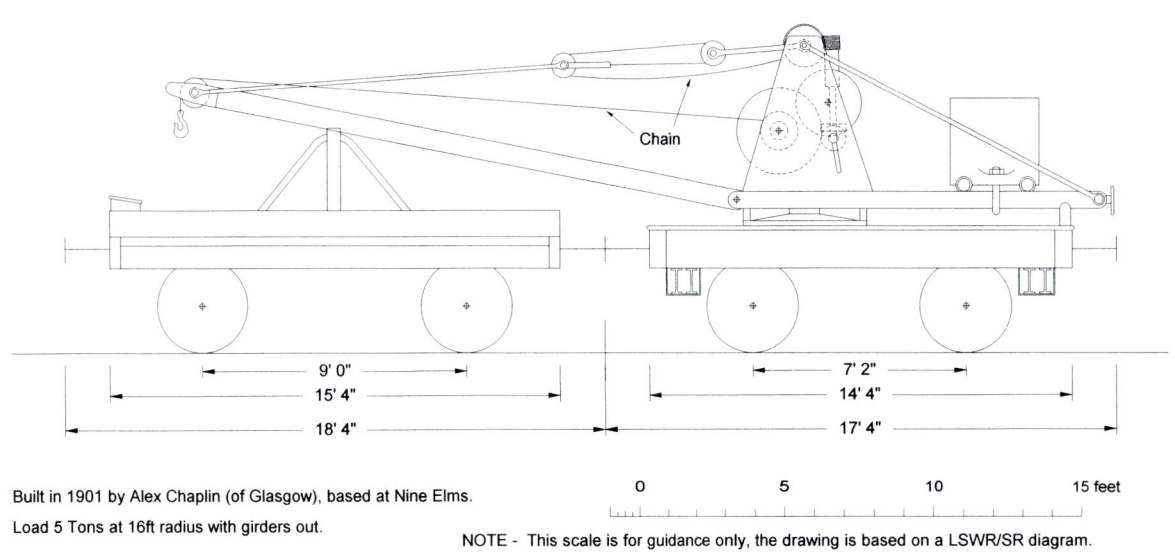

Figure 3.9. Goods crane No 4 of 1901.

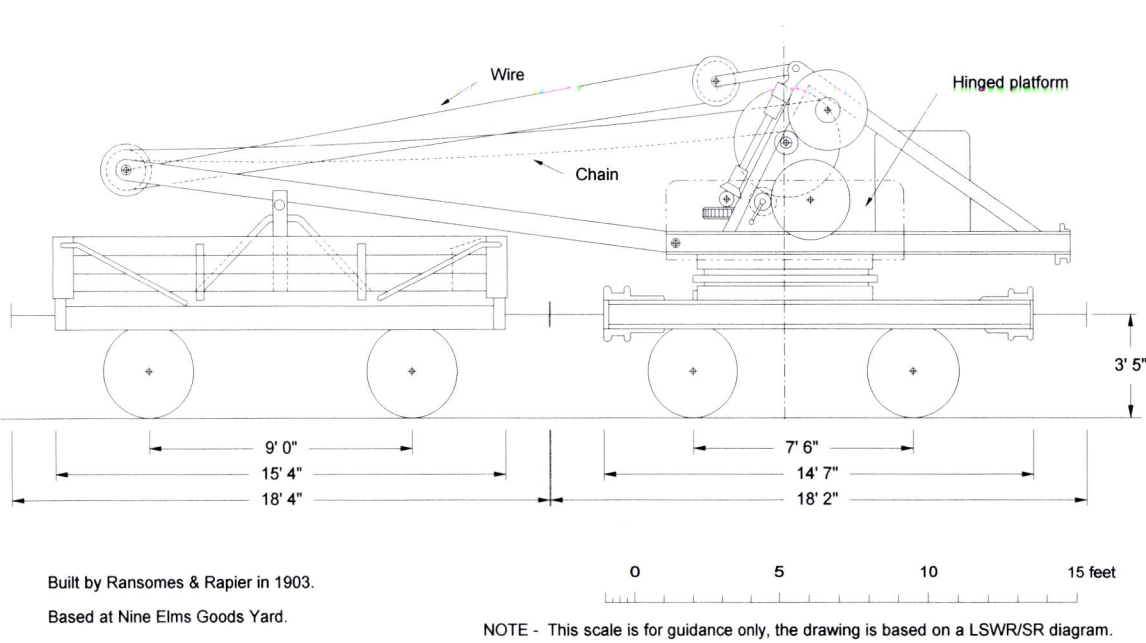

Figure 3.10. Goods crane No 1 of 1903.

TRAVELLING CRANES

Apart from what has been written so far, there are no records of the ordering or use of any other cranes. However, several other cranes are shown on LSWR and SR diagrams and hence also here. Nothing is known other than the few notes that appear on the diagrams or in the SR Service Stock Register; the locations shown are those shown in the latter document.

Taking them in number order rather than date, 5-ton goods crane number 5 was obtained from Ransomes & Rapier in 1911, and based at Exmouth Junction (figure 3.11).

10-ton goods crane number 6 (figure 3.12) was also bought from Ransomes & Rapier, but earlier, in 1901, and assigned to Feltham.

A good deal earlier was 10-ton goods crane number 7 (figure 3.13), whose builder in 1885 is not recorded; it was based at Exmouth.

10-ton goods crane number 8 (figure 3.14) came from Ransomes & Rapier in 1897, and was used at Eastleigh.

The next cranes were in other departments, and those for the Engineer's Department followed the numbering of the Goods Department.

10-ton crane number 9 was built in 1910 by the LSWR, and was used at the Wimbledon Ironworks. Although thus listed, its design looks more like a possible rebuild of a much older crane (figure 3.15).

Also used by the Wimbledon Ironworks was 3-ton Engineer's Department shops crane number 10, built by the Haigh Foundry in 1914. At the same site was 1½ton crane number 11 built around 1890. No diagram is available for either of these.

At Meldon Quarry was Engineer's Department 5-ton crane number 12, built around 1900 by Jessop & Appleby (figure 3.16).

Although the Locomotive Department probably had several cranes for coaling and other purposes, the only one recorded as a diagram is a shops crane, shown here as figure 3.17. There is no information about it, but presumably it was based at Eastleigh.

There were also some cranes used by the Carriage Department, one steam crane and three shops cranes, presumably also at Eastleigh. These had a curious and seemingly illogical system of numbering: M76, R12, 1, 2 and Y15. They are seen here as figures 3.18, 3.19, 3.20 (showing numbers 1 and 2) and 3.21, respectively.

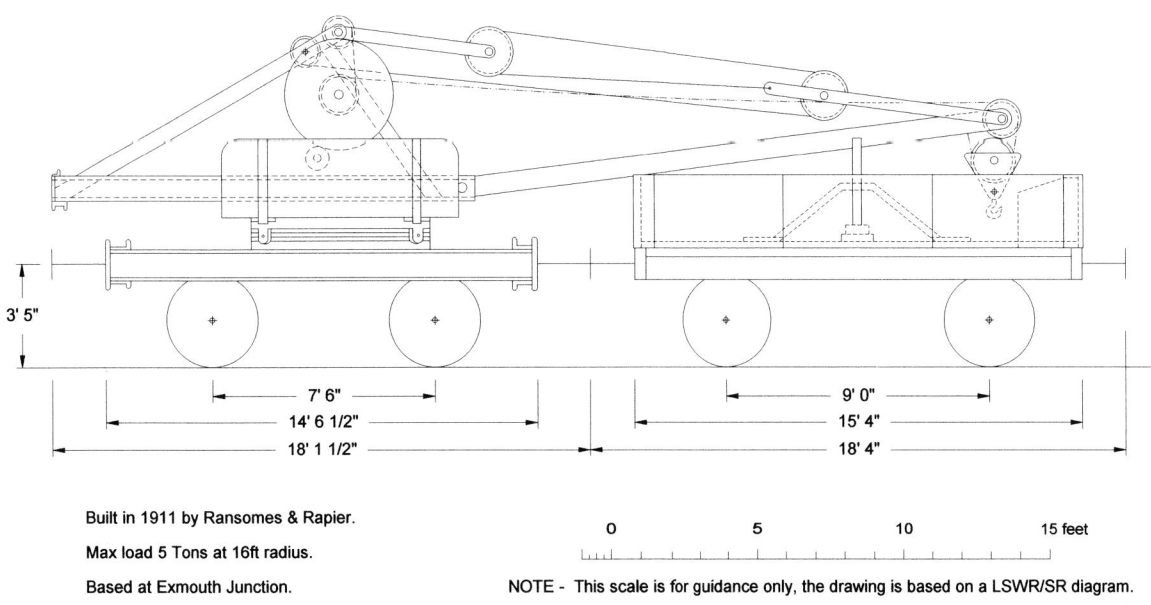

Built in 1911 by Ransomes & Rapier.
Max load 5 Tons at 16ft radius.
Based at Exmouth Junction.

NOTE - This scale is for guidance only, the drawing is based on a LSWR/SR diagram.

Figure 3.11. Goods crane No 5 of 1911.

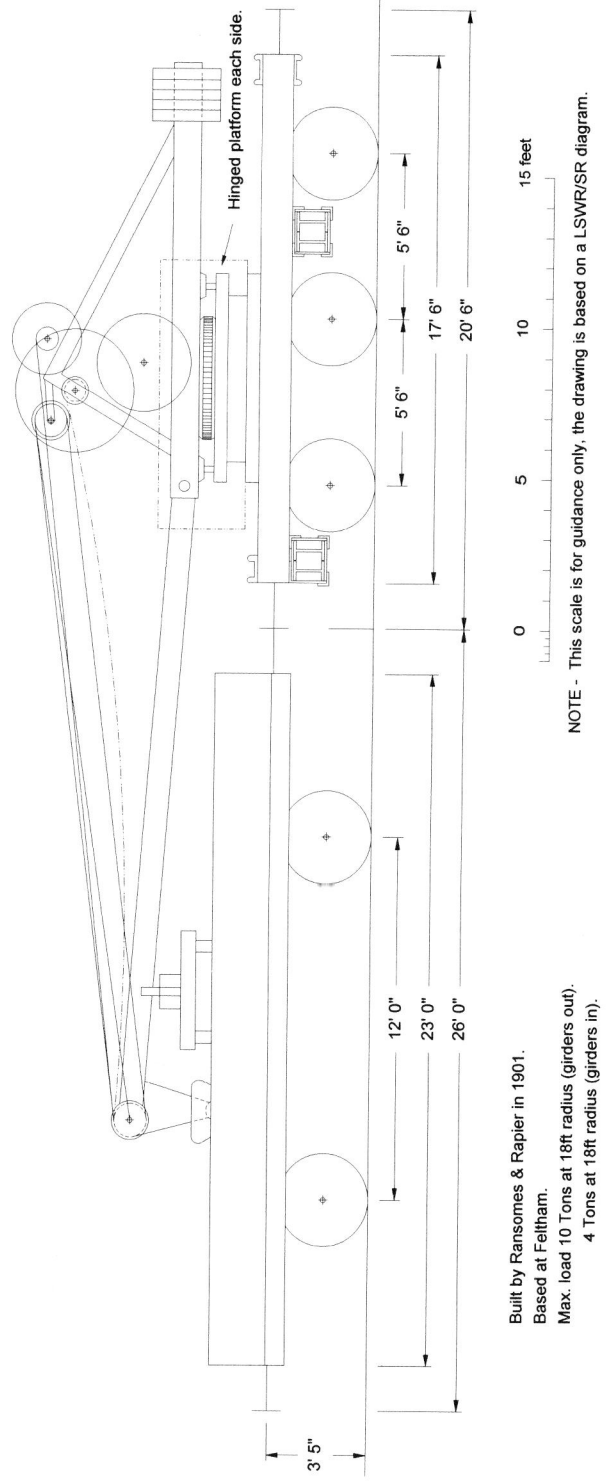

Figure 3.12. Goods crane No 6 of 1901.

TRAVELLING CRANES

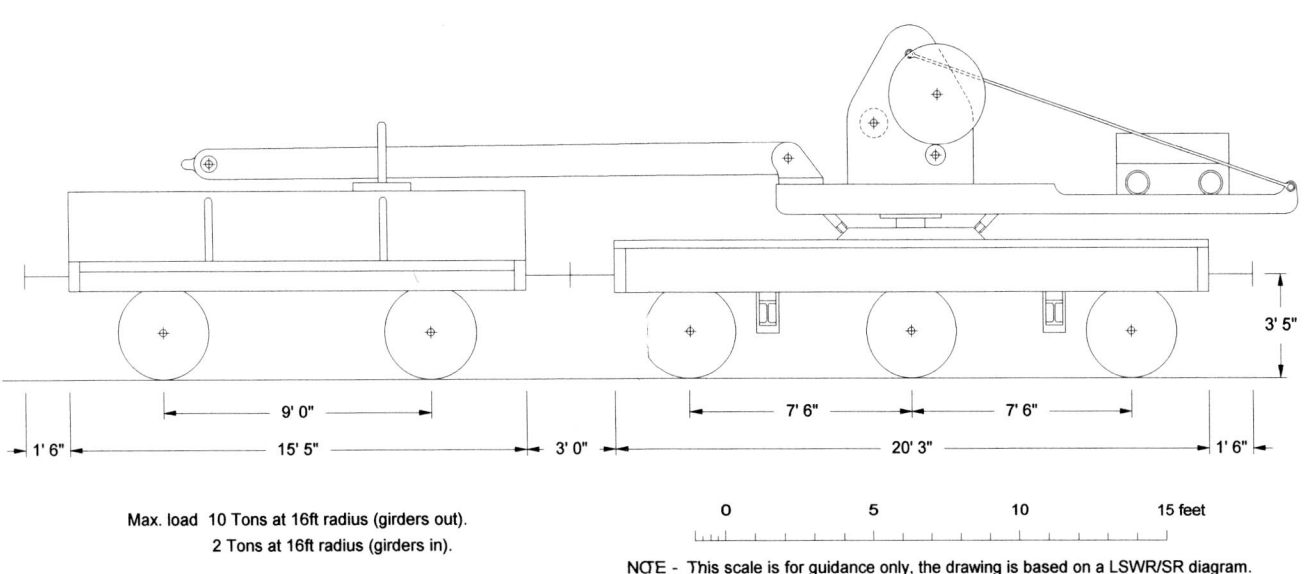

Figure 3.13. Goods crane No 7 of 1885.

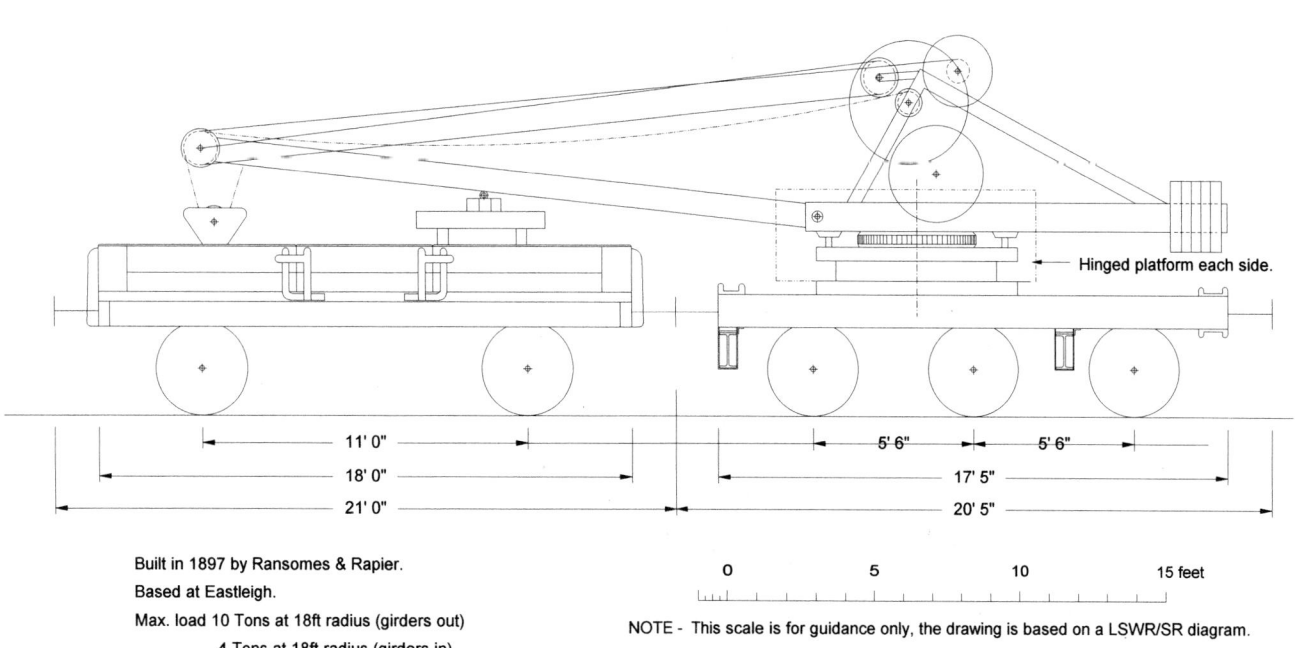

Figure 3.14. Goods crane No 8 of 1897.

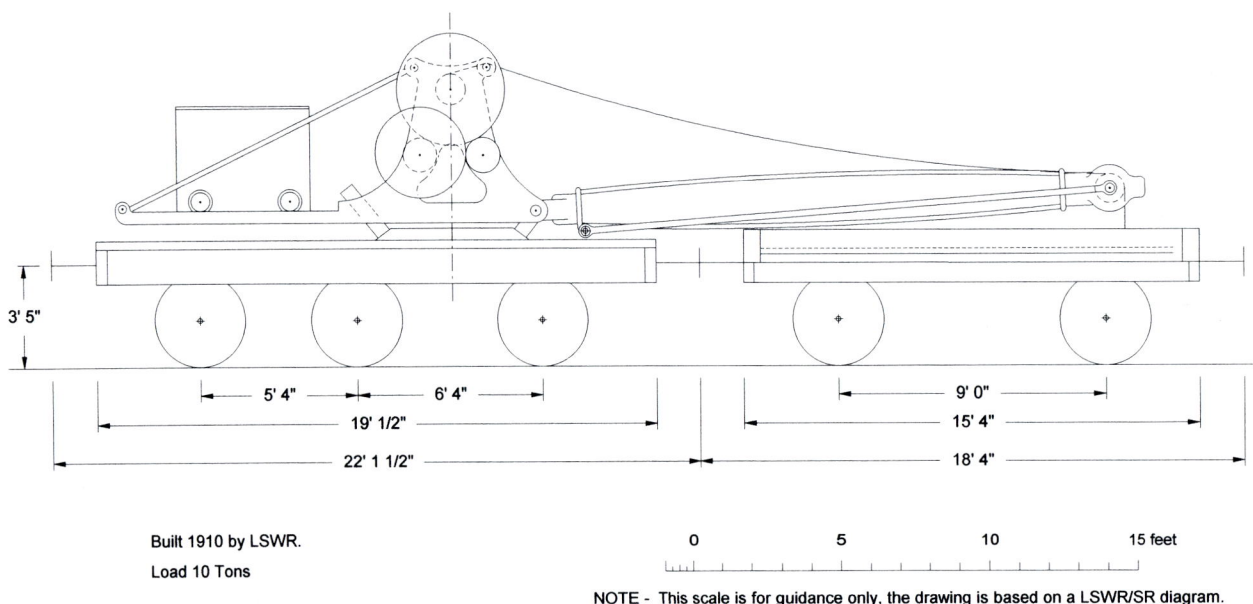

Figure 3.15. Engineer's Crane No 9 of 1910.

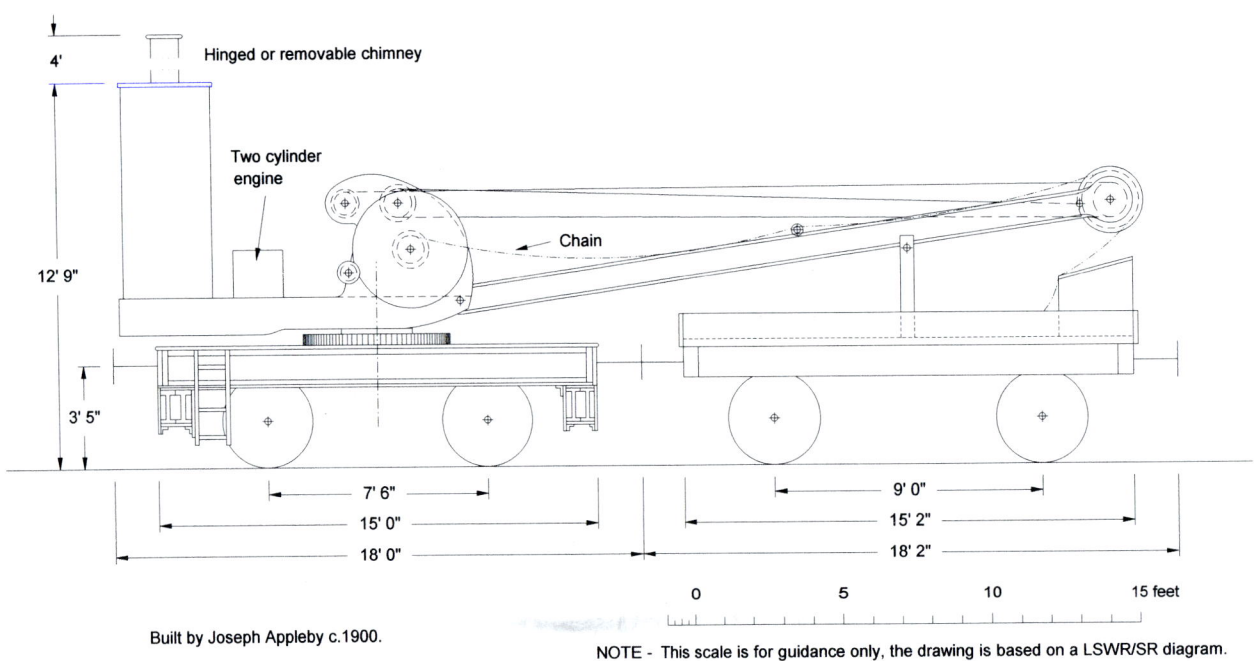

Figure 3.16. Engineer's Crane No 12 of 1900.

TRAVELLING CRANES

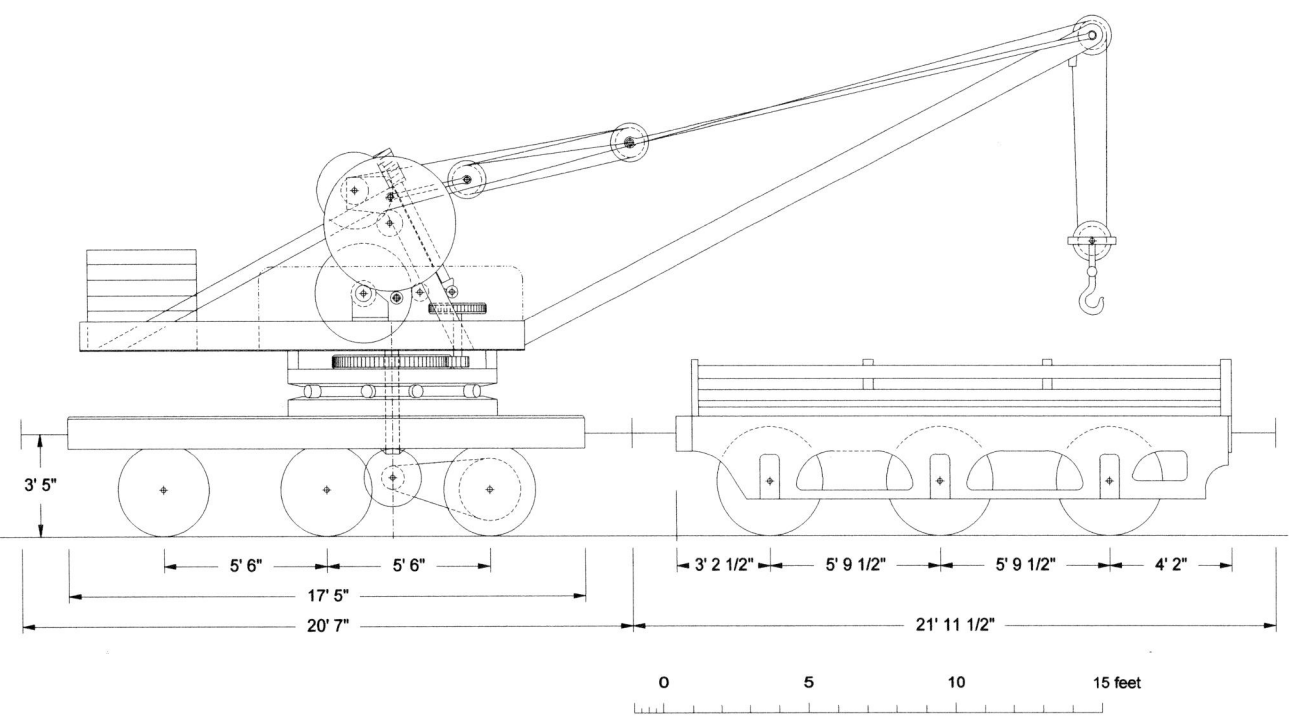

Figure 3.17. Locomotive Department shops crane.

Plate 3.17. The crane appears to be the loco shops crane or similar. Wagon 70 is a 31ft sleeper wagon of 1888. (Author's collection)

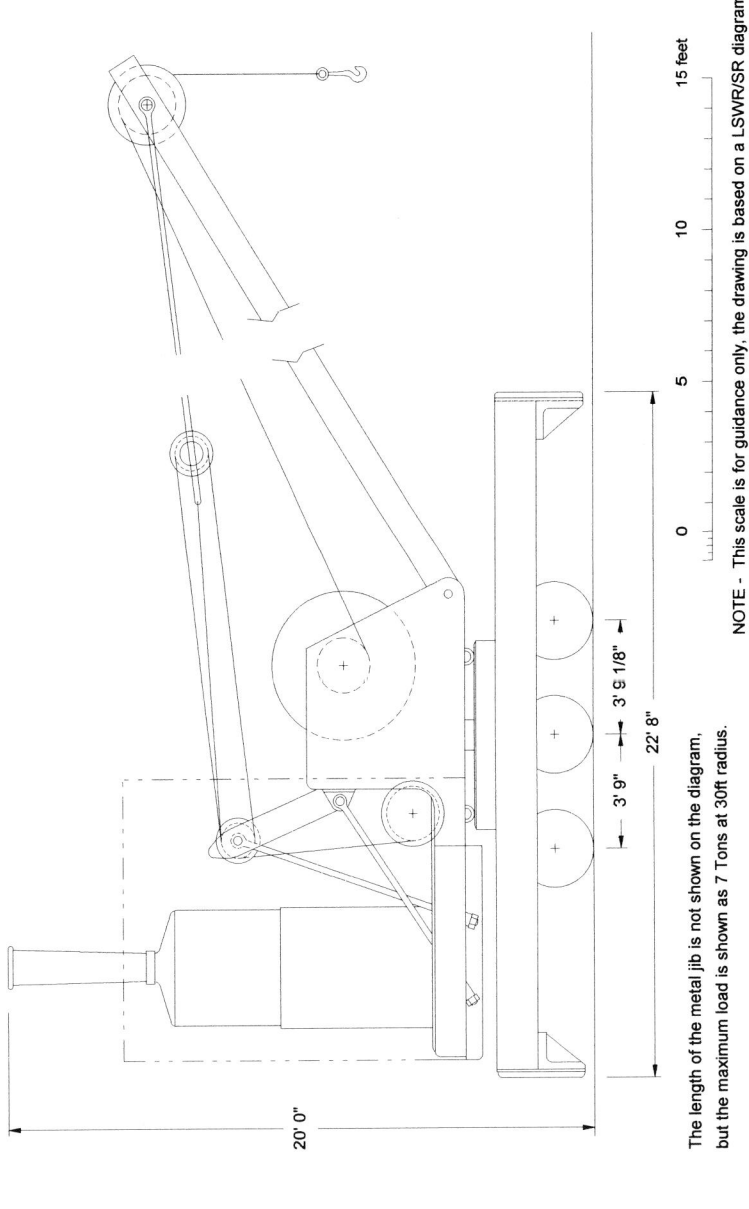

Figure 3.18. Carriage Department steam crane M76.

TRAVELLING CRANES

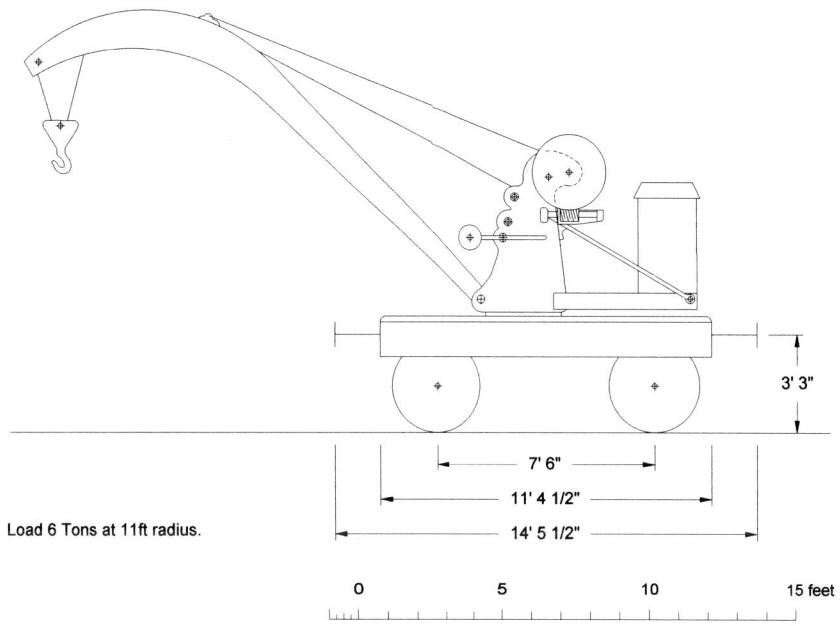

Figure 3.19. Carriage Department shops crane R12.

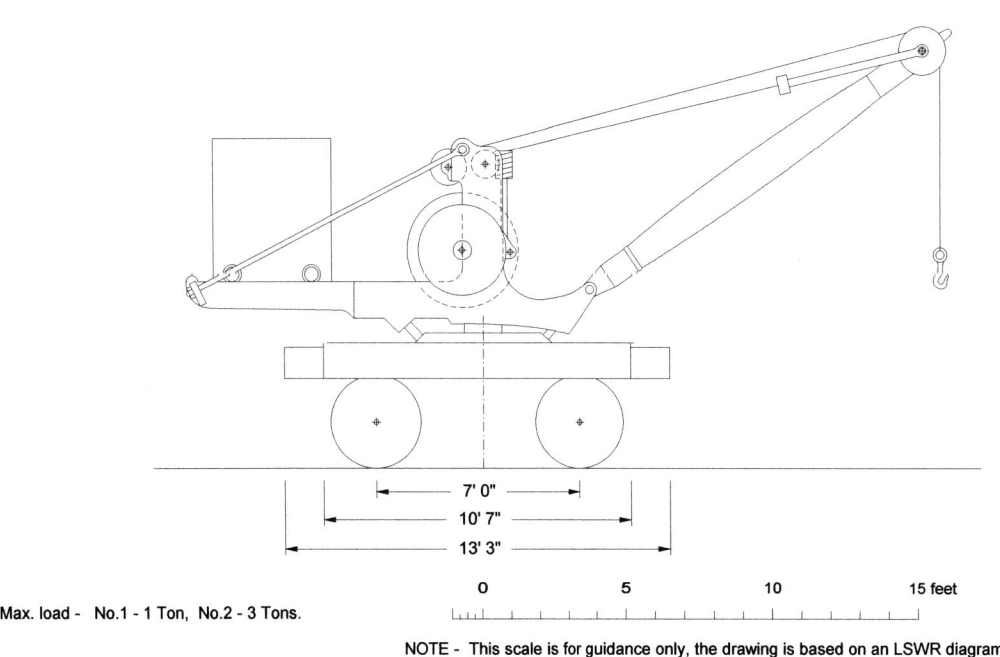

Figure 3.20. Carriage Department shops cranes 1 and 2.

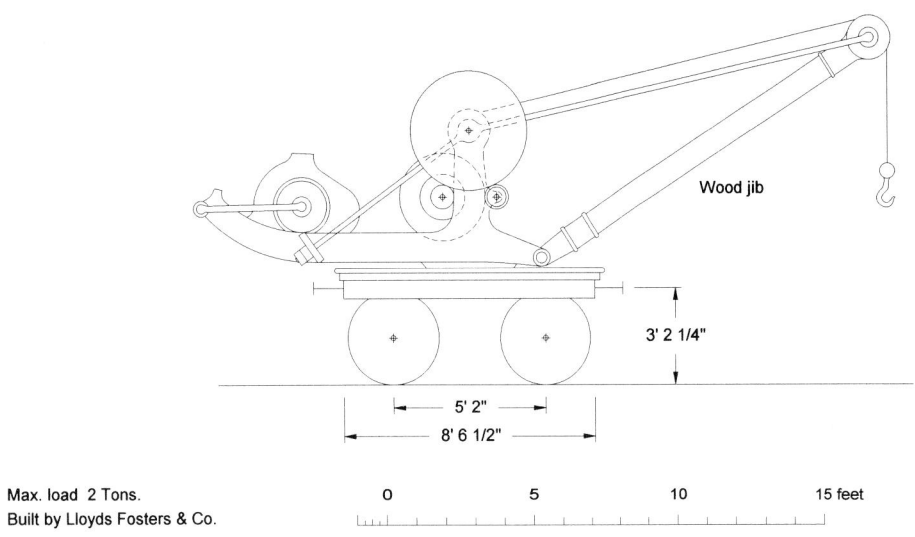

Figure 3.21. Carriage Department shops crane Y15.

Plate 3.21. Carriage Department shops crane Y15, with replacement jib. (Author's collection)

Plate 3.22. Crane 49S at Exmouth Junction in June 1948. (JH Aston)

Some photographs of other Southern Railway cranes are also shown here, but as they were on LSWR territory, readers may find them of some interest.

Crane 49S at Exmouth Junction on coaling duties (plate 3.22) has LSWR axleboxes, so it just might have been built by or for that company, its relatively low number also suggests that.

59S at the Exmouth Junction concrete works (plate 3.23) was certainly built for the SR in 1925. 198S at Feltham (plate 3.24) has the look of being "home made" for coaling work either there or at Nine Elms. By contrast, 525S at Meldon is a much more substantial machine (plate 3.25). The roof seems to have been rather battered, probably by flying rock from the blasting. 453S at Feltham is another coaling crane (plate 3.26) under which the travelling drive gear can just be seen.

Plate 3.23. Crane 59S at Exmouth Junction, June 1948. Built by Grafton c.1925. (JH Aston)

TRAVELLING CRANES

Plate 3.24. Crane 198S at Feltham in May 1948. (JH Aston)

Plate 3.25. SR 525S at Meldon Quarry, July 1948. (JH Aston)

TRAVELLING CRANES

Plate 3.26. Crane 453S at Feltham in August 1948. Built by Grafton. (JH Aston)

Plate 3.27. Crane 1582S at Sidmouth in June 1948. Built by Cowans Sheldon. (JH Aston)

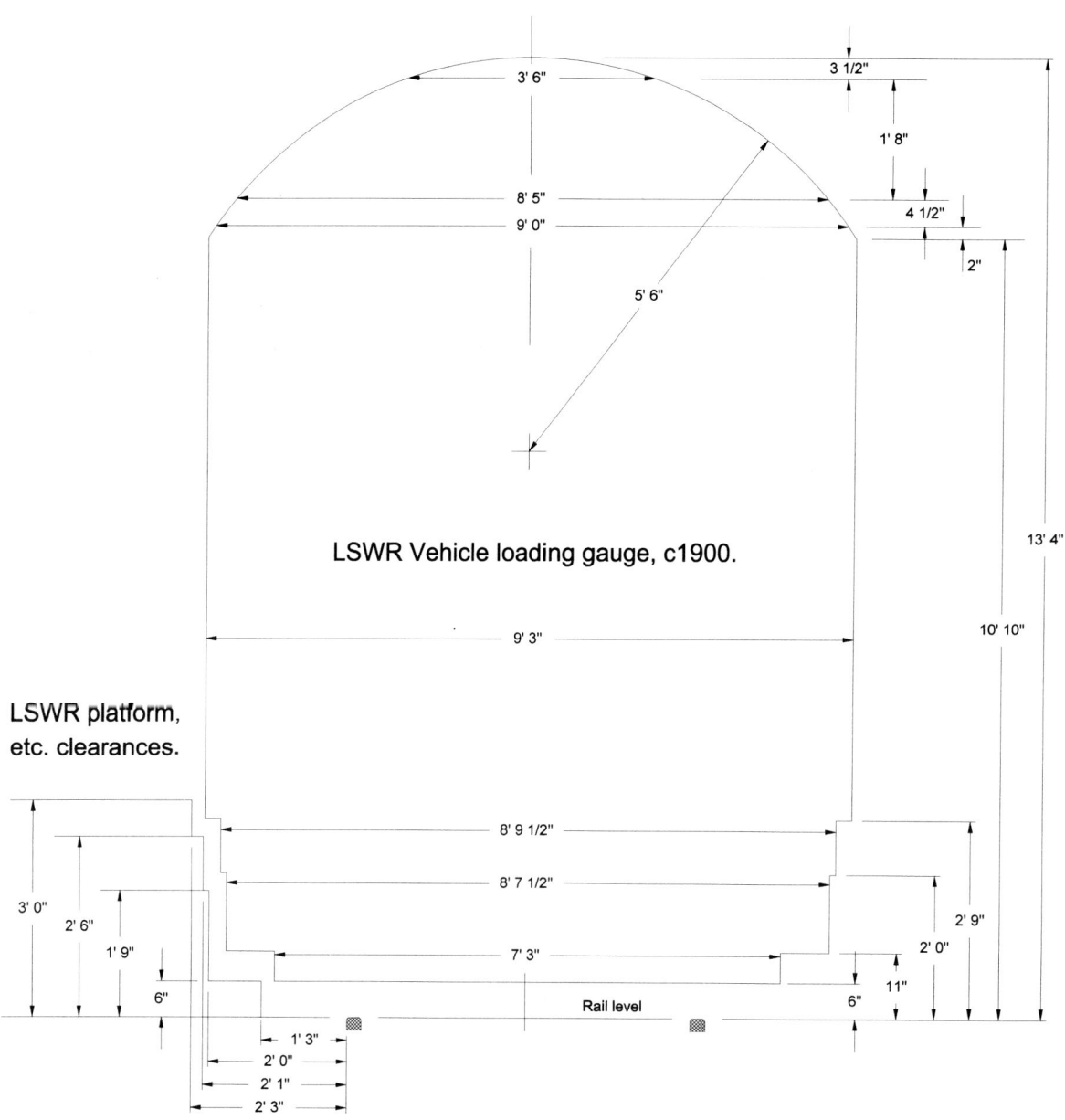

Figure 4.1.1. LSWR structure and load gauge.

CHAPTER 4
MISCELLANY

As the title implies, this chapter is for various subjects that do not clearly fall into any of the preceding chapters.

Structure and Load Gauge

Figure 4.1.1 illustrates the maximum dimensions for vehicles, including their load, and the clearances of the three types of LSWR platforms and other structures. This is taken from the *Appendix to Rules* for January 1911, but of course these dimensions had been established long before, and continued long after, that date.

Mr Peter Tatlow has very kindly allowed me to use his tracings of three patterns of LSWR loading gauges, as used in goods yards, as Figures 4.1.2a and 4.1.2b.

Road Vehicles

In an LSWR correspondence file there is a note dated 12th July 1883 that Mr Adams agreed with the Deputy Chairman that road parcels vans should be painted a standard colour in accordance with the carriage stock, as was done by the LNWR and other companies. This was to be put in hand as vehicles were repaired.

There are some dimensioned illustrations and descriptions of LSWR road vehicles in *Modern Railway Working, Volume 5* (1911) and *Railway Mechanical Engineering Volume 1* (1923), including a very detailed drawing of a three-horse road van, but the subject is not really relevant to the present work apart from what is described below. However, there are some photographs that are too good to omit, so they are included at the end of this section.

There was one case where a number of road vehicles were ordered in conjunction with matching road vehicle trucks and they were a frequently seen feature, particularly on the main line, for many years. The traffic of imported chilled meat developed rapidly from 1892, and gave rise to the introduction of pair-horse meat carts. As was mentioned in Chapter 1, in November 1892, the General Manager brought up the need to cater for the increasing Southampton to London meat traffic expected on the transfer of the Inman Line to Southampton.

It was then recommended that 50 vans of similar construction to the company's ordinary road vans, but of different dimensions and interior arrangements, should be built. They are illustrated here at figure 4.2.1, which has been prepared using typical measurements from the road vehicles register and examination of several photographs, including those shown as plates 4.2.1a to 4.2.1d, 4.2.1f and 4.2.1g. It was necessary to make some assumptions, particularly in the detail fittings. They were to be covered by a rubber cloth when travelling. 14 long van trucks as shown in plate 4.2.1e, each capable of holding two vans (one might prefer to call them carts to distinguish them from railway vans) were also recommended. These were all approved but the order for the trucks was increased to twenty a couple of weeks later.

The American Line gained a contract for increased meat consignments, and so in February 1898, it was decided to order 16 more meat carts from the Bristol Carriage & Wagon Works, accompanied by eight more long van trucks to be built at Eastleigh. This was repeated in mid-1899, when twenty carts and ten long van trucks were ordered, though where from was not specified.

The long van trucks were the 28ft ones that are shown as figure 39 and plates 121 and 122 in *Southern Wagons, Volume 1*, as well as a photograph here of one in use in SR days (plate 4.2.1e). To add a little more to the story, only a month after that approval, the order for the trucks was increased to twenty. Then, in February 1898, after the American Line entered into a contract for increased shipments of meat from Southampton to London, it was decided to build 16 more meat carts and eight more long van trucks. The carts were to be built by Bristol Carriage & Wagon Works Co. This was still an underestimate of the need, as in May 1899, a further twenty meat carts and ten long van trucks had to be authorised. As can be seen in the photographs mentioned above, when the meat carts were replaced by containers in Southern Railway days the van trucks still continued to have a very useful life.

The meat cart bodies were painted wagon brown with the lettering "South Western Railway", possibly in red on a carriage salmon background; the numerals were probably white. Wheels and underframes were finished in "oil red". The rubber sheets were off-white, whether grey or creamy is not certain; the lettering "LSWR" on them looks as though it might have been red.

The minutes only account for 74 carts as having lasted until 1920, when it was recorded that 24 were past repair and should be broken up. The remaining 50 were ordered to be converted to containers at the

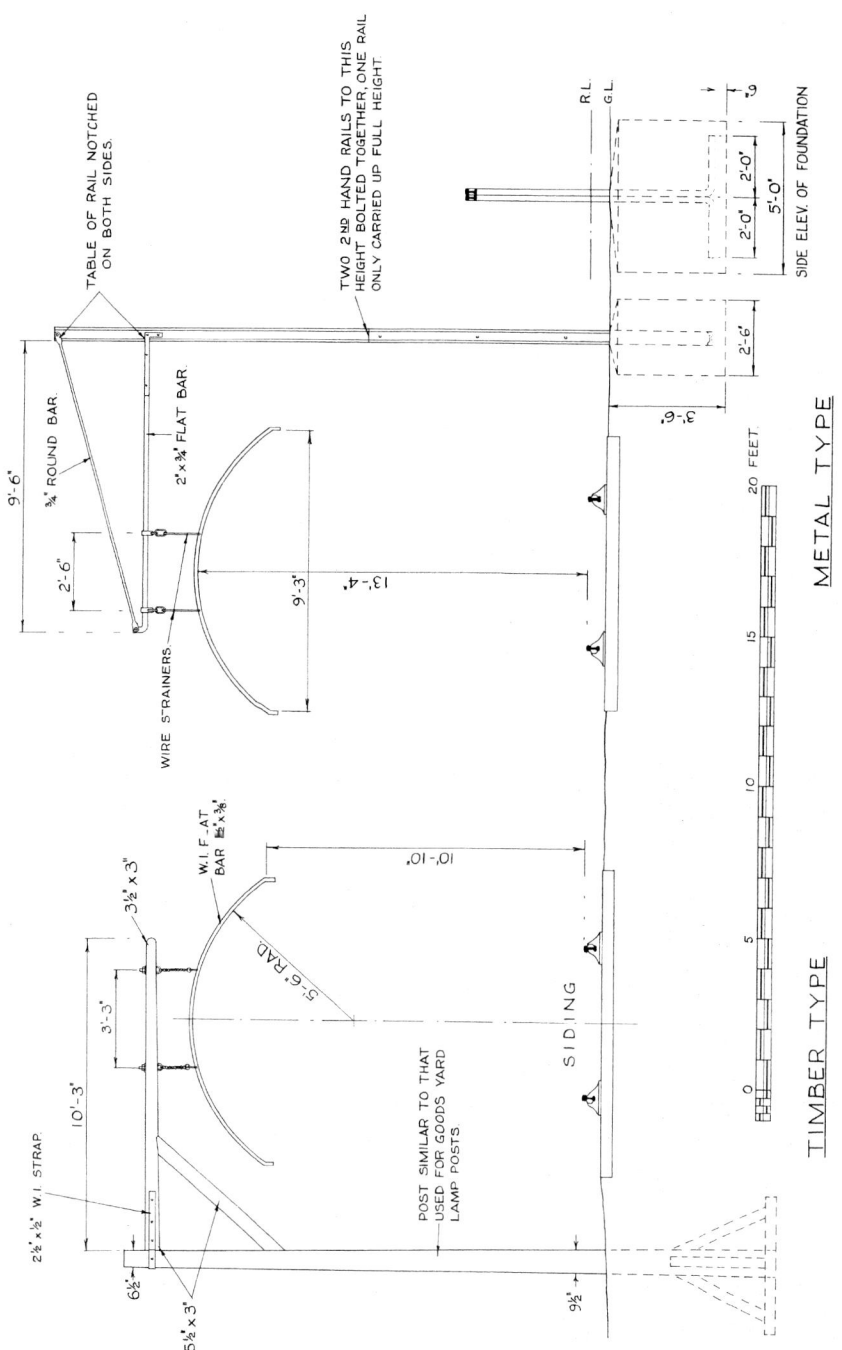

Figure 4.1.2a. LSWR loading gauges used in goods yards. (Peter Tatlow)

MISCELLANY

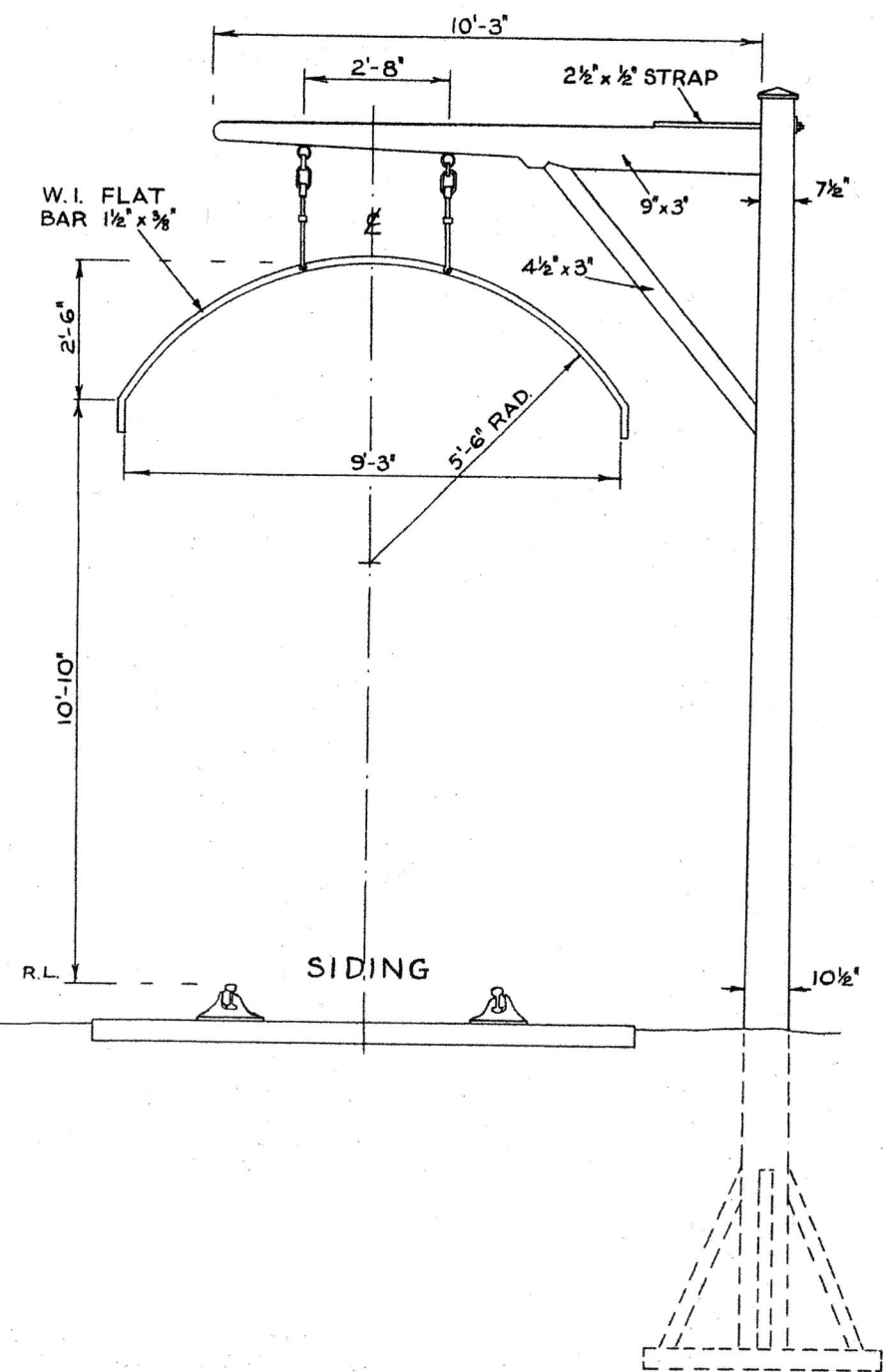

Figure 4.1.2b. LSWR loading gauges used in goods yards. (Peter Tatlow)

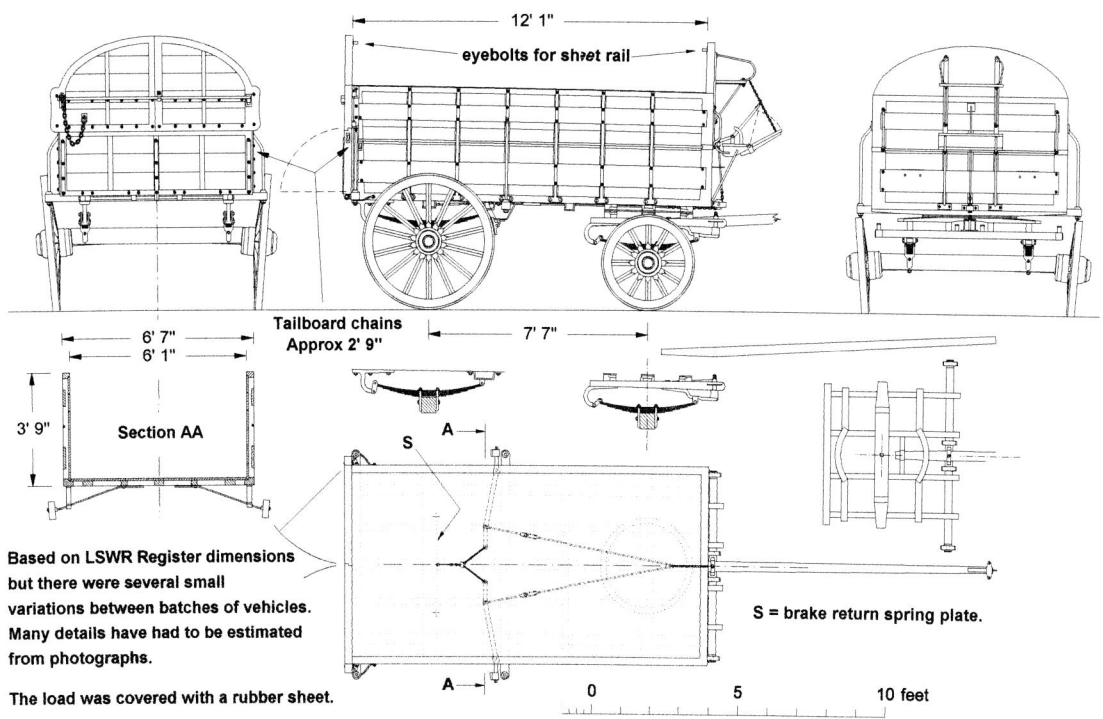

Figure 4.2.1. Road vehicles (pair-horse meat van of c. 1893).

Plate 4.2.1a. Pair-horse meat cart. (Gloucestershire County Record Office)

Plate 4.2.1b. Meat carts on 18ft road vehicle trucks. (HV Tumilty collection)

Plate 4.2.1c. L11 class No 441 with meat vans on 28ft road vehicle trucks, in Southampton Docks, bound for Nine Elms. (B Curl collection)

Plate 4.2.1d. B4 class No 89 "Trouville" in Southampton Docks with meat carts on various road vehicle trucks. (J Tatchell collection)

Plate 4.2.1e. 28ft road vehicle truck, originally built specifically to carry two meat vans. (HV Tumilty collection)

MISCELLANY

Table 4: Meat cart details from the road vehicle register

Numbers	Dates	Builder	Quantity
484 to 498	1892/3	LSWR	15
499 to 533	1893	Bristol Wagon Works	35
597 to 612	1898	Bristol Wagon Works	16
619 to 638	1899/1900	Bristol Wagon Works	20
700 to 709	1904	LSWR	10
710 to 749	1904	Gloucester Wagon Co	40
755 to 774	1907	LSWR	20
775 to 804	1907	Glover & Sons, Warwick	30
Total			186

end of 1922 at a total cost of £950. However, the road vehicle register shows that a total of 186 were built, as shown in Table 4.

Some photographs in the Hulton Getty collection (regrettably, too expensive to be reproduced here) and reputedly taken around 1918, show several types of road vehicle including some of these meat vans in use as ordinary delivery carts. The hinged rear doors had been lifted off, leaving only the normal tailboard. They can be seen loaded with a variety of ordinary merchandise, boxes, barrels, crates etc, and in one picture loaded so high with hops that it could not have been carried by rail.

The Eastleigh drawing showing the conversion to container was number E17416. This showed sling fittings on the sides and substantial beams underneath, rather like solebars, with brackets (presumably to fit onto motor road flats). One conversion, but without these beams, was the subject of the official Southern Railway photograph shown here as plate 4.2.1f, where it is seen on a pair-horse trolley, which seems a little pointless! Presumably,

Plate 4.2.1f. Meat van body converted to a container and loaded on a pair-horse trolley. (J Tatchell collection)

the intended use is as seen in plate 4.2.1g, where there are three variations in the conversions seen on Southern road van trucks.

The minutes do not record just how many of the 28ft road van trucks (LSWR drawing 869, which does not appear to have survived) were built for the meat vans, but 82 were shown in the diagram book at the end of 1922.

As mentioned above, there are some more photographs of road vehicles that may be of interest. Plates 4.2.2a to 4.2.2d show some 6-ton three-horse delivery vans built by the Gloucester Carriage & Wagon Co for the LSWR in 1897 for prices of £48 10s or £49 each. Numbered 572 to 577, they were virtually identical, although the register shows some fractional differences. They are also almost exactly as shown in the very detailed drawings published in Surrey Warner's section of *Modern Railway Working, Volume 5*, published in 1912. The bodies were 11ft 8in long, 5ft 4½in wide and 2ft 5½in high. Leading and trailing wheels were 3ft 4in and 4ft 7in diameter respectively with wheelbase 7ft 0½in and width over wheels 6ft 6½in. They were all "..fitted with appliance for protection of carmen on dickey" in mid-1906. Number 572 was renumbered by the Southern as 2074, but the others were declared redundant and sold in 1923.

Plates 4.2.3a and 4.2.3b are of LSWR delivery vehicles at St Malo. The horse-drawn delivery van appears to be to the same design as those in the Gloucester photographs.

Also included as plate 4.2.4 is a photograph of LSWR removals van number 137 at Bowerchalke, near Wilton in Wiltshire. It is not common to find a railway company actually doing removals, this was normally done by local firms, and there are several photographs of such vans loaded on railway vehicles.

It is possible that since staff moves on promotion, for example, were pretty common (and there are many such records in the archives) this van was owned by the LSWR specifically to deal with staff moves. There were almost certainly sufficient to justify it, and it would have been cheaper and easier to arrange than hiring one on every occasion. There is no entry for a furniture van in the LSWR Register of Road Vehicles (which is undated but was probably started between 1904 and 1909) but the entry for number 137 is blank, suggesting that it had recently been withdrawn. However, there were

Plate 4.2.1g. Ex-LSWR meat carts converted to containers, Alton c.1930. (P Coutanche collection/Lens of Sutton Association)

MISCELLANY

Plate 4.2.2a. LSWR 6-ton 3-horse vans, built 1897. (Gloucestershire County Record Office)

Plate 4.2.2b. (Gloucestershire County Record Office)

Plate 4.2.2c. (Gloucestershire County Record Office)

Plate 4.2.2d. (Gloucestershire County Record Office)

MISCELLANY

Plate 4.2.3a. LSWR delivery van stationed at St Malo. (J Tatchell collection)

Plate 4.2.3b. LSWR delivery services at St Malo. (J Tatchell collection)

Plate 4.2.4. LSWR Furniture van No 137 at Bowerchalke, Wiltshire. (Courtesy of Sheila Collins)

often advertisements by various removals firms in the *South Western Gazette*, including engraved illustrations of the vehicles. Some of those in 1913 for C Chapman of 100 South Lambeth Road, London, included the statement:

"To the employees of the L&SW Railway, I am offering you the use of my Pantechnican Vans when you are changing your post up and down the line by the Company. I will load and put your goods on Nine Elms with loan of van to go through. I will also send my Van to any Station to come to Nine Elms, unload in London, at an inclusive cost of 30/-. Employees! Take this opportunity and save your Furniture from Damage from packing same into Box trucks. These Furniture Vans were purchased by me 20 years ago from the South Western Railway Company. They are strong and reliable."

Clearly the LSWR had quite a substantial part in this trade in earlier years.

Goods Yard Cranes

The majority of goods yards needed a crane of some sort. In most cases, it was outdoors, and in some it was within the goods shed, whilst a few had both; these cranes varied in lifting power. The *Appendix to the Working Timetable* for January 1902 lists the stations that had cranes and weighbridges. Here are a few instances with their lifting capacity, shown in Table 5.

Table 5: Goods yard cranes with their lifting capacity	
Woking	10 tons
Alton	5 tons
Esher	None
Wareham	5 tons with another of 1 ton presumably within the goods shed
Brockenhurst	5 tons and another of 30 cwt, which was still there in mid-2002 as a feature in the goods shed, by then converted to an Italian restaurant
Seaton	5 tons
Exeter	10 tons with another of 5 tons
North Tawton	10 tons
Tavistock	10 tons
Bridestowe	None, but in mid-2002 there was still a 2-ton crane in the privately owned goods shed

MISCELLANY

A few photographs show these cranes in the distance but rarely as a feature. Mr AE West took the ones shown here of the Seaton Junction 5-ton crane (plates 4.3a and 4.3b) while the author took the ones of the 10-ton crane at Woking (plates 4.3c and 4.3d) as well as the one within the goods shed (plate 4.3e) although its capacity is not known.

Regrettably, neither of us took any measurements! Plate 4.3f shows two 23ft 10-ton double bolster wagons by the loading dock at Winchfield where the crane looks similar to the Seaton one, but the mechanism is quite different. Similar variations can be seen in other station scenes, although usually too far in the distance to be of much use for study.

Plate 4.3a. Sidmouth Junction yard crane, June 1964. (AE West)

Plate 4.3b. Sidmouth Junction crane. (AE West)

Plate 4.3c. Woking yard crane, May 1971. (GR Weddell)

Plate 4.3d. Woking yard crane, May 1971. (GR Weddell)

Plate 4.3e. Woking goods shed crane, May 1971. (GR Weddell)

Plate 4.3f. Yard crane at Winchfield with tree trunks and ex-LSWR 23ft 10-ton double bolster wagons. (F Foote)

MISCELLANY

Shunting Truck

There is no mention in official records of the construction or use of shunting trucks, but there are two works drawings (numbers 757 and 1729) but only one vehicle was recorded as having existed! The earlier drawing, number 757 (illustrated at figure 4.4a) shows truck number 336 as built in 1898. Number 336 lasted in the records well into Southern days when it received the numbers 075S in 1923, and 61321 in 1925. Plate 4.4b shows it at Exmouth Junction in June 1926, by which time it had become a different vehicle from drawing 757!

Number 336 was built in 1898 complete with a large toolbox, much resembling the GWR variety. A pencilled note on drawing 757 states, "No of wagon 336 – Box omitted from frame which went out of works Nov 1906 having been removed prior to arrival here for repairs. Tare as sent out 4-16-3". So it seems there had been some fairly serious damage in which the large toolbox may or may not have been involved. Within two years, in 1908, drawing 1729 was prepared, and it is this vehicle that appears as 61321 (ex-336) in Mr Casserley's photo taken in 1926.

The shunting truck shown in the 1908 drawing, here seen as figure 4.4b, used several parts, mainly metal, either taken from the earlier truck or identical to them. However, there are several differences of detail that appear to make it stronger and heavier than the 1898 one. The axleguards are unusually asymmetrical and clearly made as a "one-off" set, probably to accommodate the buffer spring brackets. The buffers are not the original self-contained ones and the brackets supporting the rear end of the buffer springs are more robust than on most other vehicles. There is a single side, single block, brake not seen on the original. The footguards give more protection along the length of the truck and are of much heavier steel plate, 1¼in thick instead of ⅛in. Finally, there is a note, "Holes in underframe bored to suit those existing in old plates to form pockets for scrap iron." There is no indication of any such plates on drawing 757, so they might have been added to permit making it heavier.

The photograph taken in 1926, plate 4.4b and enlargement, shows a further change to the handbrake, but the angle makes it impossible to determine just how the arrangement was revised.

Using a dose of conjecture, this is what seems to have happened. The original 336 was damaged at least once, possibly by rough shunting or derailing, the box was removed and weights were placed in pockets in the underframe to give it more substance, but even so, it either continued to suffer from the earlier damage or had a fresh accident. If so, was it of sufficient embarrassment to someone important enough to arrange for a replacement to be built without appearing in any committee minutes book? Of course, it was a low-value item so may not have been considered worth recording anyway.

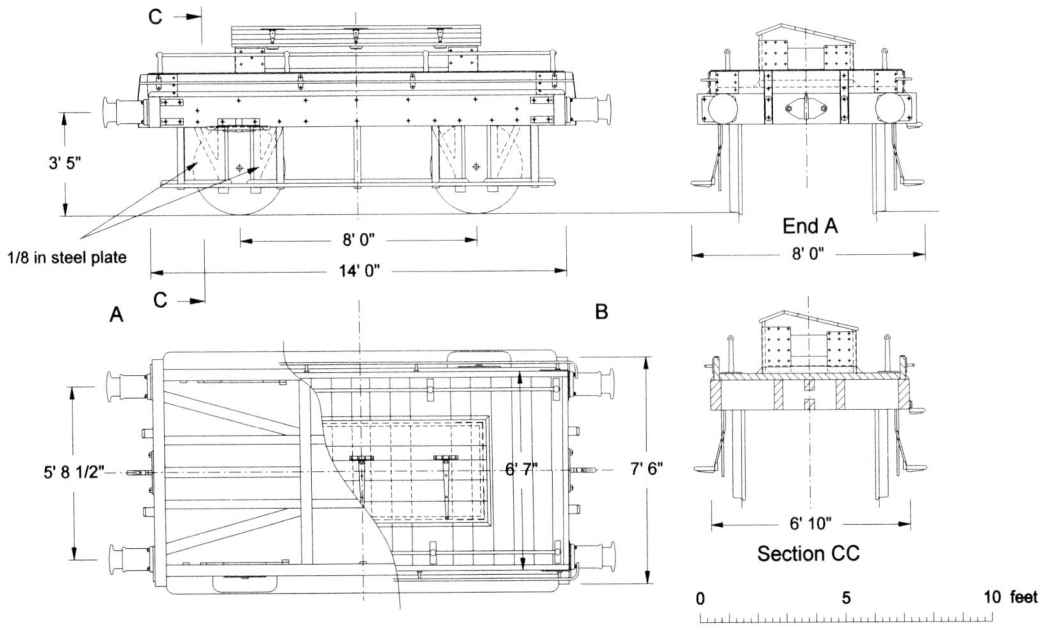

The box had been removed by November 1906.

Figure 4.4a. Shunting truck No 336 of 1898.

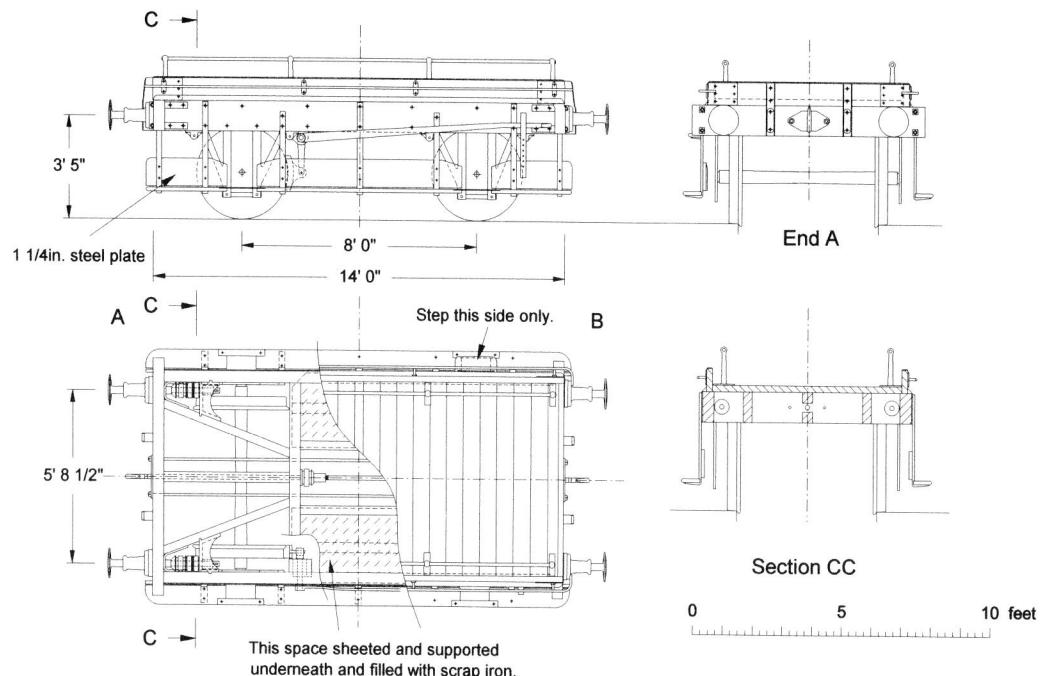

Figure 4.4b. Shunting truck No 336 of 1908.

Detail from Plate 4.4b. (HC Casserley)

MISCELLANY

Plate 4.4b. G6 class No 267 with ex-LSWR shunting truck No 336, note the altered foot protection. Exmouth Junction, June 1926. (HC Casserley)

Platform Items

Several types of barrow and trolley were used on station platforms to handle the wide variety of luggage and goods handled there. A Southern Railway painting specification of 1949 has small sketches of 26 different types, but these might be from all parts of the Southern and its constituents. Those shown here are ones that have been identified as LSWR. There are several two-wheeled barrows including the luggage barrow shown here at figure 4.5.1 and plates 4.5.1a to 4.5.1e, and the long bow barrow at figure 4.5.2 and plates 4.5.2a and 4.5.2b, as well as others with quite a short foot (or bow), a skin and hide barrow, a bacon barrow, a platform parcel barrow and a corn barrow, then an exception, a four-wheeled barrow for sheet lead. There are two sizes of wheelbarrow, one of them being a navvy barrow. Trolleys are four-wheeled and are steerable, either with a handle attached to the front axle, or by having two castoring wheels at the front. There are three variants of double ended trolley, a calf float and a couple of platform trolleys.

Plate 4.5.1a. LSWR luggage barrow, Horsted Keynes, 2003. (GR Weddell)

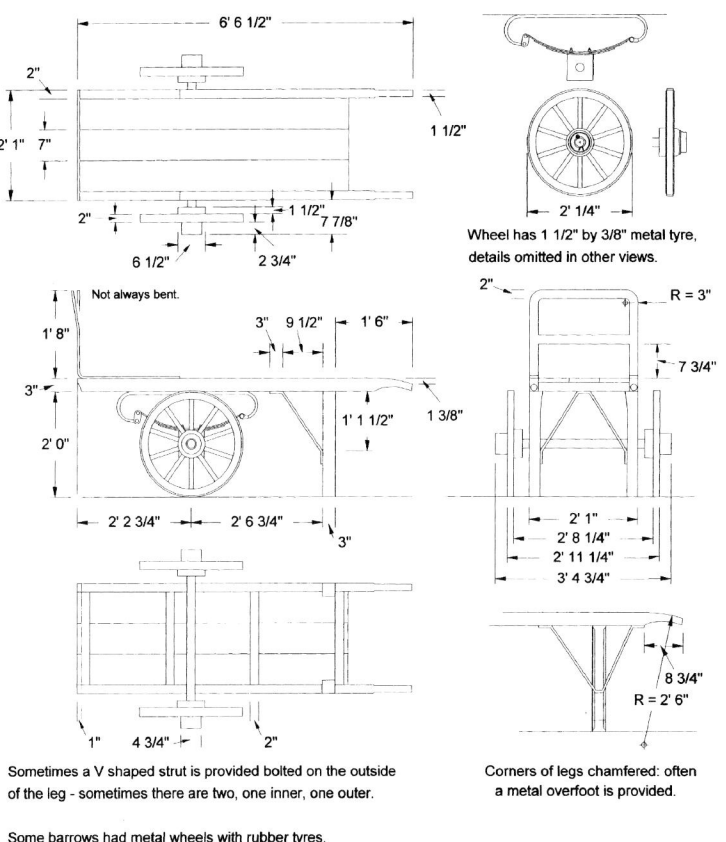

Figure 4.5.1. Platform items (luggage barrow). (For clarity, this drawing has been reproduced at 7mm scale)

Plate 4.5.1b. LSWR luggage barrow, Horsted Keynes, 2003. (GR Weddell)

MISCELLANY

Plate 4.5.1c. Luggage barrow at Frimley, 1970. (GR Weddell)

Plate 4.5.1d. Three luggage barrows at Chertsey, 1970. On the right are the wheels and body of a platelayer's trolley. (GR Weddell)

Plate 4.5.1e. Platform details at Swanage. (J Tatchell collection)

MISCELLANY

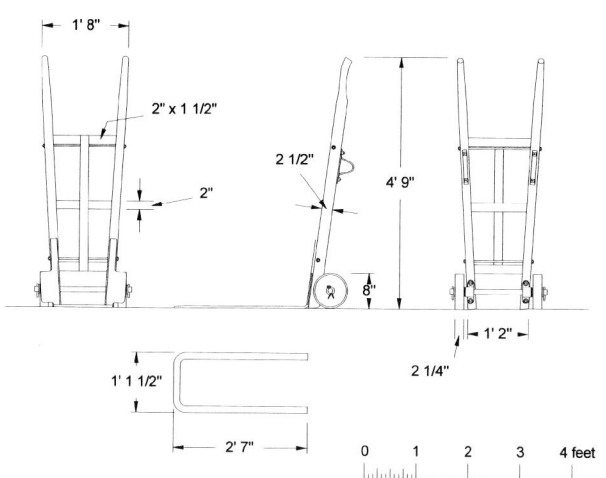

Figure 4.5.2. Platform items (long bow barrow). (For clarity, this drawing has been reproduced at 7mm scale)

Several dimensions estimated from photographs.
The name CLAYGATE was carved on the top rail of the measured example.

Plate 4.5.3. Platform trolley at Eastleigh. (J Tatchell collection)

Opposite page, left: Plate 4.5.2a. LSWR long bow barrow from Claygate, at Horsted Keynes, 2003. (GR Weddell)

Opposite page right: Plate 4.5.2b. LSWR long bow barrow from Claygate, at Horsted Keynes, 2003. Note the luggage barrow behind has steel wheels with rubber tyres. (GR Weddell)

Plate 4.5.3 shows a large platform trolley at Eastleigh. The dimensions in the specification are 7ft 6in by 3ft 10in by 2ft 0½in high with 20in wheels and a turning circle of 12ft 6in diameter, although the wheels in the photograph and the trolley height do not appear to agree with those figures.

The barrows in plate 4.5.4 at Ascot were described as platform parcel barrows. They are shown as 7ft 4½in long overall by 3ft 2in wide with wheels of 2ft 0¾in diameter. The presence of three of them suggests that there was some particular trade at Ascot that involved the sending or receiving of considerable quantities of fairly small packages, which might have fallen off ordinary luggage barrows.

Also shown as plate 4.5.5 are some notices commonly used near the ends of platforms and a gas lamp that also was fairly common on LSWR stations. Some columns had a right-handed twist, and the others a left-handed twist.

Another item conspicuous at the departure end of most platforms was a water crane. I am indebted to Mr I Smith for permitting me to use his drawing, as figure 4.5.6.

Plate 4.5.4. Three parcels barrows. (Author's collection)

MISCELLANY

Plate 4.5.5a. Coxes Lock Mill crossing (Addlestone), 1970. (GR Weddell)

Plate 4.5.5b. Brookwood, 1970. (GR Weddell)

Plate 4.5.5c. Whimple, down platform, 1970. (GR Weddell)

Plate 4.5.5d. LSWR gas lamp. (GR Weddell)

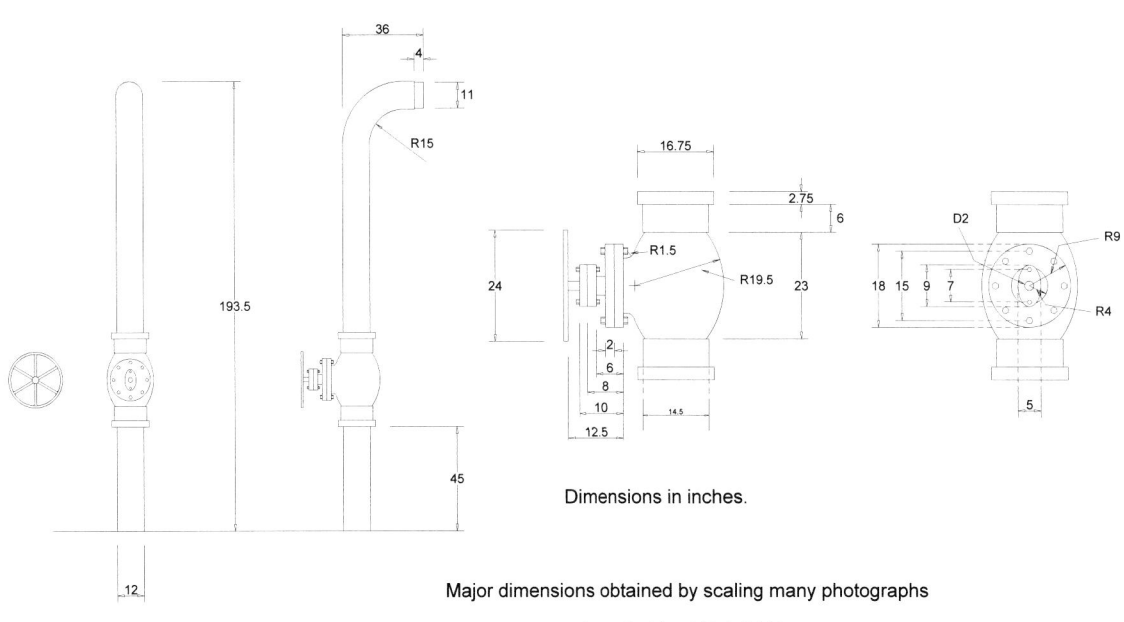

Figure 4.5.6. Water crane.

MISCELLANY

Pooley Vans

In common with many railway companies, the LSWR had long-standing contracts with Henry Pooley & Son Ltd of Temple Street, Birmingham for the examination, maintenance and repair of the wide variety of weighing machines in use on the railway. In an advert in the *South Western Gazette* in 1909, they claimed that, "$^9/_{10}$ths of the Railway Traffic of Britain is weighed on Pooley Weighing Machines".

Mr P Yarlett of the South Western Circle has provided me with the following extract from the LSWR *Appendix to the Book of Rules and Regulations* dated 25th July 1921, which is probably substantially a repeat of similar instructions from whenever the contract started. Henry Pooley & Son Ltd was operating under that name from 1897 to 1949, though the business must have been in existence before that.

"14. A contract is in force with Messrs Pooley & Son, of Birmingham, to perform all the repairs and renewals which may be required of weighing machines belonging to the Company, and to maintain them in good working order, under the general supervision of the Storekeeper. Whenever a machine is broken, or is out of repair or adjustment, it will be the duty of the Agent, or officer in charge, to send a written request as under, to do what is necessary, mentioning this Company's number in every case, and if such request be not attended to in due course, or if any of the machines be not efficiently repaired and maintained, a report thereof is to be made to the Storekeeper at Nine Elms. Stations West of Salisbury – To Messrs Pooley & Son, EXETER. All other Stations – To Messrs Pooley & Son, NINE ELMS.

"15. Messrs Pooley & Son's workmen will leave a Certificate Form with the Agent or officer in charge on each occasion each weighing machine or instrument is examined or repaired, specifying the nature of the examination or work executed, and the document is to be at once confirmed or otherwise remarked upon, and forwarded by the Agent or other officer in charge direct to the Storekeeper after making a record of the visit for reference."

In order that Messrs Pooley could carry this out, they were provided with specially adapted vans to act as workshops with testing facilities. There are two LSWR drawings for these vans. Drawing 572 is dated June 1895, and it is known that at least one van (number 207) was built to this, and survived into Southern days as their 26S. Closely based on the ordinary 18ft covered goods van, it had some small windows and a large box within the strengthened

Plate 4.6.1a. Ex-LSWR 18ft van 7774, built 1912, SR No 43219 in August 1924, converted to Pooley van No 529S in April 1931, at Wimbledon in June 1946. (D Cullum)

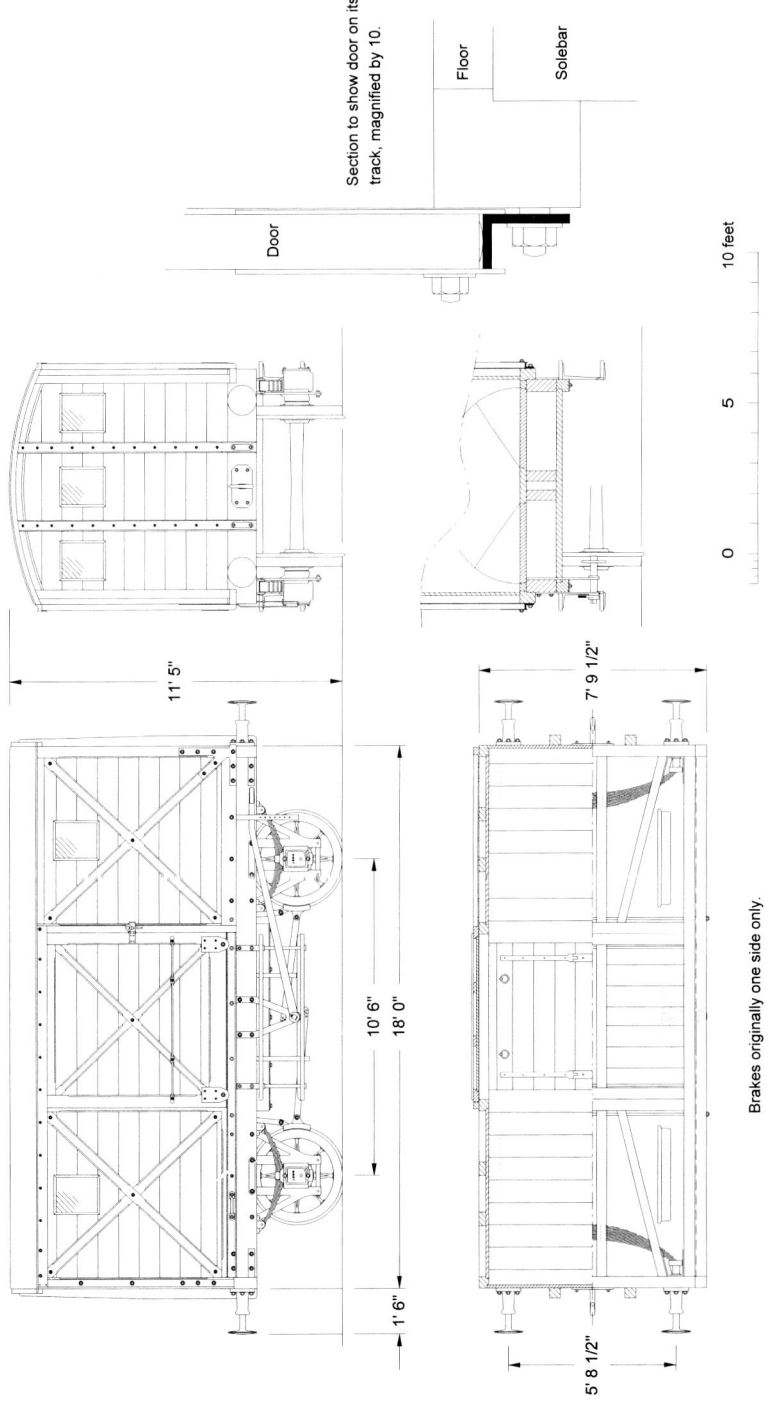

Figure 4.6.1. 18ft Pooley weighing machine van of 1895.

MISCELLANY

Plate 4.6.1b. Ex-LSWR 18ft van 1054, built 1912, SR No 42288 in April 1931, converted to Pooley van 763S in February 1934, at Padstow Quay on 5th July 1948. (JH Aston)

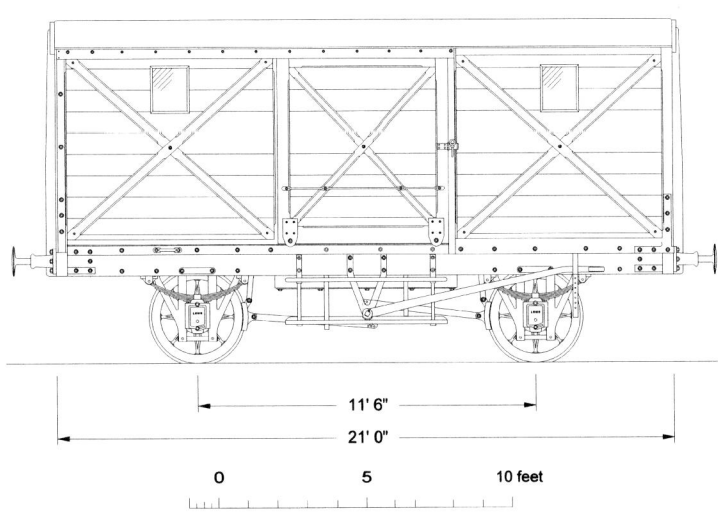

All other views and details are similar to the 18ft Pooley Van of 1895.

Figure 4.6.2. 21ft Pooley weighing machine van of 1899.

underframe for the carriage of the weights used for testing. It is illustrated here as figure 4.6.1.

Unfortunately, no photographs of the originals have come to light, but the accompanying plates 4.6.1a and 4.6.1b show Southern Railway replacements that appear to be practically identical to the drawing. From the terms of the contract, it seems likely that these vans would have been seen from time to time at practically every station on the system.

At least one rather larger van was built for Pooley in 1899 to drawing 829. Originally numbered 6501, it became SR 25S. This looked like an 18ft one stretched to 21ft, but very similar in layout and facilities. Here it is shown as figure 4.6.2 but there are no known photographs.

Engineers' Inspection Train

Information sometimes comes from unexpected sources! Recently, a member of the South Western Circle, Mr M Scott, came across an article with photographs in *The Car, Illustrated* magazine for April 1905. The article, by HG Archer, made the case for building railway inspection vehicles powered by petrol or diesel engines and used the accompanying photographs of the LSWR Engineers' Inspection Train to indicate how cumbersome was the current practice.

The train shown as plate 4.7.1 consists of a modified 22ft passenger brake van at each end, the nearer one having side lookouts, and the distant one having a caboose, as shown in figure 4.14 in *LSWR Carriages Volume 1*. Next from the left is the 1877 Directors' Saloon (figure 3.27) and then the 1877 Royal Saloon, (figure 3.28) both in that same book. Some additional information about the Royal Saloon is given in the Addendum at the end of *LSWR Carriages, Volume 3*. The brake vans had been substantially altered so as to have a viewing compartment at each end. At the extreme left edge of the picture it can be seen that the upper and top panels had been replaced by a tall window. Although not quite so obvious in this print, the same was done at the other end.

The platform view of the group of inspecting officers at Padstow (plate 4.7.2) shows how the end panels had been replaced by two huge windows. Also interesting is the pair of fold-down steps with brackets to rest on the buffer castings, similar to the end flaps on road vehicle trucks, but split to clear the brake pipe, and in this case probably provided to allow cleaning of the windows. It looks almost certain that both ends of both brake vans were treated in the same way.

The article described the two brakes as "inspection cars", the former Royal Saloon as a "resting saloon" and the former Directors' Saloon as a "refreshment saloon". The writer says that there

Plate 4.7.1. *"The Car, Illustrated" magazine, 1905.*

MISCELLANY

Plate 4.7.2. "The Car, Illustrated" magazine, 1905.

were normally three inspectors sitting, watching track and general works, however the end view seems to show the arm rests of two arm chairs, and possibly a clear view through the partitions to the windows at the far end.

This former Directors' Saloon was supplanted in its original role by the bogie one in 1885, and there has previously been little reference to its use after that. The same is true of the former Royal Saloon, although it is a reasonable assumption that, for a time at least, both may have been used for VIPs or for hire.

When the Directors went on an inspection, it was usually to attend the opening of a line or station, to have a look at the general progress on the line and, very importantly, to be seen by their employees. On the other hand, the Engineer's Department was concerned with the infrastructure, track, buildings and so on. When the Engineer's inspection team went out, it was to do a detailed examination of these features, and to provide information as a basis for orders for works to be carried out. However, with the exception of ballast trains, the Engineer rarely got any new vehicles, always older vehicles no longer required by the Traffic Department, hence the interesting formation of this train.

The only suggestion as to when the train was formed is early 1906, since that is when the saloons were cyphered to numbers 09 and 010, but there is no information at all as to how long it was kept complete.

London & South Western Railway Employés Coal Society

It was not uncommon for the staff of some railway companies to set up their own arrangements for supplying coal to their members, and the LSWR was no exception. There don't appear to be any references to this in the LSWR records in the National Archive (formerly the Public Record Office) nor, perhaps surprisingly, in the company's own newspaper the *South Western Gazette*. However, Gloucester County Council Archives have the collection of photographs of vehicles produced by the Gloucester Railway Carriage and Wagon Co Ltd, which includes at least five wagons of interest, four of which are reproduced here as plates 4.8.1 to 4.8.4. The fifth one was number 8.

All four are fairly standard RCH-type 10-ton wagons, although with very slight differences. They are either on hire or hire purchase from the Gloucester company and, with the exception of number 1, which has not received its registration plate, are registered to the LSWR. All were painted black with white lettering.

Numbers 1, 2 and 6 are marked to return empty to Manners Colliery, which was at Ilkeston,

Plate 4.8.1. LSWR Employés Coal Society wagon No 1, built November 1901. (Gloucestershire County Record Office)

Plate 4.8.2. LSWR Employés Coal Society wagon No 2, built August 1907. (Gloucestershire County Record Office)

Plate 4.8.3. LSWR Employés Coal Society wagon No 3, built September 1912. (Gloucestershire County Record Office)

Plate 4.8.4. LSWR Servants' Coal Club wagon No 6, built October 1922. (Gloucestershire County Record Office)

LSWR CARRIAGES VOLUME 4

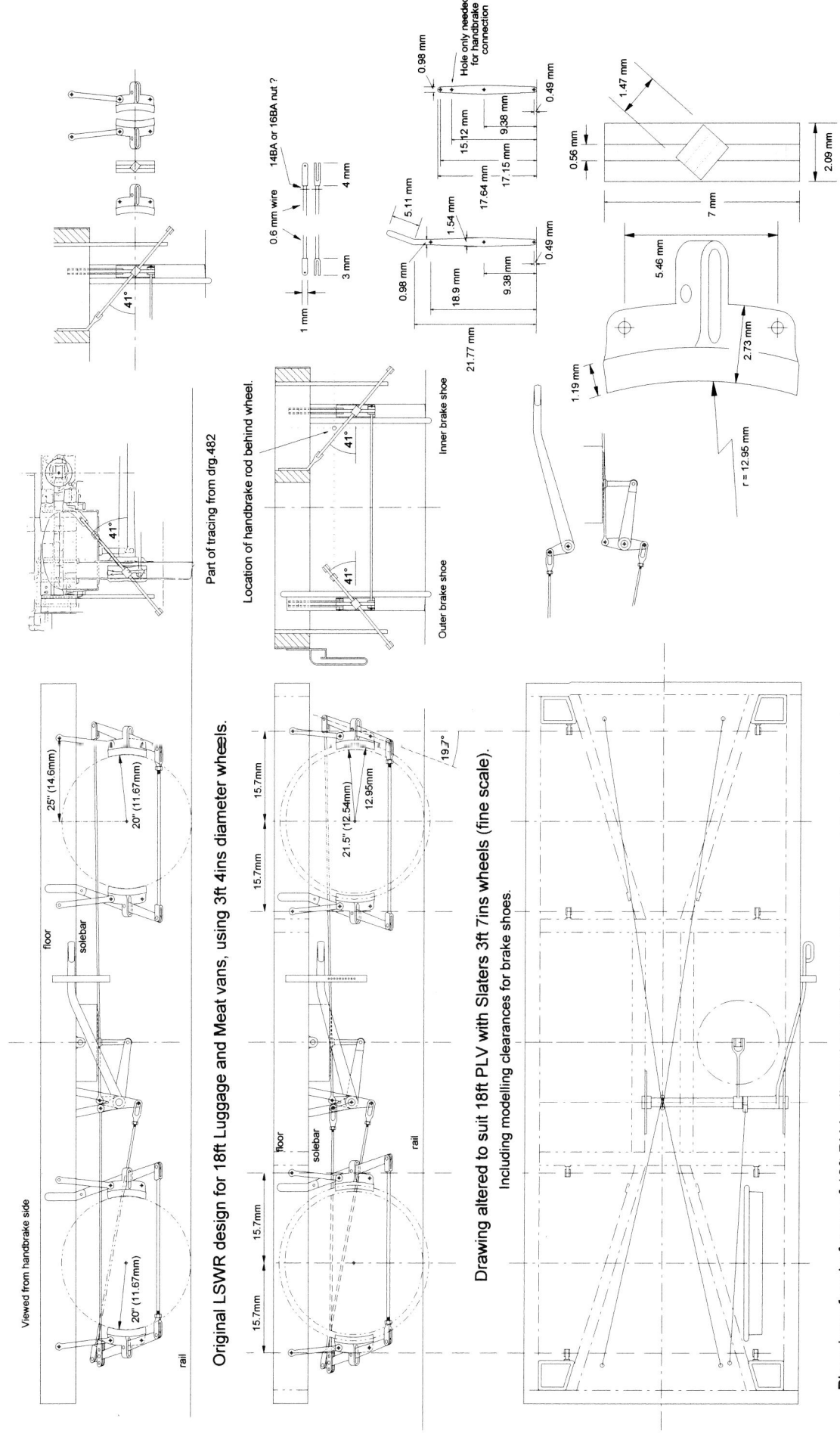

MISCELLANY

Derbyshire. Mr Len Tavender has suggested a possible LSWR connection, in that Lord Manners' family owned an estate between Christchurch and Ringwood.

Mr AG Thomas in his *Private Owners Wagons Book 3* shows a sketch of a 7-plank wagon without top doors lettered "South Western Employees Coal Fund", number 3, Nine Elms SW, painted greenish grey and lettered cream, shaded black. Unfortunately, there is no indication of the date or location of the picture from which he produced the sketch. However, this sketch suggests that the original hire of number 3 had expired, and a replacement obtained elsewhere. From the basic colour this might well have been from Stephenson Clarke who used that shade.

Skew Brakes

Several vehicles in these volumes have been described as having "skew" brake gear, and it has been shown in the various figures, but necessarily the details have been somewhat obscured. Modelmakers, in particular, probably need to know a bit more about how the rigging was arranged. Figure 4.9 attempts to provide this detail. For the commonest modelling scales and standards, an exact reduction of the full-size dimensions is not practicable, in some instances giving negative clearances. The present drawing is therefore adapted to show the rigging to suit the LSWR 18ft passenger luggage van in 7mm scale using the nearest available wheel size (in March 2006). Hopefully modellers will be able to similarly adapt the arrangement to suit other vehicles.

"Standard" Buffer Stop

An appropriate subject on which to close this series of four volumes is an LSWR buffer stop. There were at least three known official drawings, dated 1894, 1902 and 1915. All of these types were built from iron rail bent to form the necessary shapes. In the case of the 1915 drawing, this was 82lb rail, but the weight of the earlier ones is not known. The most obvious difference in 1915 was the use of only a single vertical section instead of two.

Plate 4.10.1a. Camelford

Opposite page: Figure 4.9. "Skew" brake gear.

Figure 4.10 is based on LSWR drawing 1899 of 24th March 1902, which was titled "Standard" buffer stop. The stock rail to which it was all attached was shown as 24ft but later this was increased to 30ft long. Plate 4.10.1a shows the construction quite well, although the front end of the outer rail has been greatly shortened. Plate 4.10.1b shows the detail of the special casting holding the verticals and the beam together, and plate 4.10.1c is of another example, still at Wareham in 1984. In this case the difference between the original iron rail and the modern heavier steel rail is obvious at the fishplate joint. For comparison, there is at extreme right a Southern Railway steel buffer stop with a cutout in the beam to clear buckeye couplers.

Buffers of this type can be seen in the background of many photographs taken in LSWR days. Plate 4.10.1d shows Weybridge in about 1882 with buffers of this type in the down bay. The picture of Wool at an unknown date (plate 4.10.1e) clearly has this type on the right, with what became the normal red band painted across it, while the one on the far left appears to be just a plain beam, possibly forming the face of a loading dock. Plate 4.10.1f was taken at Hampton Court shortly after the start of electric services, and both buffer stops on the right appear to be of the "Standard" type.

THE END

Plate 4.10.1b.
(A Blackburn)

MISCELLANY

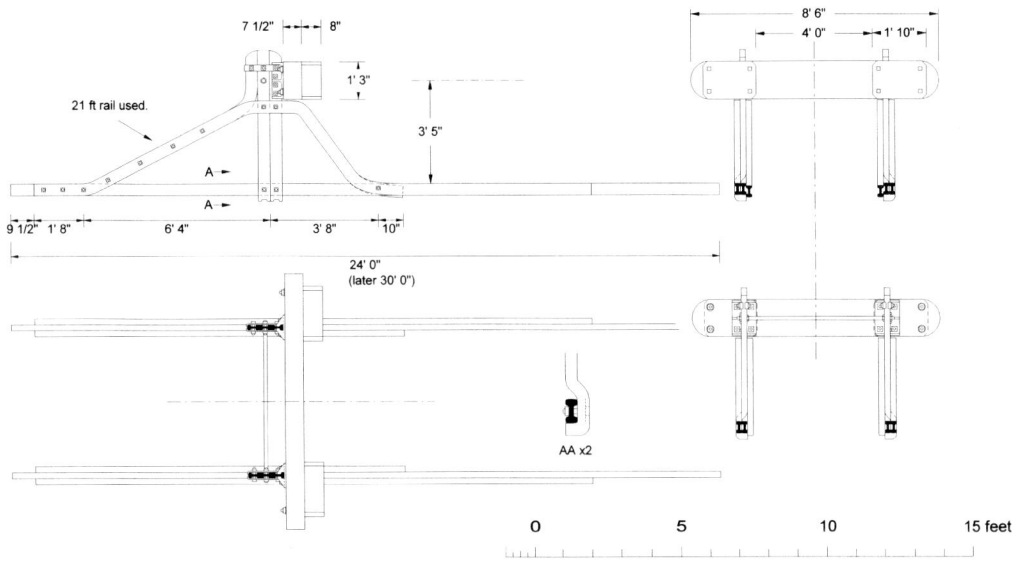

Based on LSWR Drg.1899, dated March 1902.

Figure 4.10. LSWR buffer stop.

Plate 4.10.1c. LSWR and SR buffer stops at Wareham, 1984. (A Blackburn)

Plate 4.10.1d. Weybridge c.1882.

MISCELLANY

Plate 4.10.1e. Wool.

Plate 4.10.1f. Hampton Court. (Metropolitan Vickers)

LSWR 02 No 210 at the buffer stops, Lymington.

APPENDIX TO CHAPTER 1 - GOODS VEHICLES

(Additional to lists in *Southern Wagons, Volume 1*)

No LSWR wagon numbering registers are available. The Southern Railway registers include the previous LSWR numbers of vehicles that survived after 1922, and many of these are shown in *Southern Wagons, Volume 1* but obviously this excludes the drawings in the present book.

1.17 16ft Gunpowder Vans. LSWR drawing 2203

The numbers of these vans were:

LSWR:	1296	1350	1361	1375	1379	1401	1426	1445	1904	2134	2154	6157
SR:	61201	61202	61203	61204[1]	61205	61206[1]	61207	61208	61209[1]	61210	61211	61212
Withdrawn:	1952	1955	1956	1954	1956	1954[2]	1953	1956	1956[3]	1953	1954	1952

Notes:
1. The SR numbers of 1375, 1401 and 1904 are confirmed in records, the other pairings are assumed.
2. Grounded at Woking, then moved to the Kent & East Sussex Railway.
3. Sent to the Scottish Region in March 1956 for departmental use. Withdrawn August 1980, to National Railway Museum.

No 1375 is recorded as built in 1912 with brake levers on both sides, and from photographic evidence, No 2134 had a lever on one side only. It is therefore assumed that 1426 to 6157 were the 1904 batch, with 1296 to 1401 being built in 1912.

1.23 and 1.24 18ft 2in Special Cattle Wagon. (The LSWR and SR diagram books state 18ft 3in)

All had a drover's compartment inserted during or after 1906, at an estimated cost of £10 each, and were then renumbered into carriage stock as special cattle vans, then renumbered back into wagon stock after the 1912 renumbering scheme. All were recorded at the same original cost of £143 10s 5d.

Built	No	1906 Ren	Post-1912 Ren	SR No	Withdrawn
1888	8377	1	c.6/10		
"	8378	2	c.6/10		Possibly 2/6/28
"	8379	3	c.6/10		
"	8380	4	1/14 to 8380		Replaced 1/14 by 22ft special cattle van
"	8381	5	4/14 to 8381	3671	28/11/25 (SR number probably not painted on)
1891	8833	6	7/14 to 8833	3672	29/11/24
"	8834	7	7/14 to 8834	3673	28/11/25 (SR number probably not painted on)
"	8835	8	-		Replaced 5/14 by 22ft special cattle van

1.22 18ft 8½in Special Cattle Wagon.

All had a drover's compartment inserted during or after 1906, and were then renumbered into carriage stock as special cattle vans, then renumbered back into wagon stock after the 1912 renumbering scheme. They were all recorded at the same original cost as the earlier ones, £143 10s 5d.

Built	No	1906 Ren	Post-1912 Ren	SR No	Withdrawn
1899	12464	9	9/13 to 12464	3651	8/2/39
"	12465	10	9/13 to 12465	3652	10/8/35
"	12466	11	10/13 to 12466	3653	7/7/28
"	12467	12	12/13 to 12467	3654	Unknown
"	12468	13	5/16 to 12468	3655	29/3/30
"	12469	14	3/14 to 12469	3656	16/6/28
"	12470	15	3/14 to 12470	3657	28/7/28
"	12471	16	11/13 to 12471	3658	5/2/27 (SR number probably not painted on)
"	12472	17	6/14 to 12472	3659	2/10/26 " " "
"	12473	18	5/15 to 12473	3660	15/8/31
"	12474	19	3/14 to 12474	3661	30/3/29 " " "
"	12475	20	6/13 to 12475	3662	4/4/25 " " "
"	12476	21	11/13 to 12476	3663	10/3/28 " " "
"	12477	22	6/16 to 12477	3664	9/5/25 " " "

18ft 8½in Special Cattle Wagon (continued)

Built	No	1906 Ren	Post-1912 Ren	SR No	Withdrawn
1899	12478	23			Probably sold to Brecon & Merthyr Railway c.1910
"	12479	24	7/13 to 12479	3665	29/3/39
"	12480	25	2/15 to 12480	3666	8/9/28
"	12481	26	7/14 to 12481	3667	5/2/27 (SR number probably not painted on)
"	12482	27	9/13 to 12482	3668	20/7/29
"	12483	28	7/13 to 12483	3669	16/6/28 " " "

1.25 22ft Special Cattle Van (LSWR drawing 1857, SR diagram 1043)

Built	No	Post-1912 Ren	SR No	Withdrawn
1910	1	9/14 to 12478	3678	29/3/39
"	2	12/16 to 8378	3674	10/8/35
"	3	5/15 to 8379	3675	5/6/37
1/1914		8380	3676	
5/1914		8835	3677	

1.38 China Clay Wagons

Based on the assumption mentioned in the text, the following are the likely numbers of the china clay wagons built in 1914/15.

1060, 1131, 1795, 1881, 1889, 2195, 2573, 4096, 4112, 4133, 4739, 5104, 5306, 5379, 5958, 6595, 7330, 7576, 8389, 8397, 8566, 8603, 8990, 9828, 10070.

Heavy Goods Brake Vans

The following are the LSWR numbers of the 20-ton goods brake vans that were illustrated in *Southern Wagons, Volume 1*, page 60.

3922	6533	6984	6996
3934	6535	6987	6997
4186	6539	6988	7769
4759	6978	6989	7773
4770	6979	6990	7778
6526	6980	6991	7780
6529	6981	6992	7784
6530	6982	6993	7785
	6983	6995	7787

APPENDIX TO CHAPTER 3 - TRAVELLING CRANES

These are extracts from the Southern Railway Service Register, with additions from other sources.

Key: LD = Locomotive Department, CD = Commercial Department, ED = Engineering Department
? indicates unknown or in some doubt.

LSWR No	Date	SR No	Ren	Description	Builder	Allocation
1	1880	30S	1/26	Breakdown crane, 20-ton, 8-wheel	Stothert & Pitt	LD Eastleigh
88S	?	30SM		Match truck for No 30S, 4-wheel		
				In Boiler Register, shown as Nine Elms Red Rover		
				Transferred to Eastleigh 11/19		
2	1880	31S	12/26	Breakdown crane, 10-ton	Appleby	LD Guildford
8809	1890	31SM		Match truck, ex-open wagon, 10-ton		
3	1885	32S	1/26	Breakdown crane, 15-ton, 6-wheel	Dunlop & Bell	LD Bournemouth Central
70S	?	32SM	5/24 ?	Match truck		
57450	1888	32SM		Match truck		
4	1875	33S		Breakdown crane, 10-ton, 6-wheel	Appleby Bros ?	Withdrawn 1925
63S		33SM		24ft match truck		
				In Boiler Register, shown at Eastleigh, Guildford, Exmouth Jn, Salisbury, Eastleigh		
5	1909	34S	3/27	Breakdown crane, 20-ton, 8-wheel	Stothert & Pitt	LD Exmouth Jn, later Feltham
89S	?	34SM		Match truck, 4 wheel	?	
6	1918	35S	12/26	Breakdown crane, 36-ton, 10-wheel	Ransomes & Rapier	LD Nine Elms, later Eastleigh
68S	?	35SM		Match truck, 8 wheel		
67S		36S		Tender attached to crane 35S		
7	1922	37S	1/27	Breakdown crane, 36-ton, 10-wheel	Cowans Sheldon	LD Salisbury
115S	?	37SM		Match truck, 8-wheel		
116S	?	38S		Tender attached to breakdown crane 37S		

All cranes down to here were steam-powered travelling cranes. The following were all (or mostly) hand-powered.

LSWR No	Date	SR No	Ren	Description	Builder	Allocation
25	9/1890	39S		Shops crane, 12-ton, 6-wheel	Ransomes & Rapier	LD Eastleigh
		39SM		Ex-tender frame		
1	1903	40S		Travelling crane, 5-ton, 4-wheel, 14ft 7in x 6ft 11in	Ransomes & Rapier	CD Nine Elms
963	1899	40SM		3-plank open withdrawn 24/1/31, replaced by:		
	1890	40SM		Withdrawn 21/8/37, replaced by:		
		40SM		Withdrawn 10/11/45		
2	1860	41S		Travelling crane, 3-ton, 4-wheel, 16ft 0in x 7ft 2in	Bray, Waddington Co	CD Eastleigh
4318	1890	41SM		Match truck, 10-ton, 4-wheel, ex-timber wagon 4318		
3	1860	42S		Travelling crane, 4-ton, 4-wheel, 16ft 6in x 6ft 10in	Bray, Waddington Co	CD Basingstoke
5205	1911	42SM		Match truck, ex-timber wagon 5205		
4	?			Travelling crane, 5-ton ("broken down beyond repair" - LB&SCR 12/12/1900)		
4	1901	43S		Travelling crane, 5-ton, 4-wheel, 14ft x 7ft 2in	Alex Chaplin & Co	CD Nine Elms
	1896	43SM		Match truck, 7-ton, ex-open wagon 10495		
5	1911	44S		Travelling crane, 5-ton, 4-wheel, 14ft 6in x 7ft 0in	Ransomes & Rapier	CD Exmouth Jn
	1899	44SM		Match truck, 7-ton, 4-wheel, ex-open wagon 1745 (01745)		
6	1901	45S		Travelling crane, 10-ton, 6-wheel, 17ft 6in	Ransomes & Rapier	CD Feltham
	1901	45SM		Match truck, 10-ton, 4-wheel, 23ft, ex-batten wagon 13293		
7	1885	46S		Travelling crane, 10-ton, 6-wheel, 20ft 7in x 7ft 6in		CD Exmouth Jn ?
	1890	46SM		Match truck, 7-ton, 4-wheel, 15ft 4in ex-open wagon 1177		

LSWR CARRIAGES VOLUME 4

Travelling Cranes (continued)

LSWR No	Date	SR No	Ren	Description	Builder	Allocation
8	1897	47S		Travelling crane, 10-ton, 6-wheel, 17ft 5in	Ransomes & Rapier	CD Eastleigh
114S	1905	47SM		Match truck, 8-ton, 4-wheel, 18ft open	S&DJR (LSW 15039 in 1920)	
9	1910	48S		Travelling crane, 10-ton, 19ft 1in x 6ft 11in	LSWR	ED
284	1888	48SM		Match truck, 10-ton, ex-skillet 284, 15ft 4in		ED Wimbledon Iron-works withdrawn 1931
		48SM		2-plank ballast wagon SR No 61762		
12	c.1900	49S		Travelling crane, 5-ton, 15ft x 7in	Jessop & Appleby	ED Meldon Quarry
88	1888	49SM		Match truck, ex-sleeper wagon 88, 15ft 6in x 7ft 4in		Exmouth Jn 6/48
10	1914	50S		ED shops crane, 3-ton	Haigh Foundry	ED Wimbledon Iron-works
11	c.1890	51S		ED (for internal use only), 12-ton ?		ED Wimbledon Iron-works
M76	?	52S		Carriage Department shops crane, 7-ton, 6-wheel, 22ft 8in		Carriage Department
R12	?	53S		Carriage Department shops crane		
1	?	54S		Carriage Department shops crane, 15ft 11in		
2	?	55S		Carriage Department shops crane, 15ft 11in		
Y15	?	56S		Carriage Department shops crane	Lloyds Foster & Co	
		113S		Redbridge yard crane No 3		
226S		113SM		Match truck		

Other Southern Railway cranes photographed on LSWR territory, shown in the text in plates 3.23 through 3.27.

LSWR No	Date	SR No	Ren	Description	Builder	Allocation
		198S		Steam grab crane		Feltham 5/48
		1582S		Hand crane	Cowans Sheldon	Sidmouth 6/48
	c1925	59S		Steam grab (Exmouth Jn concrete works)	Grafton	Exmouth Jn 6/48
		525S		Steam grab	Taylor & Hubbard	Meldon Quarry 7/48
		453S		Steam grab (coaling)	Grafton	Feltham MPD 8/48, Later Nine Elms

Note: Roger Kidner gives a list as at Grouping that shows these differing from above:

LSWR No	Date	SR No	Ren	Description	Builder	Allocation
1	1908	30S		Breakdown crane, 8-wheel	Stothert & Pitt	Eastleigh
4	1895	33S		Breakdown crane, 6-wheel	Appleby	Strawberry Hill